90 0852285 0

Palgrave Studies in European Union Politics

Edited by: **Michelle Egan**, American University, USA, **Neill Nugent**, Manchester Metropolitan University, UK, **William Paterson**, University of Birmingham, UK

Editorial Board: **Christopher Hill**, Cambridge, UK, **Simon Hix**, London School of Economics, UK, **Mark Pollack**, Temple University, USA, **Kalypso Nicolaïdis**, Oxford, UK, **Morten Egeberg**, University of Oslo, Norway, **Amy Verdun**, University of Victoria, Canada, **Claudio M.** Radaelli, University of Exeter, UK, **Frank Schimmelfennig**, Swiss Federal Institute of Technology, Switzerland

Following on the sustained success of the acclaimed *European Union Series*, which essentially publishes research-based textbooks, *Palgrave Studies in European Union Politics* publishes cutting edge research-driven monographs.

The remit of the series is broadly defined, both in terms of subject and academic discipline. All topics of significance concerning the nature and operation of the European Union potentially fall within the scope of the series. The series is multidisciplinary to reflect the growing importance of the EU as a political, economic and social phenomenon. We will welcome submissions from the areas of political studies, international relations, political economy, public and social policy, economics, law and sociology.

Titles include:

Ian Bache and Andrew Jordan (*editors*)
THE EUROPEANIZATION OF BRITISH POLITICS

Richard Balme and Brian Bridges (*editors*)
EUROPE-ASIA RELATIONS
Building Multilateralisms

Thierry Balzacq (*editor*)
THE EXTERNAL DIMENSION OF EU JUSTICE AND HOME AFFAIRS
Governance, Neighbours, Security

Michael Baun and Dan Marek (*editors*)
EU COHESION POLICY AFTER ENLARGEMENT

Milena Büchs
NEW GOVERNANCE IN EUROPEAN SOCIAL POLICY
The Open Method of Coordination

Kevin Featherstone and Dimitris Papadimitriou
THE LIMITS OF EUROPEANIZATION
Reform Capacity and Policy Conflict in Greece

Stefan Gänzle and Allen G. Sens (*editors*)
THE CHANGING POLITICS OF EUROPEAN SECURITY
Europe Alone?

Palgrave Studies in European Union Politics

**Series Standing Order ISBN 978- 1-4039-9511-7 (hardback) and
ISBN 978- 1-4039-9512-4 (paperback)**

You can receive future titles in this series as they are published by placing a standing order. Please contact your bookseller or, in case of difficulty, write to us at the address below with your name and address, the title of the series and one of the ISBNs quoted above.

Customer Services Department, Macmillan Distribution Ltd, Houndmills, Basingstoke, Hampshire RG21, UK

Agenda-Setting in the European Union

Sebastiaan Princen
Associate Professor, School of Governance,
Utrecht University, the Netherlands

First published 2009 by
PALGRAVE MACMILLAN

Palgrave Macmillan in the UK is an imprint of Macmillan Publishers Limited, registered in England, company number 785998, of Houndmills, Basingstoke, Hampshire RG21 6XS.

Palgrave Macmillan in the US is a division of St Martin's Press LLC, 175 Fifth Avenue, New York, NY 10010.

Palgrave Macmillan is the global academic imprint of the above companies and has companies and representatives throughout the world.

Palgrave® and Macmillan® are registered trademarks in the United States, the United Kingdom, Europe and other countries.

ISBN-13: 978-0-230-22053-9   hardback
ISBN-10: 0-230-22053-3   hardback

This book is printed on paper suitable for recycling and made from fully managed and sustained forest sources. Logging, pulping and manufacturing processes are expected to conform to the environmental regulations of the country of origin.

A catalogue record for this book is available from the British Library.
A catalog record for this book is available from the Library of Congress.

10   9   8   7   6   5   4   3   2   1
18   17   16   15   14   13   12   11   10   09

Printed and bound in Great Britain by
CPI Antony Rowe, Chippenham and Eastbourne

Contents

Figures

Tables

Preface

This book is the outcome of a research project which began when I became a postdoctoral researcher at the School of Governance, Utrecht University, in November 2002. Completing a project and a book over such a period of time owes a lot to the support and encouragement from the people with whom you work. First, I would like to thank Mark Bovens and Deirdre Curtin at the School of Governance for the opportunity that they gave me to develop this research project and carry it out. The stimulating intellectual climate they have created at the School and the sustained organizational support they gave me in doing the project have been invaluable. Without them, this book would not have been written.

While doing the research for this book I received generous help from Frank Baumgartner and Bryan Jones, whose theoretical and methodological work has been an important source of inspiration for this study. Frank Baumgartner visited Utrecht early on in the project to discuss the application of the policy agendas coding scheme to the EU. In spring 2007, I had the privilege of spending four months at Bryan Jones' Center for American Politics and Public Policy (CAPPP) at the University of Washington, Seattle. Chapter 4 is the direct result of that visit, but in a broader sense it provided an important push towards the completion of this book.

In addition, other researchers in the policy agendas network which has developed over the past years have lent their support to my project, answering questions and reading draft texts. I owe special thanks in this regard to Christoffer Green-Pedersen at the University of Aarhus, and John Wilkerson at the University of Washington. For specific questions about the application of the topics coding scheme, I could also rely on the advice from Ashley Watson and Michelle Wolf.

The coding of EU documents that forms the basis of Chapter 4 was carried out by Karin van Boetzelaer and Linda Haans, who worked as student assistants on this project during 2005. Systematic, conscientious and forward-thinking, their work has been crucial for generating a high-quality dataset.

Parts of this book have been presented as papers at conferences and meetings over the years. The comments and suggestions from the participants at those meetings formed important contributions to the evolution of the texts themselves as well as my broader argument about agenda-setting in the EU. Paul 't Hart's encouragement and incisive comments throughout the project have contributed greatly to various chapters and the overall book. In addition, drafts of specific chapters have benefited from the comments by Gerard Breeman, Dirk de Bièvre, Bas de Wit, Andreas Dür, Dian Hoskin, Dave Lowery, William Paterson, Sarah Pralle, Gerald Schneider, Marie-Jeanne Schiffelers, Arco Timmermans, Femke van Esch, Marianne Van de Steeg, Sophie Vanhoonacker, Kutsal Yesilkagit and an anonymous reviewer for Palgrave Macmillan.

Chapter 2, which outlines the theoretical framework underlying this study, is based on my article 'Agenda-Setting in the European Union: A Theoretical Exploration and Agenda for Research', published in the *Journal of European Public Policy* (vol. 14, no. 1, 2007, pp. 21–38). Parts of that article appear in the chapter, although it has been revised, expanded and updated.

I would like to express my gratitude to the people that I interviewed for my case studies. The time they took to answer my questions and discuss their work with me formed an important input into the case study analyses presented here. Without their generous help, this type of research could not be done.

Finally, a special thanks goes to my partner Marieke and our daughter Sara. Marieke has been with me during this whole project. Apart from spending four wonderful months in Seattle together, she has been a constant source of encouragement while writing this book. Nothing quite sets one's personal agenda as becoming a parent. Little Sara gave us this pleasure in April 2008 and we have happily let her dominate our agendas since. Five months old, she is starting to pull books off our bookshelves. Hopefully, one day she will pull out the book her father wrote, then perhaps to read it.

Utrecht, September 2008

1
Studying Policy Agendas in the EU

1.1   The challenge of agenda-setting

'If you want a policy to be adopted, you first have to get decision-makers to talk about it.' This could be a very brief summary of why 'agenda-setting' has become such an important topic in political science and policy studies. Agenda-setting is not concerned with the actual decisions that are taken, but with the issues that decision-makers devote attention to: the issues they talk about, think about, write about and take into consideration.

At first sight, this may seem to be a rather inconsequential activity. After all, why should we be interested in what people talk about if the talk does not lead to policy activities or decisions? However, this is too narrow a concept of what policymaking and politics are about. To begin with, agenda-setting is a necessary condition for decision-making: only if issues are talked about, can they be subject to decision-making. This implies, vice versa, that if an issue does not occur on the agenda, it will not be subject to decision-making. As a result, the agenda is of prime importance for political actors. Those who want to change an existing policy first have to get that issue on the agenda, that is, attract the attention of decision-makers to it. Conversely, those who are happy with the status quo will try to keep the issue off the agenda: that is, prevent decision-makers from talking about it, because no agenda attention for an issue is the best guarantee that the status quo will be maintained. Students of agenda-setting have noticed that the best time to win a political battle is before an issue even appears on the agenda.

In addition, agenda-setting is important because it largely determines the terms in which an issue is discussed. Issues normally reach the agenda in certain terms (cf. Rochefort and Cobb 1994). For example, during the 1990s, protection of personal information reached the agenda of many Western countries because of the threats posed to it by the growth of the Internet and e-commerce (Princen 2002: 277–8, 293). After 11 September 2001 ('9/11'), it also came onto the agenda, but this time as an impediment to effective anti-terrorism policies. In both cases, protection of personal information came onto the agenda because it was seen to be problematic, but the reason why it was seen as such differed greatly. These terms in which the issue was placed onto the agenda initially set the stage for subsequent debates: in the 1990s it was about the expansion of personal information protection, and in the 2000s about relaxing protection. Any political actors opposed to these policy changes face an uphill battle, in which they first have to convince others that the terms of the debate are wrong – not an easy feat once a certain problem definition gains a foothold in policy debates.

Therefore, the form and content of the political agenda are highly relevant for understanding policymaking. In domestic political systems, agenda-setting has received considerable attention in the political science literature. In the US, agenda-setting studies can be traced back to the seminal work by Schattschneider (1960), which was followed by a series of studies on the topic that continues to date (Baumgartner and Jones 1993; Cobb and Elder 1972; Kingdon 2003 [1984]). In other Western countries, studies of agenda-setting are more recent but have become an established part of the literature (Albæk et al. 2004; Baumgartner, Green-Pedersen and Jones 2006; Considine 1998; Green-Pedersen 2007; Soroka 2002).

In the literature on international organizations, by contrast, agenda-setting has remained an understudied subject. For reasons that will be discussed more extensively later in this book, the international relations literature usually fails to distinguish agenda-setting as a separate process and instead has focused on decision-making as one single process. Even in the European Union (EU),[1] which of all international organizations arguably represents the most strongly integrated political system, scholars have devoted most attention to decision-making processes. Only in recent years has agenda-setting arisen as a specific focus in the literature, but then mainly in the form of scholarly articles on specific aspects of agenda-setting, or as part of broader studies of European integration (Harcourt 1998; Peters 1994; 2001; Pollack 1997; 2003; Princen and Rhinard 2006; Tallberg 2003).[2]

Despite the relative scarcity of specific studies on the topic, there is ample reason to assume that agenda-setting processes are relevant in the context of the EU. After all, the EU deals with some issues but not others, and these choices are far from self-evident. Quite the contrary: a whole series of political actors, ranging from member state politicians to private interest groups, try to get the EU to take up some issues or to drop others, testifying to the contested and highly political nature of agenda-setting processes in the EU. Moreover, and partly as a result of all this political activity, the EU shows clear changes in the content of its agenda over time, both in terms of a long-term evolution of its agenda and short-term 'waves' of interest in some issues at the expense of others.

This book seeks to understand these agenda dynamics in the EU. More specifically, it seeks to answer the following question: what determines the content of policy agendas in the EU? Related to this: Why are some issues on the EU agenda and not others? What determines the long-term evolution of the EU agenda? And what determines the short-term dynamics around specific issues?

1.2   Why study EU agenda-setting?

It was argued above that agenda-setting is a crucial part of policymaking processes that merits systematic study in its own right. However, this does not answer the more specific question as to why we need a book on agenda-setting in the EU. The emphasis in this question is twofold: why do we need a book on *agenda-setting* in the EU (when a lot is already known about decision-making in the EU), and why do we need a book about agenda-setting *in the EU* (when we already know quite a bit about agenda-setting in other political systems)? This section will pinpoint more clearly the added value of studying agenda-setting in the EU, and the contributions that this book seeks to make to debates in the literature on the EU. These potential contributions can be divided into three main areas: our understanding of EU policymaking; our understanding of the process of European integration; and normative debates about the EU. Each will be discussed in turn.

1.2.1   Understanding EU policymaking

First, understanding agenda-setting will aid our understanding of EU policymaking more generally. As argued above, struggles over the political agenda are an important element of policymaking processes. Determining which issues are to be considered is no less political than decision-making on given issues. These agenda struggles cannot be understood by looking only at decision-making over issues which have made it onto the agenda; it is equally important to look at the reasons why these issues have made it onto the agenda while others have not. In this way, agenda-setting studies offer an opportunity to study what Bachrach and Baratz (1962) have called the 'second face of power'. The first face of power is the power to influence decision-making on a given issue: this is the kind of power that is the focus of decision-making studies. The second face is the power to keep issues off the agenda: normally, this will not show up in studies of decision-making processes, but it can be studied by analysing the political agenda as a whole and the agenda-setting processes underlying it.

To give a sneak preview into what is to come later in this book: it is interesting to understand why the EU has chosen the specific instrument of a ban on tobacco advertisements to discourage smoking, but an important preliminary question is why the EU has actually chosen to deal with the issue of smoking from among the wide range of possible issues that it could have taken up. In a similar vein, it is equally interesting to understand why the EU has hardly been involved in the regulation of health insurance or health facilities. The answers to these questions are less self-evident than they may seem when we take the existing status quo for granted: understanding exactly why the EU takes up some issues and not others will enhance greatly our understanding of the way that it makes policy. This is the reason why it is useful to study *agenda-setting* in the EU.

In addition, we need a specific study on agenda-setting *in the EU*, because the way in which the EU makes policy differs greatly from what we know from domestic political systems in the Western world. Having begun as an international organization, the EU has evolved gradually into a political system that combines elements of classic diplomacy (bargaining between representatives from different states) and elements of 'domestic' political systems (exemplified by a set of strong institutions at the European level, such as the European Commission, the European Parliament and the European Court of Justice (ECJ)). We will go into the specifics of EU policymaking later in this book, but for now it is important to note that these differences are likely to have an impact on the type of issues that the EU takes up and the processes that lead to the formation of policy agendas. Specifying exactly what these differences are, and how consequential they are for agenda-setting in the EU, is an important objective of this book.

1.2.2   Understanding the process of European integration

In addition to our understanding of EU policymaking, studying agenda-setting in the EU may contribute to our understanding of the process of

European integration. A core interest of EU scholars has been to explain how European integration has developed, and what has driven the integration process. In this endeavour, the concept of 'integration' has been defined in various ways, for example in terms of a shift of 'loyalties, expectations and political activities toward a new centre' (Haas 1968: 16), or as 'the process by which the horizontal and vertical linkages between social, economic, and political actors emerge and evolve' (Stone Sweet and Sandholtz 1997: 304).

In policymaking terms, we may say that the extent of European integration can be equated with the range of issues that the EU deals with, and the way in which it deals with those issues. In other words, the extent of European integration can be equated with the EU's political agenda. Therefore, a decision to deal with a certain issue is not only relevant for the substance of policies but also for the scope of EU activity. By taking up new issues the EU expands its scope, while by dropping issues the scope of activity contracts. Hence, understanding agenda-setting is directly relevant for understanding European integration.

Traditionally, two broad approaches to explaining the process of European integration have dominated. The intergovernmentalist approach has stressed the role of member states in European integration: put simply, it argues that decisions by member states, based on their national interests and the power balance between them, determine the extent and speed of integration as well as the room for manoeuvre for EU institutions. This approach tends to focus on the main episodes of treaty formation in EU history in order to explain the process of European integration (see e.g. Moravcsik 1998). In so doing, it tends to downplay the importance of daily policymaking processes, assuming that the scope for daily policymaking is determined by the parameters set in the EU treaties. However, this assumption is questionable. In a number of fields European integration has developed without any concomitant change in European treaties. Examples include competition policy, where a strong EU regime has been set up on the basis of two concise provisions in the original Treaty of Rome, and market integration, where in the late 1970s the ECJ provided new impetus to the integration process through a number of landmark decisions on mutual recognition of regulatory standards. There is no reason to assume *a priori* that the sum of these daily decisions is less important in understanding the process of European integration than the 'history-making events' of treaty-making.

An alternative approach to European integration, which takes a greater interest in daily policymaking processes, is neo-functionalism.

Neo-functionalists accord a greater role to supranational political actors, such as the European Commission, ECJ and transnational interest groups. Along this line of reasoning, integration in one area will lead to pressures to integrate in another area, a process known as 'spill-over' (Haas 1968: 283ff.; Lindberg 1963: 10–11). For example, stimulating the mobility of workers among member states out of economic considerations may lead to calls for coordinating pension systems or health insurance (since workers otherwise may experience financial problems or problems of coverage when they want to work in another member state). In addition, as the EU becomes involved in a wider range of policy areas, political actors from the member states will focus their political activities and allegiances increasingly on the European rather than member state level (Haas 1968: 13–14; Lindberg 1963: 9–10). This shift in loyalty will create a transnational political elite that in turn will politically strengthen the EU further. In both processes, a special role is played by transnational policy entrepreneurs, such as the European Commission, which will seek actively to promote European integration.

Thus neo-functionalism avoids a narrow focus on episodes of treaty-making in explaining European integration. At the same time, the main weakness of the approach is the rather deterministic logic underlying it: both functional and political spill-overs are supposed to lead to ever-increasing European integration. As a result, neo-functionalism has difficulties accounting for periods of stagnation in European integration, and therefore, the approach in its pure form has lost most of its appeal. Nevertheless, important tenets of neo-functionalism are reflected in later approaches to studying the EU (cf. Rosamond 2000: 97). This is particularly true of neo-functionalism's focus on daily policymaking processes within the EU and the role that it accords to supranational actors in the process of European integration. Studying agenda-setting in the EU may shed new light on this debate by carefully tracing and analysing how issues come onto, or disappear from, the EU agenda, and thereby affect the extent of European integration.

1.2.3   Normative implications

Besides the theoretical interests outlined above, the study of agenda-setting has normative relevance. To begin with, the EU is seen often as biased toward a neo-liberal agenda (e.g. Scharpf 1997; 1999): it is then claimed that its policies are geared primarily to economic interests and much less to 'social' interests. Also, the EU's 'roots' in economic integration would lead it to view issues through an 'economistic' perspective, focusing on market liberalization rather than other social values. Tying in with this claim about the EU's policies, it is often argued that economic interest groups dominate EU decision-making at the expense of public interest groups. Moreover, much has been written in the past decade on the EU's 'democratic deficit'. This deficit arises because of the limits to popular participation and popular representation in EU politics (see e.g. Follesdal and Hix 2006; Mair 2005; Stein 2001). As a result, EU policymakers operate in relative isolation from public opinion and popular demands, leading to the allegation that EU policymaking fails to live up to basic standards of democracy and responsiveness.

To an extent, these are claims about the EU's agenda: they state that it is biased toward economic issues and that it is largely unresponsive to public opinion and popular demands. By systematically studying the EU's political agenda and processes of agenda-setting in the EU, these claims can be critically tested: does the EU indeed have a market-oriented agenda? To what extent does the EU agenda reflect popular demands, or is it driven by the specific interests of policymaking elites? Has this changed over time, and if so, in what direction? Which factors underlie such developments, if they have occurred? In so doing, this study complements existing studies by looking at the output side of the agenda-setting process: that is, at the actual agenda content. After all, one can argue that when it comes to democracy in the EU, the 'proof of the pudding is in the eating'. What matters in terms of agenda biases, democracy and popular representation is how the EU performs in translating citizen demands into policies.

By contrast, most of the existing literature looks at the input side or relies on an analysis of the institutional characteristics of the EU's decision-making process. In analysing the input into policymaking, some studies have surveyed the activities of interest groups and the conditions under which they gain access to the EU institutions (Beyers 2004; Bouwen 2002; Mahoney 2004). Although these studies have given a fascinating insight into the actual relations between political actors in the EU, they ignore the influences on agenda-setting that operate outside of explicit contacts between political actors. Analysing the political agenda as it eventually comes out of the agenda-setting process overcomes this limitation. Other input-oriented studies have looked at social movement activity and political protest (Imig and Tarrow 2001), while others have analysed citizen attitudes towards the EU and voting behaviour in European Parliament elections or in regard to European issues (Franklin 2001; Marks and Steenbergen 2004; Schmitt 2005). These studies also offer important insights into the political context within which EU policymakers operate, but they remain silent on what this eventually means for the EU's policy outputs.

Institutional analyses have highlighted the relatively weak position of the European Parliament in EU decision-making and the fact that elections for the European Parliament do not translate into a governing coalition at EU level (Follesdal and Hix 2006). Other studies have identified gaps in the transparency and accountability arrangements within the EU (Arnull and Wincott 2002; Harlow 2002). Since the existence of certain institutional characteristics is assumed to be a precondition for democratic politics, their absence is seen as proof of current gaps in the EU's democratic credentials (Lord and Beetham 2001). Here, an analysis of EU policy agendas can lead to an empirical assessment of the implications of all this for the responsiveness of EU policymaking.

1.3   Three central themes

The next chapters of this book will provide a detailed analysis of the factors that underlie the agenda-setting dynamics in the EU, and will present a range of data and cases to support this analysis. Running through the analysis are three central themes (or premises) that inform the argument developed in this book.

1.3.1   The EU as an evolving integration scheme and a functioning political system

One of the 'grand debates' in the literature on the EU concerns the nature of the EU as a political entity or, as it is often called, the 'nature of the beast'. Is the EU an evolving economic and political integration scheme, which means it is in the process of being formed but has not reached any stable 'equilibrium' yet? Or is it a functioning political system whose main concerns in many respects parallel those of well-established political systems at the domestic level?

This question is of interest, because the answer to it has important implications for one's focus and assumptions about the way in which EU politics works and should be analysed. If the EU is seen as an evolving integration scheme, the main focus is on the factors that drive European integration forward. The search for these factors dominated much of the EU literature well into the 1980s, structured by the debate between neo-functionalists and intergovernmentalists alluded to above. The other approach, which sees the EU as a functioning political system, leads to quite a different set of questions (cf. Hix 1999: 1) which have become more popular among EU scholars since the late 1980s. In this approach, the focus is no longer on the process of European integration, but on the policymaking and decision-making that take place within the existing EU institutions. The questions that are asked in this approach are largely similar to those traditionally posed in (domestic) policy studies, and relate to the actors and processes through which decisions are taken and implemented.

Even if a debate has been waged on which of these two approaches is most useful for analysing the EU, one can claim that they *both* apply, but to different issues and policy areas. In some policy areas, the EU has become a well-established policymaking institution that almost routinely produces policies and decisions. For these policy areas, the EU can be seen as a 'functioning political system'. However, in other areas, the EU is in the process of establishing a presence and carving out a role for itself. In these areas, the major questions relate to issues of European integration, and the EU is best seen as an evolving integration scheme.

Both types of policy areas coexist in the EU and arguably give rise to different types of agenda dynamics. In evolving areas, the main question is how to get the EU involved in an area in which it was hitherto absent, and in which EU involvement is not (yet) self-evident. Placing an issue on the EU agenda involves placing it on that agenda for the first time. In well-established areas, the main question is how to get an issue that is already part of the EU agenda higher onto that agenda, or how to draw attention to formerly neglected aspects of that issue. EU involvement is (already) more or less self-evident, so the debate becomes one of what exactly the EU should be doing in that area and how it should prioritize its various activities.

This book will analyse both types of agenda dynamics by looking at the process in which new issues are placed onto the EU agenda (in Chapters 5 and 6), and at the process in which existing issues struggle for higher agenda status (in Chapter 7). One of the key aims of the analysis is to find out to what extent these two types of agenda dynamics differ, and to what extent they are in fact similar. Together, they will provide a more comprehensive picture of agenda-setting processes in the EU.

1.3.2   Agenda-setting as a combination of venues and frames

Despite the differences between the two types of agenda dynamics sketched above, and the wide variety in agenda-setting processes in general, the analysis in this book will start from one central theoretical assumption, which is that agenda-setting dynamics can be explained best by looking at the combination of venues (or institutional decision-making arenas) and frames (or issue definitions) that, in turn, determines the participation of actors in decision-making processes. (This assumption builds on studies of agenda-setting in a domestic context and will be discussed in more detail in Chapter 2.)

In its most elementary form, agenda-setting theory stresses that *what* is being talked about depends on *who* is doing the talking. In other words, the agenda (i.e. the range of relevant issues) is determined largely by the scope of participation in a decision-making process (Cobb and Elder 1972: 102–3; Schattschneider 1960: 2ff.). For example, if asked about the most important policy priorities, a group of environmentalists is likely to come up with a different set of issues than a group of industrialists. A collection of Italian parliamentarians will stress a different set of issues than a collection of Swedish parliamentarians, even if some issues may appear on both lists. Therefore, the key to controlling an agenda is to control participation: if you know what issues you want to get high onto the agenda and what positions the various actors take on those issues, you may try to involve those actors in the decision-making process that are supportive of your cause and to exclude others.

The inclusion and exclusion of actors is affected crucially by the institutional decision-making arenas in a political system. These arenas are never neutral as to the actors they include or, in broader terms, the interests to which they are receptive. As Schattschneider's (1960: 71) famous dictum goes, 'organization is the mobilization of bias', and by organizing political decision-making, some interests are 'organized in' while others are 'organized out'. Political systems, and specific political institutions within the same political system, differ as to exactly *which* interests are organized in and out. This can be illustrated by Parrish's (2003) analysis of the rise of sport as a policy issue in the EU. Parrish discerned two leading perspectives on sport in EU policymaking: as an essentially economic activity falling under the EU's internal market; and as a sociocultural phenomenon requiring a specific regulatory regime. Among the EU institutions, the first perspective found a receptive ear at the European Commission's Directorate-General (DG) Competition and the ECJ. By contrast, the second perspective was taken up by the Commission's DG Education and Culture and the European Parliament.

These differences in receptiveness are the result of institutional differences between venues. First, venues differ in terms of the *task* that they are supposed to look after, and they will be interested primarily in issues that are potentially relevant to that task. Second, venues have the *authority* to deal with some issues but not others. For example, DG Competition has the authority to initiate cases against perceived anti-competitive practices. However, it has no authority to regulate the sociocultural aspects of a sector if there is no link with competition, so it would make little sense for it to take up the issue of sport in those terms. Third, venues differ in terms of their *composition*. DG Competition is the domain of economists and competition lawyers, who are knowledge-able and care about competition issues. This makes them more inter-ested in, and receptive to, issues that relate to competition policy. By contrast, DG Education and Culture harbours officials who know and care about cultural issues.

The various EU institutions form what Baumgartner and Jones (1993: 31ff.) have called 'venues' for policymaking: formal decision-making arenas in a political system. Institutional frameworks are important because they define which venues are available and define for each venue: (a) what specific tasks, authority and resources it has; (b) who participates in it; and (c) the procedures according to which it comes to a decision. Political systems are likely to differ on these three points and therefore are likely to differ in their relative receptiveness to issues. The 'trick' for prospective agenda-setters is to get their issue into the 'right' venue.

In the EU, differences between venues are relevant at two levels. First, the EU as a whole differs from member states and other international organizations in terms of its policymaking processes, institutional remit and the actors that it includes. This makes it relatively more receptive to some issues and interests than to others, which affects the types of issues that are likely to end up on the EU agenda. Second, the EU itself consists of different institutions that form alternative venues for dealing with issues: the European Commission is a different venue from the European Parliament and, on an even more disaggregated level, the Commission's DG Enterprise represents a different venue from DG Health and Consumer Protection. As a consequence, agendas differ between those venues. These differences and shifts between venues are important drivers behind agenda dynamics and shifts in the overall EU agenda.

Whether an issue is likely to be taken up in a given venue depends on the way in which that issue is defined: in other words, the 'issue image' or 'issue frame'. Almost any issue can be defined in more than one way, as in the example of the two perspectives on sport regulation given above. Therefore, an important key to understanding why issues come onto an agenda is formed by the process in which issues are defined. This process inevitably involves a choice between different possible definitions, in which some aspects are highlighted at the expense of others. So, what we can observe is a process with two sides to the equation. On one side, political actors actively seek to 'sell' their issues to decision-making venues by framing them in certain terms. On the other side, decision-making venues are more receptive to some issues than to others (and sometimes are even actively looking for issues themselves). If and when the two sides 'fit', an issue has a good chance of making it onto the agenda – otherwise, it does not.

Together, the two elements of venues and images form a clear and elegant framework for understanding agenda-setting processes. At the same time, they are formulated at a rather abstract level that applies to a wide range of situations and political systems, without pinpointing specifically what it is about venues and images that makes for certain agenda-setting processes. Therefore, an important task of this book is to specify more precisely the conditions under which issues are likely to come onto, or fall off, the EU agenda. In so doing, an important additional task is to specify how exactly agenda-setting processes in the EU differ from those in other political systems, where the general theoretical framework was developed.

1.3.3   The EU as one among a series of linked arenas

So far, this chapter has spoken of the EU as an isolated political institution within which agenda-setting processes take place. In the end, the focus of this study is on explaining the EU's agenda and not that of other institutions. However, if we want to understand why issues come onto the EU's agenda, we should be careful not to narrow the scope of our investigation to EU institutions alone. EU policymaking is closely linked to policymaking processes in EU member states and other international organizations, whereby these other international organizations include both regional organizations within Europe and those that operate on a global level. As a result, often the occurrence or rise of an issue on the EU agenda can be understood only by looking at developments elsewhere, in venues outside formal EU institutions.

The history of European integration shows many examples of issues and even whole policy areas that were developed outside the EU to be 'imported' onto the EU agenda later. The EU's policies in the area of 'justice and home affairs', for example, were developed in separate initiatives outside the formal EU framework and subsequently incorporated into the EU Treaties. This is the case for the Trevi group, which was created in 1975 to develop joint policies for combating terrorism and cross-border crime and laid the groundwork for the creation of the EU's 'justice and home affairs pillar' in the Maastricht Treaty of 1992. Another example is the Schengen Agreement, a treaty from 1985 which abolished restrictions on travel between a limited number of member states and was incorporated into the Amsterdam Treaty of 1997. To take an example from an entirely different field, the 'Bologna process' of harmonizing the organization and structure of higher education in Europe has been developed outside formal EU institutions. At the same time it has clear links with the EU agenda in a stricter sense, if only because the European Commission plays a facilitating role in the process.

Agenda issues may derive also from the work of other formal international organizations. Rhinard (2002: 78) showed that officials from the European Commission's DG Environment 'used' the Organisation for Economic Cooperation and Development (OECD) in order to build up expertise and ideas for the regulation of genetically modified organisms in the EU. Dostal (2004) argued that the OECD has played a similar role in the field of social policy. For issues related to human rights, the Council of Europe often has played a frontrunner's role vis-à-vis the EU.

The role of other international venues is not limited to the rise of new issues on the EU agenda. In many issue areas, policymaking on 'going concerns' takes place in several venues at the same time. Consider, for example, trade policy, which is dealt with simultaneously in the World Trade Organization (WTO), the OECD and the EU (as one of the world's leading trade blocs). European security issues are dealt with by the United Nations, NATO, the Organization for Security and Co-operation in Europe (OSCE) and the EU. Intellectual property rights are the subject of regulation within WTO, the World Intellectual Property Organization (WIPO) and the EU. Hence, the EU is part of a dense web of international institutions that influence each other (see more generally Oberthür and Gehring 2006). The reason why issues are developed outside the EU to be imported subsequently onto the EU agenda is closely linked with the above discussion of venues and images. Each international organization represents a different venue, with specific characteristics that make it more receptive to some issues and images than to others. As a result, it may be easier to get an issue on the agenda of another organization first, then to use the outcomes in that other organization in the process of agenda-setting in the EU. The OECD, for example, is an organization that focuses mainly on the development of non-binding best practice in expertise-driven consultative processes. This makes it perfectly suited for building consensus on issues before they enter the more contested arena of EU decision-making (cf. Princen 2006).

Similar dynamics are at play in the relationship between the EU and its member states. For the advocates of a certain issue, the EU may offer a new potential venue to promote their preferred policy and therefore they have a choice between working at the domestic level or at EU level (or doing both simultaneously). Whether they will attempt to bring an issue to EU level depends to a great extent on the prospects of success: that is, on the relative receptiveness of the EU to an issue compared to their domestic political system. To give an example, during the 1970s women's groups turned to the EU as a venue to develop policies for the equal treatment of men and women in the workplace. In most EU member states, attempts to bring this issue onto the agenda had been hampered by pre-existing policy arrangements and vested interests that militated against government activity in this field. At the EU level, by contrast, these political impediments were much weaker and EU institutions even welcomed the opportunity to play a role in this new policy area. EU legislation and policy initiatives in this field subsequently led to the inclusion of gender equality in domestic policy agendas and provided an important impetus for action in the EU member states themselves (Mazey 1998). Hence, the choice by women's groups to bring this issue to EU level was a result of the greater receptiveness of the EU to their cause compared to their national governments. Conversely, the reason why an issue does not come onto the EU agenda may be that venues in the member states themselves offer better opportunities for addressing them.

Apart from these either/or choices between the EU and member states, it is not uncommon for issues to be taken up at various levels at the same time. Take the issue of obesity – the health problems caused by overweight – which has gained prominence on health agendas since the early 2000s. In February 2005 it became the subject of a national action plan in Spain (Government of Spain 2005), to mention only one of many countries which have addressed the issue. The European Commission published a Green Paper on obesity in December 2005 (European Commission 2005c), while in May 2004 the World Health Organization (WHO) adopted a 'Global Strategy on Diet, Physical Activity and Health' which focused on obesity (WHO 2004b). Thus the issue arose at the national, European and global levels at the same time. The reason for this is that different venues complement each other in terms of what they can do and in the specific aspects of issues which they are most receptive to, and that debates at one venue tend to input into or strengthen the debates at other venues.

As a result, the specific agenda dynamics going on at EU level cannot be understood in isolation from what is happening within EU member states and other international organizations. The links between processes within the EU and processes within other venues are a recurrent theme in this book, in particular in the case studies of Chapters 5 to 7. This allows us both to understand where issues came from in those specific cases, and to specify more clearly what differentiates the EU from other international venues in terms of agenda-setting dynamics and the factors that affect those dynamics.

1.4　The main argument

The main argument to be developed and presented in this book specifies the conditions under which issues will rise on the EU's political agenda. In so doing, it distinguishes between three types of agendas, only two of which can be said to be truly EU agendas. The rise of issues on the EU agenda proceeds through each of these three types of agenda, and the conditions for successful agenda-setting are different for each one.

To begin with, issues become the subject of debate in transnational policy networks. These networks consist of policy experts from domestic governments and international organizations, as well as academics and journalists. For an issue to rise within these networks, two conditions have to be met. First, there has to be a certain convergence of policy debates among the participants in these networks. For practical purposes, this often means that there has to be a degree of convergence in domestic policy debates. Second, there needs to be a strong network within which members of the policy network can exchange ideas. These policy networks are often broader than the EU member states *per se*, and may include members from European non-member states and from other Western countries, such as Canada and the US. Members of a policy network read the same publications and meet each other at conferences and other occasions. As a result, they may develop shared perspectives on what the important issues are and the policy options to tackle them. When this happens, the issue can be said to be on an international policy agenda, but it is not yet on any EU agenda. However, being discussed in transnational policy networks forms an important precondition for this to happen.

In the next step, an issue may move from the agenda of transnational policy networks to the EU agenda. This occurs when EU policymakers are receptive to the issue and the terms in which it is discussed in the transnational policy network. Whether this will happen depends crucially on the institutional characteristics of (venues within) the EU, and the way in which the issue is framed. If these elements 'match', EU policymakers will pick up the issue and initiate a policy debate within the EU proper. In so doing, EU policymakers need not only be passive 'recipients' of issues that are brought up by other political actors; EU officials (most prominently within the European Commission) can take the initiative themselves, stimulating EU-wide debates and initiating policy proposals. Finally, issues can enter the EU agenda through the activities of other international organizations in which the issue is developed first.

At this point, the issue has reached that part of the EU's political agenda where ideas are floated and perspectives developed. Following John Kingdon (2003 [1984]: 4), we may call this the EU's 'governmental agenda', which can be distinguished from the set of issues that are considered for active decision-making, the EU's 'decision agenda'. For an issue to move from the governmental to the decision agenda, the issue has to overcome two types of potential blockades. The first type occurs when competing policymakers within the EU challenge the substance of the proposals put forward by proponents of the issue, and thus are able to keep it off the decision agenda. This type of blockade we may call a 'horizontal blockade'. The second type is in a way more fundamental and occurs when member state governments are reluctant to allow the EU to play a role on the issue. Then, the agenda struggle revolves around the more principled issue of what the appropriate role is for the EU, quite apart from any considerations on the substance of the issue. This can be called a 'vertical blockade'.

Issues differ in the extent to which they are likely to move from one type of agenda to the other. As a result, as will be shown in Chapter 4, the EU agenda is structured differently in different policy areas. Moreover, as Chapters 5 to 7 will show, the strategies that political actors employ, and the success of these strategies, vary depending on the type of issue and the type of 'blockade' to which the issue gives rise.

1.5   Plan of this book

This book is divided into eight chapters. After this introductory chapter, Chapter 2 continues with a discussion of theoretical approaches toward agenda-setting. It defines more precisely what is meant by the concept of 'agenda' and reviews the existing literature on both agenda-setting in domestic contexts and EU policymaking, in order to formulate the theoretical framework that will guide the further exploration of EU agenda-setting dynamics. Chapter 3 turns to the methodological aspects of studying agenda-setting. It explains and justifies the combination of quantitative and qualitative methods that is used in this book, as well as the more specific choices made within those methods.

The next four chapters focus on the empirical analysis of agenda-setting processes in the EU. Chapter 4 presents a quantitative analysis of the development of the EU agenda over time in two issue areas: environmental policy and health policy. It compares the EU agenda with the agenda of the US federal government in these two areas, and links these outcomes with the institutional characteristics of, and developments in, the EU.

Chapters 5 and 6 take a look at the micro-level dynamics of 'agenda expansion', or the entrance of new issues to the EU agenda. They discuss the processes and strategies that underlie concrete attempts at placing a new issue on the EU agenda. Chapter 5 does so by analysing two issues in the field of public health that political actors have tried to place on the EU agenda, albeit with varying degrees of success: smoking policy and alcoholism policy. By analysing these cases, more insight will be gained into the strategies used during agenda-setting processes and the conditions under which they are successful.

Chapter 6 delves further into the limits to agenda expansion in the EU by tracing the fate of another issue which has attracted attention in recent years: health care organization and financing. Although the European Commission has attempted to carve out a role for the EU (and itself) in this area, member state governments have been reluctant to cede authority. As a result, the issue has remained largely confined to the EU's governmental agenda and has not made it onto the its decision agenda. This allows us to specify further what the limits are to agenda-setting in the EU.

Chapter 7 goes on to discuss agenda-setting around recurring policy issues. It turns to the micro-level again by analysing agenda dynamics around a typically recurring issue: fisheries policy. The crucial debate in this area in the past 10 to 15 years has been the attempt to shift the focus of attention toward the environmental and conservation aspects of fisheries. In unravelling the attempts to do so, this chapter will shed more light on the agenda struggles surrounding recurring issues and the conditions under which such issues are likely to rise on the EU agenda.

Finally, Chapter 8 returns to some of the broader questions that were introduced above. It begins by reviewing the conclusions that can be drawn from the empirical analysis; the remainder of the chapter is devoted to sketching the implications of these conclusions for the debates introduced in section 1.2. First, it formulates a number of lessons for the study of EU policymaking more generally. Second, it discusses the relevance of studying agenda-setting for our understanding of European integration processes. Finally, it returns to the normative questions on agenda biases and democracy in the EU raised above. In so doing, it hopes not just to contribute to the substance of these debates, but also to prove the benefits of adopting an agenda-setting perspective in studying the EU.

2
Understanding Agenda-Setting Dynamics

The introductory chapter sketched the outlines of this book and its main arguments about agenda-setting. This chapter will clarify the concepts used in analysing agenda-setting processes and develop a framework for understanding agenda-setting in the EU, which will structure the empirical analysis in later chapters. Since the definition of 'agenda' is central to any attempt at explaining what shapes it, first the concept of agenda itself will be discussed: what is an agenda, and what types of agenda can be discerned? Because agendas comprise issues, this chapter then turns to the concept of 'issue': what is an issue, and where does it come from? Having clarified the conceptual foundations of agenda-setting theories, the chapter will discuss the factors that cause issues to rise and fall on agendas. As the literature on agenda-setting in the EU (or international politics in general) is very limited, it will start from models of agenda-setting which have been developed in the context of domestic political systems. Finally, it will apply the insights from these theories to the EU, taking into account the specific characteristics of EU policymaking.

2.1 What are policy agendas?

2.1.1 Agendas and attention

An agenda is usually defined as the set of issues that receive serious consideration in a political system (Cobb and Elder 1972: 86; Kingdon 2003 [1984]: 3). Let us take a further look at some of the main elements in this definition. To begin with the 'serious consideration' part, agendas are about the *attention* given to issues. The existence of agendas is the result of a simple fact of life: people cannot attend to an infinite number of things at the same time; in fact, they only can attend to quite a limited number of things at the same time because their time, energy, expertise and attention spans are limited. In studies of public opinion, for example, it was found that normally no more than five to seven issues are considered to be prominent problems in public opinion polls at the same time. Therefore, the number of problems that 'the public' consider to be important is limited and, as further research showed, it is also remarkably stable over time (McCombs and Zhu 1995). This means that for any new issue to rise in public attention, another issue has to fall (see also Hilgartner and Bosk 1988: 58–61; Zhu 1992).

The same is true for institutions, such as parliaments or government bureaucracies. Although such institutions can process vastly more issues than any single individual could, they still have to deal with limits in time and manpower. Moreover, the most important issues in any political institution typically have to go through a limited number of persons (Kingdon 2003 [1984]: 184ff.). For example, each proposal by the European Commission has to go through the responsible commissioner and then the full college of commissioners. Similarly, all decisions that require approval by the Council of Ministers have to be scheduled to go through a Council meeting at some point. As a result, the potential number of top issues at any given point in time is severely limited.

There are several ways to reduce the burden of agenda items in these bottlenecks in the political system. This is illustrated well by the way in which the Council of Ministers works. Although formally the Council of Ministers is a single institution of the EU, in practice it consists of a range of 'configurations' depending on the issue at stake. So, if a decision needs to be taken on agricultural subsidies, this is done in the 'Agricultural Council of Ministers', which comprises all member state ministers of agriculture. If, by contrast, the issue is monetary policy, it will be debated and decided upon in the Economic and Financial Affairs Council (also known as 'ECOFIN'). Officially, there are a total of nine Council configurations, but within each of these the actual participants may vary further, depending on the specific issue at hand.

As another way of easing the burden on the Council's agenda, all Council decisions are prepared in a meeting of the permanent representatives of each EU member state, the Committee of Permanent Representatives (COREPER). The decisions in COREPER, in turn, are prepared in literally hundreds of more specialized Council working groups, which include civil servants that specialize in a specific subject from the member states. If a proposal is agreed upon in a lower-level meeting, it is not discussed at the higher-level meeting. As a result, only about 15 per cent of all items on the Council of Ministers' agenda are debated by the ministers. The other 85 per cent have been agreed upon already in COREPER and/or the relevant Council working group, so they can be adopted without discussion in the Council of Ministers (Hayes-Renshaw and Wallace 2006: 77).

Similar ways of delegating actual decision-making to meetings at lower levels also exist in the European Parliament and the European Commission. Such organizational arrangements vastly expand the scope of agendas in those institutions, because people need not occupy themselves with all issues that are discussed or all decisions that are taken within a given time period. Nevertheless, even though the number of issues that are processed can be expanded, it will never be infinite, and this is especially true of the truly 'big issues' that require attention from the top institutions in the political system (cf. Talbert and Potoski 2002).

An important implication of thinking about agendas in terms of attention is that agenda-setting is a matter of degree, rather than a matter of simply being 'on' or 'off' the agenda. Therefore, much of the political struggle around agenda-setting is concerned with moving issues higher up the agenda or pushing them down (cf. Tallberg 2003: 5). Still, the terms 'on' and 'off' the agenda are used to denote the distinction between those issues that receive 'considerable' or 'serious' attention, and those that receive only little or token attention (cf. Cobb and Elder 1972: 87).

2.1.2 Types of agendas

An agenda was defined above as attention being given 'in a political system'. This raises the question of *who* exactly is giving this attention in the political system, and the answer has been the basis for discerning different types of agendas. At the most general level, the literature distinguishes between three different types of agendas. The 'political' or 'formal' agenda is the set of issues that are seriously considered by decision-makers. The 'public' or 'systemic' agenda consists of issues that are seriously considered by 'the public' (as in the research on public opinion polls cited above). Finally, the 'media agenda' refers to issues that are covered in the media. Each of these agendas has been the subject of extensive study. Moreover, since they need not completely overlap, an important theoretical concern in the agenda-setting litera-ture is whether and how these types of agenda influence each other (cf. Soroka 2002). If we are interested in understanding policymaking (as we are in this book), the type of agenda that is ultimately most relevant is the political agenda, because it contains the issues on which policy will actually be made. Hence, throughout this book there will be a focus on the EU's *political* or *policy* agenda and what determines the relative attention given to issues in the EU's decision-making institutions.

The choice of political agendas leads us to a further level of differentiation between agendas, because the question then becomes: *who within government* is paying attention to issues? For example, we may expect each of the EU's main policymaking institutions (Commission, European Parliament and Council) to have its own agenda, which may not be identical to that of the other institutions. Moreover, even within the institutions there may be further differentiation by specialized agendas that are restricted to the specifics of a given policy area. For example, the agenda of the European Commission's Directorate-General for Transport (DG Transport) is likely to be different from that of DG Environment.

A more analytical distinction can be made between agendas that are closer to, or more remote from, actual decision-making. Kingdon (2003 [1984]: 4) distinguished a broader 'governmental agenda' of issues that are discussed by policymakers in a given period of time from a narrower 'decision agenda' of issues that are up for active decision-making. This distinction is relevant, because the mechanisms that lead issues onto the governmental agenda may be different from those that lead them onto the decision agenda.

2.1.3   Agendas and issues

Having discussed the concepts of 'attention' and 'political system', one element in the definition of 'agenda' remains: the 'issues' that make up that agenda. An 'issue' can be defined as 'a conflict between two or more identifiable groups over procedural or substantive matters relating to the distribution of positions or resources' (Cobb and Elder 1972: 82). The key definitional move here is the identification of 'issues' with 'conflict'. In day-to-day parlance, issues are identified often in terms of topics, such as 'crime', 'unemployment' or 'the greenhouse effect'. However, politically speaking, these topics only become issues when political actors have different ideas about what should be done about them. Therefore, issue definition involves the identification of dimensions on which there is conflict between political actors, thus agenda-setting may concern both the identification of conflicts over new topics, and the creation of new conflicts over old topics. Given the centrality of issues for the formation of agendas, an important question is: where do these issues come from? The next section will turn to this question.

2.2 Two perspectives on issue formation

An issue was defined above as a conflict over a stake. These conflicts are the stuff that politics are made of, no matter whether we are talking about the Arab–Israeli conflict in the Middle East, debates on social insurance reform in Western welfare states, or the siting of a new road in local politics. Since agendas consist of issues, an important question is: where do these issues come from? Or: why do political actors define something as a political issue?

Following a distinction made by Mansbach and Vasquez (1981: 87ff.), two sources of issues on international agendas can be discerned: the international environment, and the actors themselves. The international environment creates agenda issues when international actors are confronted with threats or opportunities 'occasioned by factors not directly associated with the behaviour of actors' (Ibid.: 88). In addition to these external sources of agenda issues, actors may create them purposefully by 'creat[ing] a new stake, reviv[ing] an old one, or alter[ing] the values ascribed to an existing stake' (Ibid.: 90).

These two 'sources' of issues conform to two perspectives on agenda-setting. The first approach sees issues as arising from the international environment in which states operate. In this approach, issues are external to the political process in the sense that they are determined outside of that process. This approach has dominated the international relations literature, which explains why agenda-setting is analysed rarely as a separate process. The second approach sees issues as arising from the interests and activities of political actors. Political issues are internal to the political process because the struggle over agendas is integral to the policymaking process itself. This approach borrows from work on domestic and comparative policy studies, which takes the political nature of issue formation as a given. This section will explain in more detail what each approach entails, what their strengths and weaknesses are, and why an approach that looks at the political construction of issues offers a better basis for understanding agenda-setting in the EU than one which assumes that issues are determined outside of the political process.

2.2.1 Issue formation as external to the political process

As previously mentioned, international relations scholars have traditionally tended to see the formation of issues as external to the political process. This can be illustrated by looking at two approaches which have long dominated the international relations literature: neo-realism and international regime theory.

Neo-realist thinking begins from the assumption that the international system is decentralized and anarchic: that is, there is no central authority which can formulate and enforce binding rules, so states can rely only on their own activities. Given the anarchic system, which does not curtail the use of force by any one state, states have to worry above all about their survival. Survival is an overriding concern because if a state is conquered or becomes dependent on another state, all other forms of policy become impossible. The implication of this is that there is a clear hierarchy of issues, with security on top (Waltz 1979: 88–93). This hierarchy is not the outcome of political choices by individual states, but is dictated by (the structure of) the international system: because it is decentralized and anarchic, states have no choice but to accord highest priority to security issues in their dealings with other states. Other issues, such as environmental protection or human rights, may be topics of international debate and decision-making, but only insofar as geopolitical concerns leave room for them. Therefore, the distinction between 'high politics' and 'low politics' is crucial in neo-realist thinking, whereby neo-realist theory focuses exclusively on high politics, leaving aside issues of low politics, because the high politics issues are prior to, or more fundamental than, the low politics issues. In this approach, agenda-setting is not conceptualized as a separate process, since the international system determines the type and hierarchy of issues as well as the outcome of conflict; hence it makes little sense to speak about 'agenda-setting' as a separate process (cf. Keohane and Nye 2001 [1977]: 28).

Neo-realism has great merits as a theory of international conflict and can be used to understand a wide range of phenomena in international politics. However, it is less useful for explaining agenda-setting in the context of the EU, except perhaps for a limited range of issues that relate to fundamental decisions about the process of European integration and security policies. Most of the debate and policymaking within the EU is about much more mundane issues such as market regulation, environmental protection and police cooperation: these are issues that neo-realists typically think of as 'low politics', and outside the scope of the theory. Yet in the EU, these issues arguably make up most of the policymaking activity and deserve an analysis in their own right. Therefore, if we want to understand why these issues arise, we need other theoretical tools.

Another approach, which is able to account for a wider range of issues, can be found in the literature on international regimes. This literature is interested in explaining the conditions under which states will cooperate and what determines the characteristics and success of international regimes, normally defined as the 'principles, norms, rules, and decision-making procedures around which actor expectations converge in a given issue-area' (Krasner 1982: 185). The EU, or distinct clusters of EU policy, can be seen clearly as 'international regimes' in this sense. International regime theory has been applied to a wide range of issue areas from security issues to environmental politics. Also, it does not assume a fixed hierarchy between issues or issue areas. At a given point in time, one issue may be more important for states than others, but which issue does may vary over time.

An important part of the literature on international regimes adopts a functionalist perspective on international cooperation (e.g. Abbott and Snidal 2001: 346 ff.; Keohane 1984: 80–3; Krasner 1982: 191–2; Young 1999: 24–5). This perspective asserts that international cooperation will arise in response to international collective action problems. These problems are twofold. On the one hand, countries may seek to coordinate policies in order to reap economies of scale. The clearest example of this type of international action is technical standardization: if all countries use the same technical standards for, say, telecommunications, communication across borders will be facilitated. On the other hand, countries face problems arising from cross-border externalities. When activities in one country affect another country (be it negatively, as in environmental pollution, or positively, as in the provision of public goods), countries have an incentive to come to joint solutions. Examples include pollution of rivers that cross borders, or the management of fish stocks in international waters (see Abbott and Snidal 2001 for a more detailed typology).

Thus, this type of explanation of international cooperation states that the level of policymaking is determined by the scope of the problems to be addressed, and therefore would predict that EU policies arise in response to European (or at least supranational) problems. Certainly, this literature does not claim that international collective action problems automatically lead to international policies, let alone effective international policies. In fact, much of the literature on international regimes is devoted to fleshing out the conditions under which states are able to overcome international collective action problems. For example, in his classic study on international economic regimes, Robert Keohane (1984: 80–3) explicitly used functionalist arguments to explain the existence of international regimes, but also offered a careful discussion of the conditions that need to be met in order for states to reap potential joint benefits.

At the same time, functionalist explanations do assume that international policies will *not* arise if there is no international collective action problem. Therefore, a functionalist approach may be better suited to explaining why issues are being considered in the international arena than whether or not states reach agreement on those issues. In other words, functionalist explanations relate more to agenda-setting than to decision-making on actual policies, even if the regime literature itself does not make an explicit distinction between agenda-setting and decision-making.

Functionalist explanations of agenda-setting are similar to neo-realist explanations in the sense that both see issues as emanating from the environment of actors. It is not so much the political process among actors that defines issues, but that issues present themselves to those actors. Explanations based on cross-border externalities and international collective action problems provide an elegant approach to international agenda-setting that is able to explain a range of international policies. Also, they can account for a wider range of policies than the high politics in which neo-realists are interested. Still, they suffer from three important problems. First, they tend to present international collective action problems as pre-given or pre-defined, thereby ignoring the contested nature of what constitutes an 'international collective action problem' and the political process that leads to the identification of these problems. Second, they may explain why issues are 'on' or 'off' the international agenda, but they have more difficulties accounting for the rise and fall of issues on that agenda – in particular when the changes in agenda status are not linked directly to the 'objective' severity of problems. Third, they fail to explain why the international agenda contains issues that do not present clear cross-border externalities. There are many examples of issues on the EU agenda that are not clearly linked to cross-border externalities such as human rights, working time, occupational health and safety and the fight against smoking and non-contagious diseases. If we want to understand why these issues come onto the EU agenda, we need to look beyond external factors and delve into the process in which issues are defined and selected for decision-making. That is, we have to study issue formation as internal to the political process.

2.2.2   Issue formation as internal to the political process

The rise of seemingly 'domestic' issues on international agendas has been explained with reference to the political activism of domestic groups and officials that turn to the European level in order to achieve political objectives that they cannot achieve 'at home'. As Keohane and Nye (2001 [1977]: 28) observed in their work on 'complex inter-dependence', '[d]iscontented domestic groups will politicize issues and force more issues once considered domestic onto the interstate agenda'. International organizations, including the EU, then simply become alternative loci of decision-making for groups, politicians and civil servants seeking the most favourable place to push for their preferred policies.

These processes have been observed widely in the literature on the EU. Mazey and Richardson (2001) and Richardson (2000) have argued that European interest groups often try to 'Europeanize' an issue if it increases their chances of success. Wendon (1998) has shown how the European Commission has sought actively to create new European ven-ues in order to stimulate the development of European social policies. More generally speaking, the whole multi-level governance literature is predicated on the idea that subnational governments and private actors will turn to the EU in order to bypass their national governments (Bache and Flinders 2004: 2–3; George 2004: 118ff.; Hooghe and Marks 2001: 4, 78). On a similar note, the literature on political contention and political protest has argued that social movements and interest groups will turn to the European level when and insofar as the 'political opportunity structure' at EU level is more favourable than at domestic level (Imig and Tarrow 2001; Marks and McAdam 1996; cf. Princen and Kerremans 2008). Similar processes have been identified at the global level (Botcheva and Martin 2001: 12ff.; Keck and Sikkink 1998).

This is not to say that all issues have an equal chance of making it onto the international agenda. In fact, there are strong institutional and political reasons why issues that are more self-evidently cross-border in nature stand a better chance of reaching the agenda of the EU or other international organizations. However, if we want to understand how these dynamics work, we need to analyse further the process that leads to agenda formation and the reasons why political actors try to move issues onto international agendas.

A systematic treatment of the way in which issues are shifted from one decision-making institution to another can be found in Frank Baumgartner and Bryan Jones' theory of venue shopping, which was developed in the context of US politics. Baumgartner and Jones (1993) argue that fundamental policy change often occurs when actors suc-ceed in shifting debates and decision-making on an issue to new venues which are susceptible to different kinds of arguments than the venue(s) that originally dealt with the issue. They focus on venues within the

US federal government, but a similar argument can be made about the choice between domestic and EU institutions. For example, just as actors may try to shift an issue from the president to the US Congress or from one congressional committee to another, they may seek also to shift an issue from the national to the European (or even global) level in order to have their preferred policy adopted (Guiraudon 2000; Pralle 2003).

Additionally, venue shopping is relevant in relation to different international organizations or institutions within the EU. Actors that want to place an issue onto the international agenda have a choice between a range of venues that typically bring different views to bear on the issue. Chad Damro (2006) illustrated this point nicely in his analysis of the way in which the European Commission DG Competition 'shops' between different alternative venues for developing cooperation agreements in the international enforcement of competition policy, eventually choosing the venue that is most receptive to its perspectives. Adam Sheingate (2000) applied the venue shopping framework to the reform of the EU's agricultural policies, which was set in motion when proponents of reform were able to shift policymaking to venues outside the EU's agricultural community.

Therefore, agenda-setting in the EU and other international organizations can be seen as a combination of 'horizontal' and 'vertical' forms of venue shopping. Baumgartner and Jones' venue shopping theory provides a good starting point for exploring these agenda dynamics further. However, before we do so, we need to be more specific about two questions: what motives do actors have for turning to the international level in order to promote 'domestic' causes, and under what conditions is the EU an attractive venue for their attempts?

2.2.3   Motives for shifting issues to the international level

Political actors may have different motives for moving essentially domestic issues up to a European or international venue. Three different motives for this can be discerned: circumventing domestic constraints, providing a 'level playing field' and missionary zeal. First, political actors may want to internationalize an issue in order to change a domestic status quo. Shifting debates to international venues involves the inclusion of entirely new actors, which may open up the possibility of reaching outcomes that are not feasible at the domestic level. The outcomes of international policymaking then can be transported back into the domestic political system in order to break a deadlock and tilt the political balance towards the political actor's preferred policy option. Keck and Sikkink (1998: 12–13) called this the 'boomerang effect'. In this way, actors can circumvent political constraints that prevent the direct adoption of policies at the domestic level. As an example of this strategy within the EU, Guiraudon (2000) showed how member state immigration officials were able to circumvent domestic courts and rival government departments by partly shifting policymaking on immigration issues to the EU.

Second, providing a level playing field becomes relevant when differences in policies between countries lead to differences in production costs for firms located in those countries. In those cases, governments and firms from a highly regulated member state may seek to 'Europeanize' the regulatory standards of that member state in order to raise the costs for competing firms in other member states, and to protect their own standards (Héritier et al. 1996: 12). A good example of this process were the pleas by the German and French governments for a minimum corporate tax rate throughout the EU, due to their fear that firms would relocate to low-tax countries. Similar considerations, whether openly or as hidden motives, may lie behind the support from governments and firms for EU-wide standards in other fields.

Finally, some groups and officials may want to internationalize a policy out of idealistic or missionary considerations, because they believe that people in other countries would benefit from that policy or, in a stronger form, because they believe that those policies represent universal rights that people should enjoy, regardless of their nationality. The latter, rights-based motive is particularly strong when it comes to the international protection of human rights (cf. Keck and Sikkink 1998) and related issues such as workers' rights (Langille 1997), or the position of women (Joachim 2003). As David Vogel (1995: 197ff.) has pointed out, this motive was behind attempts by Non-Governmental Organizations (NGOs) to stop the export of dangerous chemicals to developing countries, while Ethan Nadelmann (1990) analysed a range of 'global prohibition regimes', ranging from piracy and counterfeiting of foreign currency to slavery and human trafficking, which evolved largely as a result of 'moral proselytism' and cosmopolitan views on the part of the groups that pushed for them.

In actual cases of European policymaking, it is difficult to distinguish between these motives. Many policies are supported by coalitions of actors who support the same policy but for different reasons (Vogel's 'Baptist-bootlegger' coalitions; see Vogel 1995: 20–2). One and the same actor may even act out of a combination of different motives when pushing for a policy at the European level. Moreover, political actors from member states may be joined in their quest by actors from EU institutions, which have an institutional interest in expanding their competences and the EU's range of activities. In this sense, EU institutions are not just passive venues, waiting for issues and demands from other political actors to come their way, but active players who try to promote issues themselves by taking initiatives and developing policy debates.

2.2.4   The attractiveness of the EU as a policy venue

Although political actors may have various reasons for bringing an issue to the international agenda, they will not necessarily try to bring any issue to the EU's agenda. Whether or not the EU is the most attractive venue for a political actor depends on what the EU can 'do' for the actor. This, in turns, depends on the instruments that the EU has at its disposal. In terms of instruments, the EU is limited mainly to regulatory activities. Its expenditure hovers around 1 per cent of European Gross Domestic Product (GDP), considerably less than government expenditure in each of its member states. In 2002, almost 80 per cent of the EU's budget was spent on just two policy areas, agriculture and regional policy (Nugent 2004: 372). With the exception of these areas, the EU does not have the budgetary means to finance the large-scale provision of public goods; therefore, the budgetary battles that are central to many domestic political systems are absent from most policy areas in the EU.

The EU's regulatory instruments differ widely between and within policy areas. In some areas, the EU can adopt legislation that is binding on its member states. In those cases, the EU has a relatively effective enforcement mechanism which allows the European Commission as well as private parties to put pressure on non-compliant member states (Keohane et al. 2000; Tallberg 2002). Still, the EU has neither its own police force nor, in most policy areas, its own inspection capacity, so member state governments remain crucial for actors seeking to have policies effectively enforced. In other areas, the EU can issue only non-binding guidelines and recommendations, or simply provide a framework for debate and the exchange of ideas.

Although the availability and non-availability of certain instruments has a great impact on the EU's attractiveness for political actors, this should not be taken to imply that binding decisions are always more attractive than non-binding decisions, as this also depends on the objectives of the political actor. If the purpose is to change the status quo, international non-binding standards may have an important agenda-setting function: signalling an international consensus around a given policy can be a valuable outcome to a political actor as a reinforcement of claims for binding decisions made elsewhere.

As a result, the EU may be an attractive venue in principle for a wide range of actors and issues, but all this depends on what the actor wants to achieve and whether the EU can help to achieve that objective. Moreover, apart from the instruments that the EU has at its disposal, it is also important for actors as to whether the EU is receptive to the type of issues and claims that they seek to put forward. This relates to the key to successful agenda-setting: getting decision-makers to pay attention to the issues in which you are interested. It is to the factors that determine this agenda success that we now turn.

2.3   Agenda-setting in domestic politics: Conflict expansion, framing and institutions

The previous section discussed the reasons why political actors bring an issue to the EU agenda (or by extension, the agenda of any international organization). However, this is only one side of the story: an actor may want to place an issue (high) onto the EU agenda, but this does not mean that it will succeed in doing so. The literature on domestic agenda-setting forms a good starting point for identifying potentially relevant factors in this process of placing an issue onto the agenda. Below, it will be argued that the main insights of this literature can be summarized in three key concepts: conflict expansion, issue framing and institutional opportunities and constraints. Subsequently, these three concepts will be applied to the EU, showing how they can be used to explain agenda-setting. In doing so, it will be shown that the insights derived from domestic political systems require modification in order to fit the specific (institutional) characteristics of the EU.

2.3.1   Conflict expansion in domestic agenda processes

In the agenda-setting literature, a central place has been accorded to conflict expansion. When conflicts are confined to only a few participants, some of them may benefit from involving a wider circle, because the balance of support is likely to be different from that among the initial participants. The key to getting an issue high onto the agenda is to expand conflict to increasingly wider circles of participants, from a narrow circle of experts to the 'public at large' (Baumgartner and Jones 1993: 83ff.; Cobb and Elder 1972: 103ff.; Schattschneider 1960: 3). For example, in direct dealings with industry, an environmental group is unlikely to get much done in terms of limiting the use of genetically modified crops. However, by publicizing and politicizing this issue, the environmental group may be able to raise public awareness of and support for its cause, thus forcing the issue higher onto the public agenda. This in turn may induce decision-makers to take up the issue for consideration and, in the end, decision-making.

The process of conflict expansion has been analysed in greater depth by Cobb and Elder, who claim as a general 'rule' of agenda-setting that 'the greater the size of the audience to which an issue can be enlarged, the greater the likelihood that it will attain systemic agenda standing and thus access to a formal agenda' (Cobb and Elder 1972: 110). In this process of expansion, they discern four types of publics that are increasingly more remote from the initial conflict (Ibid.: 105ff.), starting with groups that identify with one of the parties in a political conflict, via groups that are interested in specific issues and groups that are generally informed about and interested in political issues, to 'the general public'. The further we move away from the original conflict, the larger the circle of potential participants, but also the more difficult it becomes to mobilize them.

Take the hypothetical example of a political actor (be it a politician or someone working for an interest group) that wants to draw attention to problems in quality of health care. First, they can address the people who are in charge of developing health care policies: this may be enough to start a discussion on the issue and build momentum for policy change. If it is not, the political actors can try to involve a somewhat wider audience, including academics specializing in health care issues, people in the health care sector and politicians who may be interested in their cause. If this still does not yield sufficient political pressure for the desired policy changes, they can try to mobilize public opinion, for example by claiming that patients risk death because of maltreatment. Initially, they may target an audience of well-educated and politically interested voters (what Cobb and Elder call 'the attentive public'), but eventually they may try to reach out to all potential voters in an attempt to raise the issue to agenda prominence.

As political actors seek to expand conflicts further, they will have to make greater efforts to involve people. In the example above, health care specialists will have an automatic professional interest in the quality of health care, while people with ill friends and family will also be triggered by claims that the quality of health care systems is not up to par. By contrast, for people who are not confronted with health issues in their professional or personal lives, it will be much less self-evident that they should be interested, let alone be actively involved, in a political struggle to reform health care. Therefore, agenda success depends on the degree of conflict expansion necessary to tilt the balance of political forces, and the success at actually mobilizing the people necessary to achieve that level of conflict expansion.

2.3.2 Framing in domestic agenda processes

The key element in conflict expansion is the way in which an issue is defined or 'framed' (Baumgartner and Jones 1993: 25ff.; Kingdon 2003 [1984]: 173; Rochefort and Cobb 1994). By defining and redefining an issue, the line between the proponents and opponents of a proposal may be drawn differently. In his classic study of agenda-setting in the US, Kingdon (2003 [1984]: 173) gave the example of mass transport:

> When a federal program for mass transit was first proposed, it was sold primarily as a straight-forward traffic management tool. If we could get people out of their private automobiles, we could move them about more efficiently, and relieve traffic congestion in the cities, making them more habitable. When the traffic and congestion issues played themselves out in the problem stream, advocates of mass transit looked for the next prominent problem to which to attach their solution. Along came the environmental movement. Since pollution was on everybody's minds, a prominent part of the solution could be mass transit: Get people out of their cars and pollution will be reduced. The environmental movement faded, and what was the next big push? You guessed it: energy. The way to solve the country's energy problem, so reasoned the advocates of mass transit, was to get people out of their cars when commuting.
>
> (Kingdon 2003 [1984]: 173)

Thus, proponents of greater investments in mass transport tried to 'sell' their programmes as solutions to traffic congestion, environmental pollution and energy dependence respectively, depending on the problem that prevailed in political debates at the time. By linking mass transport to issues that were 'popular' at the time, they tried to gain support from actors that cared about those other issues and thereby tilt the balance of support for new initiatives in mass transport.

Conversely, keeping an issue off the agenda can be achieved by linking existing policies to taken-for-granted notions. A good example of this is the widely shared notion in most European countries that the death penalty goes against basic conceptions of human dignity. Another way of achieving the same effect is to link the alternatives of challengers to generally abhorred notions. A clear example of this strategy in the US is the identification of proposals for universal health insurance with the introduction of 'socialized medicine'. In both cases, supporters for changing the status quo have a difficult time finding support for causes that are placed so clearly outside of the political 'mainstream', and serious challenges to the status quo are made extremely difficult.

In terms of the framework laid out by Jones and Baumgartner (2005: 31ff.), the key to issue framing is to highlight some dimensions of an issue and downplay others, even if all of them are relevant in principle. This type of selective issue framing is a ubiquitous characteristic of political processes, since it is difficult for people to consider all sides to an issue at the same time. As a result, they will focus on one side of the issue at the expense of others, and major shifts in issue perception often concern shifts from one dimension to another. Hence, agenda-setting is about giving information that highlights the particular side (or as Jones and Baumgartner call it, 'attribute') of the issue that will make people look favourably upon it.

Whether a reframing strategy is successful depends, first, on whether the link between 'problem' and 'solution' can be made convincingly, and second, on political 'events' that may shift the balance of power in the political system. Examples of such events include a change of government due to elections, and a major crisis or highly publicized external event (a 'focusing event'; Birkland 1998; Kingdon 2003 [1984]: 94–100). Such events may turn the political tide and open up room for the consideration of proposals that were previously out of bounds. Consider, for example, the way in which 9/11 has changed the political debates on crime and privacy protection in many Western countries, opening up room for far greater law enforcement efforts and intrusion in the privacy of individual citizens than were considered appropriate before.

2.3.3   Institutional opportunities and constraints in domestic agenda processes

Besides issue framing, conflict expansion is related to institutional factors. Decision-makers operate within an institutional framework that is more favourable to some interests than to others. In the words of Schattschneider (1960: 71), 'organization is the mobilization of bias'. Some interests have easier access than others, and the institutional set-up of political and governmental institutions makes them more receptive to some types of argument than others. Since 'types of argument' are crucial in agenda-setting, this implies that political and governmental institutions are also more receptive to some issues than to others. As a result, the rise of issues on the political agenda depends on the availability of institutionally favourable conditions within the political system.

The link between framing and institutions is a central part of Baumgartner and Jones' theory of agenda-setting. They argue that an integral part of venue shopping consists of the construction of an 'image' that associates a given policy issue with certain values and symbols. For example, in the field of nuclear energy, opponents succeeded in changing the image of the technology from one of economic progress and cheap energy to one of potential disaster and environmental degradation. In this way, they were able to involve a new set of venues that dealt with environmental protection rather than energy production or economic development, thereby effecting a major policy change (Baumgartner and Jones 1993: 59ff.).

Venues are more receptive to some issues than others because the way in which these venues are set up and operate tends to favour certain participants and viewpoints. Suppose, for example, that environmental groups want to convince decision-makers to ban an industrial substance that they say is dangerous. In this case, environmental agencies or ministries are more likely to be receptive to their arguments than agencies or ministries that are entrusted with economic development. First, environmental agencies have an institutional *task* to look after environmental quality, hence they will be interested in issues that are potentially relevant to that task. Economic development agencies, by contrast, are tasked to promote economic activity. A ban on a certain industrial substances is likely to have a negative impact on such activity, or at best will be neutral to it; in either case, it does not tie in well with what they are supposed to be doing. Second, environmental agencies have the *authority* to deal with these kinds of issues. Even if an economic development agency were to find merit in the environmental groups' arguments, it would make little sense for it to take up that issue: after all, it is not well placed to deal with that particular type of issue. Finally, the *composition* of environmental agencies is likely to be different to that of economic development agencies. Environmental agencies harbour more people who know about environmental issues and, importantly, who care about them. Economic development agencies will be composed of people who are knowledgeable and care about economic issues: as a result, they will be less inclined to take up an environmental quality issue (unless, of course, the environmental groups succeed in convincing them that stricter environmental policies actually would be good for innovation and economic development – but this argument is often difficult to sustain).

2.4   Agenda-setting dynamics in the EU

Summarizing the argument outlined above, agenda-setting can be explained as the interplay between venues and framing that determines the scope of participation in a policy process, and thereby the types of issues and arguments that are likely to be taken up. Figure 2.1 presents this visually.

We may expect similar dynamics to occur in the EU. However, at the same time we need to take into account the specific characteristics of the EU political system and EU policy processes. These specific characteristics relate to each of the three elements of agenda-setting processes discussed above. By combining these general insights with more specific insights on the EU, we arrive at a theoretical understanding of the conditions under which issues will rise on the EU agenda. Moreover, this theoretical understanding enables us to specify how EU agenda-setting processes differ from agenda-setting processes in domestic political systems.

2.4.1   The ambiguities of conflict expansion in the EU

In Cobb and Elder's analysis, conflict expansion is essentially linear: it moves from narrower to wider circles of participants. The 'losing' side in an agenda-setting process has an incentive to expand conflict in an attempt to involve new participants who may tilt the balance of support and opposition. Along this line of reasoning, moving an issue from one level of government to a 'higher' level of government is simply another way of expanding the scope of conflict. Thus, according to Elmer Schattschneider, moving an issue from the state to the federal level in the US is just another way of expanding conflict by involving a wider range of participants, since the size of the public is much larger at the federal rather than state or local level. As he notes, 'one way to restrict the scope of conflict is to localize it, while one way to expand it

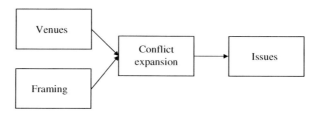

Figure 2.1   A theoretical model of agenda-setting

is to nationalize it' (Schattschneider 1960: 10). As he argues: 'It follows that debates about federalism, local self-government, centralization and decentralization are actually controversies about the scale of conflict' (Ibid.: 11).

However, in the EU, the link between agenda-setting and conflict expansion is far more ambiguous. The idea of conflict expansion as a driving force behind agenda access is linked closely to polities in which direct accountability to 'the public' plays an important role, and in which political actors operate in a somewhat integrated 'public sphere' of debate on political issues. In such polities, involving the public is a viable strategy, since there is 'a public' to begin with, and decision-makers are likely to take account of what this public thinks.

Nevertheless in the EU both the existence of an integrated public sphere and the direct accountability of decision-makers to the public cannot be taken for granted. Even though there is evidence of a convergence of public debates on important issues within the EU (Van de Steeg 2006), it is still very difficult for political actors to appeal to a European public: newspaper and broadcasting systems are firmly national in scope, and the national level remains by far the most important level of reference for European citizens when it comes to political issues. As a result, the member state level dominates the European level as a focal point for citizens' political loyalty and interests. Furthermore, decision-makers at the European level are less directly accountable to (national or European) publics than domestic decision-makers in most democracies. The European Parliament is elected directly, but studies show that these elections remain dominated by national issues (Franklin 2001; Schmitt 2005). Political parties, which are important channels to the political agenda in many member states, are much weaker and less integrated at the European level. The national representatives in the Council of Ministers are indirectly accountable through their domestic parliaments, but European issues tend to be rather unimportant in parliamentary affairs. The Commission is not accountable to any public, or at best only indirectly through the European Parliament's powers to dismiss it.

Therefore, EU decision-makers are much less likely to be vulnerable to public mobilization than domestic decision-makers: this is borne out by several strands of empirical research on the EU. Research on social movements and political protest in the EU has shown that political protest is targeted overwhelmingly at national governments, even when European issues are at stake. This literature explains these findings by referring to the unfavourable 'political opportunity structure' that exists for social movements and political protest at EU level (Imig and Tarrow 2001). Similarly, studies of interest representation have argued that strategies of 'outside lobbying' (public mobilization) are used less often at European level than in EU member states. Interest groups tend to rely on 'inside lobbying' (information exchange and persuasion in direct contact with decision-makers), which again points at the relatively limited role of public mobilization at the European level (Marks and McAdam 1999: 103; but see Beyers 2004 for important qualifications).

As a result, venue shifts to and within the EU result in changes in participation that involve elements of expansion and contraction of conflict. Shifting a new issue to the European level leads to an expansion of conflict in the sense that participants from other countries (seen from the perspective of any one domestic political actor) become involved in an issue. This may lead to a change in the way that an issue is discussed, and thereby to a different agenda priority. For example, for an interest group from a member state with weak environmental policies, shifting an issue to the European level may be favourable because it leads to the involvement of actors from member states with stronger environmental policies. At the same time, the shift to the European level may lead to a contraction of conflict, since public mobilization becomes more difficult and less relevant. For some actors, this contraction may be advantageous, since decision-making at EU level tends to be divided among functional lines. For example, immigration officials from a number of EU member states were able to agree on more stringent policies at EU level than were feasible domestically, because at EU level they could decide among themselves and did not have to deal with other government departments that supported a more liberal approach to immigration (Guiraudon 2000).

Shifts between venues within the EU are more similar to the conflict expansion dynamic in domestic systems. Such shifts take place if an already existing EU policy is placed on the EU agenda again: following the conflict expansion and venue shopping logic, they will include attempts to involve new institutional venues within the EU. Adam Sheingate (2000) analysed these dynamics in the reform of EU agricultural policy. The key to policy reform, according to Sheingate, was to shift the focus away from issues of agricultural production to the 'externalities' produced by those policies: budgetary constraints, environmental degradation and problematic trade relations with the US. By refocusing the problem definition (a good example of reframing an issue), new sets of actors in the EU became interested and involved in agricultural policy, in this case most prominently officials who dealt with trade and external relations (Ibid.: 354–55). This in turn raised the issue on the EU political agenda (and put pressure on the EU's agricultural community to liberalize existing policies).

This process is similar to those found in domestic systems in the sense that it involved a broadening of participation from a single policy community, centred on the European Commission's DG Agriculture and the Agricultural Council, to a wider set of participants that included trade and external affairs officials at the EU and member state levels. At the same time, the process was dissimilar in the sense that public mobilization played a minor role. Even if the circle of participants was expanded, the expansion was characterized by shifts between policy-making elites in different policy areas rather than from policymaking elites to wider circles of 'the public'.

Hence, the general notion that participation is crucial in agenda-setting processes is as valid in the EU as it is in domestic political systems. However, in the EU, the key shifts in participation revolve around shifts between policymaking elites in different areas. If we want to understand EU agenda-setting processes, we have to focus on the framing strategies and the institutional characteristics of venues which characterize such shifts.

2.4.2 Framing of issues in the EU

As argued above, issues and proposals are not pre-given or pre-defined, but their definition is highly contested in political processes. In a way, contestation about what issues are 'really' about can be seen as the essence of political processes (cf. Stone 2002). With the 'constructivist turn' in international relations theory, this also has become a much more accepted proposition in studies of international and European policymaking (see for example Joachim 2003, for the case of international women's rights; Mörth 2003, for the case of European defence policy; and Sell and Prakash 2004, for the international regulation of intellectual property rights).

In the context of the EU, we may expect framing processes to be affected by the EU's specific tasks and remit. For issues that are new at European level, framing processes involve an additional dimension over the dimensions discussed in domestic contexts. In bringing issues to the EU agenda, framing not only involves the nature of problems and solutions, but also the appropriateness of the EU as a level of government. Actors have to argue not only that certain substantive aspects of an issue are more important than others, but also that European action is needed to address them. In short, they have to construct a story about why the issue is European in scope. The arguments used in doing so need not be directly related to the reasons why actors push an issue, but in any case actors need to be able to justify their claims in terms of the 'Europeanness' of the issue. In principle, debates about the appropriate level also may arise in domestic debates, in particular in federal states, but the authority and remit of the EU are much more contested than those of the national government in a well-established federal state. Hence, while the literature on domestic agenda-setting focuses mostly on the framing of substantive policy issues, the EU context also requires an analysis of the framing of scales (cf. Leitner 1997).

Apart from the scale aspects of issue framing, we may expect the EU to favour certain frames over others. The EU's origins and core tasks in the field of market integration between its member states may lead to a greater receptiveness to issues and arguments which can be linked to the reduction of trade barriers and creation of an internal market. In the field of EU health policy, for example, Guignier (2004: 100ff.) argued that the EU favours arguments framed in economic terms, inducing what he calls an 'economicized' approach to issues. Thus, presenting an issue in economic terms, or simply highlighting its relevance for economic development, will increase its chances of being picked up.

2.4.3   Institutional opportunities and constraints in the EU

The discussions above showed how the EU's institutional set-up affects processes of conflict expansion and framing. In addition, agenda-setting in the EU is affected by its combination of many access points and demanding decision-making rules. As Guy Peters (1994; 2001) has noted, the existence of many access points to the EU policymaking process makes it relatively easy to get an issue onto the agenda of at least one participant in that process. There will always be at least one member state, one European Commission Directorate-General, or one party group in parliament that will be receptive to a certain issue. Yet problems arise for any prospective agenda setter when the issue has to spread to a wider range of decision-makers, since there are many of them and the EU's decision-making procedures create a relatively large number of 'veto players' that can block a proposal at some point in the process. In this regard, Peters draws a stark contrast between the ease of gaining agenda access and the difficulty of decision-making and implementation.

However, arguably the EU's demanding decision-making rules also exert an influence on agenda-setting. As mentioned previously, agenda-setting is not merely about getting issues 'on' or 'off' the agenda, but about getting them 'high' or 'low' on the agenda. It may be easy to get *someone* at EU level to consider an issue, but it is more difficult to get an issue *high* onto the political agenda of the EU as a whole. Therefore, successful agenda-setting in the EU requires a considerable degree of consensus among important actors about the need to address the issue, even more so on the EU's 'decision agenda' than on its 'governmental agenda'.

There are several ways in which such a consensus may arise. First, the views of policymakers from different member states may converge around a given approach. Such a convergence can be aided by the strategic framing of issues in ways that make them more attractive to a wider range of actors. In this way, issues can come onto the EU agenda 'from below' (Princen and Rhinard 2006), through the gradual convergence of member state practice and policy around a given approach. Of course, such a convergence need not lead automatically to a place on the EU agenda, but if political actors see benefits in moving an issue to the EU level, the existing consensus will reduce potential opposition to its inclusion on the agenda and make it easier to agree on a common approach.

Second, an issue may affect a wide range of member states, making it more salient for a larger number of actors. This is one reason why issues with cross-border aspects have a better chance of making it onto the EU agenda than issues without clear cross-border aspects. Not only do cross-border effects enhance the legitimacy of EU action and offer a ready argument for the 'Europeanness' of issues, but they also increase the scope of affected actors, and thereby the political salience and palatability for actors, in a wider range of member states.

Third, an external event with transnational repercussions (such as the Chernobyl nuclear accident or 9/11) may focus the attention of policymakers in a range of member states and EU institutions. Even though public mobilization is a much less relevant process at EU level, focusing events can trigger public opinion in several member states, whose governments may then seek EU action in response to the event or simply in order to be 'seen doing something' (cf. Princen and Rhinard 2006 for the impact of 9/11 on EU bioterrorism policy). Moreover, focusing events also may have a direct effect on policymakers because for them, the event may lead to greater visibility of hitherto relatively obscure issues and problems.

Each of these three mechanisms may lead to broader support for EU action, and hence higher agenda status for a given issue. In the absence of these mechanisms, we may expect issues to linger in the lower ranges of the EU's political agenda.

2.5   Factors and processes in EU agenda-setting

A theory of EU agenda-setting has been outlined above that builds on insights from studies on domestic politics, while specifying the ways in which the EU operates differently to domestic polities. Wrapping up the argument, four crucial factors can be identified in explaining the rise of issues on the EU agenda: two of these are related to the reasons why actors raise issues at EU level; the other two relate to the factors that determine their success in doing so.

First, for an issue to come onto the EU agenda, a political actor needs to be sufficiently motivated to challenge the status quo in a given policy field, which can be either an existing EU policy or existing policies in a member state or other international organization. In the latter case, changing EU policy is not the ultimate objective of the agenda-setting effort, but it serves as a means to changing policies elsewhere.

Second, whether or not the EU is an attractive venue for the political actor that wants to challenge the status quo depends on the instruments that the EU has at its disposal in relation to the objectives pursued by the political actor. This follows from the strategic considerations of the actors challenging the status quo: they want to change something, so they will turn to the venue which can help them to achieve that goal. In many cases, binding EU legislation (either in the form of directives or regulations) is the greatest prize to be won at EU level, because it overrides member state law. However, in other cases the EU may be equally useful as a venue for raising the salience of issues, developing alternative approaches, funding studies and building networks of support for policy change. Yet, if the actor is interested in something that the EU cannot deliver (for example, disbursement of unemployment benefits or direct funding of government services), there will be little reason for the actor to invest a lot of time and effort in getting the issue onto the EU agenda.

Third, moving to the factors that determine agenda success, an issue has a greater chance of rising on the EU agenda if those who promote the issue can frame it in ways that appeal to relevant participants in the EU policymaking process. This framing effort involves both a substantive element (explaining why something should be done about the issue) and a scale element (explaining why the EU should be doing something). The more appealing the frame is to a wider range of relevant policymakers, the higher the issue will come onto the EU agenda.

Finally, the success of attempts at agenda-setting and framing depend on the existence of receptive venues at EU level. As previously

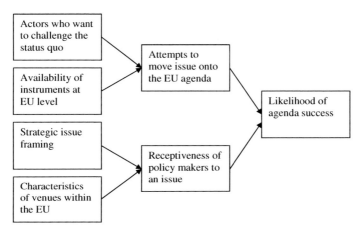

Figure 2.2   Theoretical framework for explaining EU agenda-setting

mentioned, agenda-setting processes in the EU can be seen as a combination of 'vertical' venue-shopping (between venues at different levels of government) and 'horizontal' venue-shopping (between the various institutional venues within the EU). Because every venue is relatively more receptive to some issues and arguments than to others, the existence (or absence) of favourable venues will increase (or decrease) the chances of successfully 'selling' an issue to the EU. In addition, EU policymakers may try to place an issue on the EU agenda themselves, thus playing an active role in the agenda-setting process.

These factors and their interrelationships are summarized in Figure 2.2. On the basis of this framework, and the more specific theoretical insights discussed above, we can turn to an empirical study of EU agenda-setting processes. In so doing, first we need to answer the question: how we can assess empirically the content of agendas and the dynamics of the processes underlying them? This question is the focus of the next chapter.

3
Assessing Agendas and Agenda Dynamics

When studying agenda-setting processes empirically, there are two things that need to be assessed: the content of policy agendas, and the dynamics that produce those agendas. The assessment of both is far from straightforward. This chapter outlines and explains the ways in which both agenda content and agenda dynamics are studied in this book. The next section begins with the choice to focus on two specific policy areas: health and environment. Then, it will discuss the way in which the content of EU policy agendas has been assessed. Finally, it discusses the methods used to study the dynamics underlying the formation of these policy agendas.

3.1 The choice of health and environmental policies

A preliminary choice, which affects all subsequent methodological choices, has been to limit the study to two policy areas: health and environment. Limiting the scope of empirical study is necessary because examining agenda processes in-depth requires a firm grasp of the substantive policy issues and debates in the areas under study. As has become clear from the discussion of framing in Chapter 2, agenda processes revolve around policy debates and the representations of policy issues in those debates. In order to understand these debates and the shifts that occur in the terms in which they are conducted, one needs quite an intimate knowledge of the issue area, prior developments in it and the context within which the debate is waged.

At the same time, policy areas may differ in their specific agenda dynamics. Therefore, the choice was made to compare two policy areas that differ on a number of key characteristics that are relevant to agenda-setting. Environmental policy is a well-established policy area in the EU.

Although a separate legal basis for environmental policy was included first in the European Economic Community (EEC) Treaty by the Single European Act 1986, legislative and policymaking activity in this area goes back to 1973, when the EU adopted its first Environmental Action Plan (cf. Hildebrand 2002; McCormick 2001: 42ff.). In the second half of the 1970s and the first half of the 1980s, a vast array of environmental standards was adopted, making the introduction of the formal legal basis more a codification of existing policy activity than the establishment of a new policy area.

At the moment, EU environmental policy comprises hundreds of regulations, directives and decisions which span almost all types of environmental problems. The role of the EU in environmental policy, and in most specific environmental issues, is no longer controversial. Therefore, environmental policy is a good area in which to study agenda-setting in the EU as a 'functioning political system' (see Chapter 1). This is illustrated by John McCormick's (2001: 63–4) analysis of EU environmental legislation. The number of environmental laws adopted each year between 1958 and 1999 shows a strong rise, particularly in the early 1990s, which is accounted for mainly by amendments to existing laws rather than the adoption of new ones. As a result, the proportion of new laws fell to below 50 per cent in the 1990s, and in some years it was only 20 per cent of all laws adopted (cf. Weale et al. 2000: 61–2; Zito 1999: 28).

By contrast, health policy is a new policy area in the EU (cf. Hervey and McHale 2004: 72ff.; Moon 1999: 148ff.). A legal basis for EU health measures was introduced only in the Maastricht Treaty of 1992, and even then it remained heavily circumscribed. The first Health Action Plan was set out in a Commission communication published in 1993 (European Commission 1993), even if a number of specific health issues had been taken up in earlier decades. The Treaty of Amsterdam of 1996 expanded the formal legal basis for EU health policy somewhat, but even though the provisions on health policy encourage the EU to take initiatives to improve public health, they still explicitly prohibit the harmonization of member state legislation aimed at protecting and improving human health (see Article 152(4)(c) EC Treaty). Therefore, the role of the EU in health policy is much weaker and more contested than it is in environmental policy. Moreover, most of the agenda struggles in health policy are about getting issues onto the EU agenda for the first time. Hence, health policy is a good example of agenda-setting in the EU as an 'evolving integration scheme' (see Chapter 1).

These differences are relevant to the factors that affect agenda-setting processes (as discussed extensively in Chapter 2). In terms of framing, we may expect health issues to require more arguments for EU involvement than environmental issues. This is so for two reasons. First, the EU's legal competencies are much more limited in health policy than in environmental policy, so greater care needs to be taken to construct an argument for EU action. Second, arguably, the EU's expertise and political legitimacy are lower in health policy than in environmental policy, simply because the EU has been involved in the latter area for a longer time. Therefore, we may expect the character of framing processes to differ between the two areas: in environmental policy, it will be focused more on substantive debates, while in health policy it will involve debates about both the substance of policy and the EU as the proper 'level' to deal with them.

Similarly, the institutional venues available for health and environmental policy differ. Institutionally, the European Commission's health policy units used to be part of other policy areas, in particular health and safety at work. Only since 1999 has there been there a separate Directorate-General for Health and Consumer Protection ('DG Sanco') (Guignier 2004: 110–11). Even then, within this directorate-general, health is covered by one directorate while three deal with animal health and food safety issues, and yet another deals with consumer protection. DG Environment, by contrast, has existed as a separate Directorate-General since 1981 (at the time, under the name 'DG XI'), and environment has been a full portfolio for one commissioner since 1989 (McCormick 2001: 52). Currently, it comprises seven directorates dealing with various different environmental issue areas. The same difference is visible in the institutional set-up of the Council of Ministers. Environment alone forms one of the Council's nine official 'configurations', whereas health is part of a Council configuration on 'employment, social policy, health and consumer affairs'.

Thus health policy and environmental policy differ in terms of the tasks, authority and composition of venues (the three aspects of venues discussed in Chapter 2). Therefore, we may expect the receptiveness of EU venues to health and environmental issues to differ, which should have consequences for the content of policy agendas as well as the dynamics and strategies underlying the formation of those agendas. This is not to say that the two policy areas are static or undifferentiated in this regard – quite the contrary. The picture of EU environmental policymaking painted above refers to the situation in the last decade or two. In the early years of EU environmental policy (well into the 1980s), many of the characteristics that now apply to EU health policy, such as a lack of a separate legal basis and a weaker position within the EU institutions, also applied to EU environmental policy (cf. Hildebrand 2002).

Similarly, not all health issues are institutionalized equally weakly at EU level. Some issue areas have a longer pedigree than others. Examples include the regulation of medicines (which is closely linked to the creation of an EU internal market and goes back to the mid-1960s; see Hervey and McHale 2004: 284ff.; Permanand and Mossialos 2005: 50ff.) and the fights against cancer and AIDS (which date back to the mid-1980s). We may expect agenda-setting on these issues to be closer to that on most environmental issues than agenda-setting on newer and less well-established health issues. This variation also allows for valuable comparisons within the field of health policy, which will be argued below in a discussion of the selection of issues for the case studies within the two policy areas.

3.2 Assessing agendas

Since agendas are about the attention given to issues, measuring the content of policy agendas implies measuring the attention given to specific issues at certain points in time or during certain periods. Studies of agenda-setting that focus on one specific issue often use qualitative indicators to determine the 'importance' of that issue: whether important proposals were made on the issue, whether interview respondents said the issue was important, or whether the issue seemed to command a lot of attention in the media and/or political institutions.

This approach is often sufficient to identify whether a given issue has 'come onto the agenda' or not. Ideally, the agenda status of issues should be assessed in relation to other issues: after all, as was stressed in Chapters 1 and 2, the attention for issues is relative to the attention given to other issues. Hence, if we want to assess agendas, we should have a measure of the attention given to some issues in comparison with the attention given to others. One way of doing this is by simply asking a large number of participants in policymaking processes about which issues they think top the agenda at a given point in time. By doing this annually for four consecutive years, Kingdon (2003 [1984]) was able to track waxing and waning attention for specific health and transportation issues in the US in the late 1970s. The advantage of this method is that it taps into the perceptions of people who are involved in the policymaking process about what is important: the perception of policymakers is what agendas are about.

At the same time, this method has a number of disadvantages. First, it is difficult to develop measures of agenda content over longer periods of time using interviews unless one is able to repeat the interviews for 20 or 30 years. As a result, the results from interviews tend to be limited to a few years at most, whereas students of the policy process typically see policy processes evolving over periods of 10 or 20 years or more (Baumgartner and Jones 1993: 39–40; Sabatier and Weible 2007: 192).

Second, interview methods work best when applied in the context of a single policy area. Within these policy areas, participants often have a reasonably good overview of which issues are 'hot' and which are not. Policymaking tends to be organized in terms of different policy areas, and each have their own networks, government institutions, interest groups and experts (cf. Considine 1998: 299–300). As a result, they are the logical frames of reference for those who are involved in policymaking. The flipside to this argument is that policymakers will find it much more difficult to assess the attention given to issues in their area compared to the attention given to issues in other areas. The most knowledgeable observers will be able to identify a number of 'big issues' or indicate how much attention is given to broad issue areas (such as 'unemployment', 'economic development', 'the environment' or 'defence'), but they will find it much more difficult to compare the attention given to specific issues in one policy area with that given to specific issues in another (e.g. water pollution versus gay rights).

Third, the answers that interviewees give to questions about important issues make sense during a specific time period and within a specific political system, yet they are much more difficult to compare over time or between political systems. When asked which issues are important, interviewees will respond in the terminology prevailing at the time. For example, over the past few years participants in EU policymaking might have said that 'the Lisbon Strategy' is important, or 'the Services Directive', or 'the formation of a rapid reaction force'. These are issues that make perfect sense in the EU during this time period, but suppose there was a series of interviews going back to the early 1980s: how would we compare these answers with the answers given then, when no one had heard of the 'Lisbon Strategy', the 'Services Directive' or a 'rapid reaction force'? Without a single unified conceptual framework, comparisons between periods are difficult to make. The same is true if we want to compare policy agendas in the EU with those in, for example, Canada or the US, which each have their 'own' issues with accompanying policy-specific jargon.

An alternative way of assessing agendas is to count how often specific issues occur in policy documents. The assumption underlying this approach is that normally, issues that command more attention will be the subject of more policy documents and/or mentioned more often in those documents. If this is true, then attention can be inferred from policy documents. The most systematic use of this approach has been made in Frank Baumgartner and Bryan Jones' policy agendas project (Baumgartner, Jones and MacLeod 1998; Baumgartner, Jones and Wilkerson 2002). As part of this project, more than 100,000 documents going back to 1945 in US government have been coded. The unifying element in this coding exercise is the topic code, which defines the specific topic that is addressed in a document or statement. Baumgartner and Jones' original coding scheme consists of some 225 subtopics, which are grouped into 19 major topics ranging from health policy to foreign policy, and from employment issues to transportation. In principle, a wide range of documents can be (and have been) used for this type of research, including press releases, parliamentary questions, proposals for legislation, parliamentary hearings, minutes of meetings, speeches by government officials and budgets (see John 2006: 980, for an overview of the various types of documents to which the coding scheme has been applied).

This study has applied the policy agendas topic coding scheme to the EU, using Commission and European Parliament documents. This method has four distinct advantages, the first three of which mirror the disadvantages of the interview methods outlined above. First, coding documents allows us to cover large periods of time and, insofar as documents are available, to do so retrospectively. Second, it is possible to assess the attention given to issues across a wide range of policy areas. For example, if one codes parliamentary questions, the figures tell us something about the relative importance of issues within, but also between, policy areas. Third (and perhaps most importantly for this study), the uniform coding scheme allows a comparison of results between time periods and between political systems. For example, Green-Pedersen and Wilkerson (2006) compared long-term agenda dynamics around health policy in Denmark and the US, using data about US and Danish documents that were coded on the basis of the policy agendas topics coding scheme. In this way, we can gain more insight into how the attention for issues develops over time as well as the issues to which particular political systems devote relatively much or little attention. Finally, using the same topics coding scheme enables an assessment of not only which issues receive a lot of attention, but also those which do not. As stated previously in Chapters 1 and 2, agenda-setting is not only about what comes onto the agenda, but also about what is left out. If we want to know to what extent a political system is biased towards certain types of issues, we need to assess not only the issues that receive attention but those which do not. Using a single coding scheme across different political systems allows us to do so in a systematic way because some specific topics will command less attention in one political system than in another. Of course, the topic coding scheme itself is not universal in the sense that it includes every conceivable issue that could ever come up. However, by using a topics coding scheme developed in the US, we can be sure that it includes all types of issues commonly taken up by modern governments in the Western world. Comparing the EU against this baseline gives a clearer picture of the issues that the EU devotes relatively much and relatively little attention to, respectively. It offers a way around the problem of 'observing events that did not happen', which is central to assessing Schattschneider's 'mobilization of bias' and Bachrach and Baratz's 'nondecision-making'.

However, this is not to say that the method is a panacea. In particular, two crucial assumptions underlying the approach require more careful scrutiny: the assumption that attention is reflected in (numbers of) documents, and the assumption that the application of a single topics scheme allows for comparisons between different times and places. The idea that attention is reflected in official documents is plausible but not self-evident. Kingdon, for example, found no correlation between the number of hearings in US Congress devoted to a certain issue, and the answers of interviewees to the question of which issues were most important. He explained this by pointing out that hearings may be held to satisfy a specific and small constituency or because of routine renewals (Kingdon 2003 [1984]: 243–4). This may apply also to EU documents. For example, members of the European Parliament may ask a question simply to satisfy a constituency back home without really seeking high agenda status for the issue as such. Moreover, counting documents implies that all documents of a certain type are counted as one, whereas it is clear that some documents are much more important in terms of agenda status than others. For instance, the massive 'REACH' proposal to overhaul EU chemicals policy (COM (2003) 644) counts as one document, as does the proposal relating to restrictions on the marketing and use of certain polycyclic aromatic hydrocarbons in extender oils and tyres (COM (2004) 98). Still, most observers would agree that the former commanded more attention among EU policymakers than the latter.

Therefore, we should be careful about using coded documents to make strong claims about the agenda status of specific issues at specific points in time. Nevertheless, coded documents do give an idea of the range of issues that were discussed and developments in that range over time. In that sense, the issues that are the subject of official documents reflect the range of legitimate concerns in a political system, and the ordering of concerns on that agenda. Therefore, this study will use coded documents to trace the development of EU policy agendas over time and in comparison with the US. However, they will not be used as the sole source for making claims about the level of attention for a specific policy issue at a certain point in time.

The second assumption that merits closer attention relates to the use of a single coding scheme to code documents from different eras and political systems. The idea behind this scheme is that it allows for comparisons because the same concepts are used to classify different (types of) documents. In applying the scheme, two issues came up. The first concerns consistency of application: in moving from an abstract coding scheme to concrete coding decisions, coders need to make choices about what to put where. These choices are not always self-evident, because in reality, documents do not always conform to the neat categories developed on paper, and sometimes they can be coded plausibly under more than one heading. If different coders do this differently, the codes that are applied to various documents do not have the same substantive meaning, which is a problem for comparison. These potential problems were dealt with in three ways. First, the coding instructions included not only the definitions of the topic categories but also a set of rules on how to apply the coding scheme. These rules conformed to the coding rules developed for the US coding scheme (cf. Baumgartner, Jones and MacLeod 1998). Moreover, as the documents were coded by two student-assistants, intercoder reliability was ensured by supervising the codes they assigned and by discussing 'hard cases'. Finally, in order to ensure comparability with applications of the coding scheme in other political systems, specific coding issues were discussed with researchers from the US and Denmark, so that consistency in application of the coding scheme could be achieved.

The more fundamental issue regarding the application of the coding scheme concerns the context-specificity of political issues. There is no single, 'objective' definition of political issues that holds for all times and places, and distinctions that make sense in one political system may not make sense in another. For example, in the US, abortion is defined primarily as a legal rights issue (more specifically as a privacy rights issue), whereas in other countries it may be seen as a predominantly medical issue. A coding scheme that is based on single topic codes will not be able to pick up on these differences in definition and shifts in the way that issues are framed.

This concern is justified. However, it is an argument for a careful use of the results of the coding scheme rather than against the coding scheme as such. Four points can be made to substantiate this claim. First, although the coding scheme may run into problems when it comes to studying specific political issues (as in the example of abortion above), this is much less the case when we are interested in overall developments in broader policy areas. Here, too, there may be differences between political systems in where an issue is perceived to 'belong', but there are also many issues which are viewed more or less in the same terms. For example, air pollution is an issue in both the US and the EU, as is the approval of new medicines or tobacco control. So, even if there is scope for debate on certain issues, for many others the coding system provides a good ordering scheme that allows us to compare attention for issues between different countries and/or the EU.

Second, the coding scheme is not as rigid as it may appear. In principle, three types of changes can be made to the topics without disturbing comparability: a subtopic code can be moved from one major code to another; a subtopic code can be divided into more specific subtopics; and two or more subtopics can be combined into one. In all of these cases, the data from one coding scheme easily can be made comparable to those from another scheme by recombining certain categories. In Chapter 4, where the EU data are presented, some of these things will be done in order to allow for the specificities of EU policies without loss of comparability. The only thing that cannot be done is to create a new subtopic that spans only part of a subtopic in another coding scheme, because in that case it is impossible to reconstruct subtopics that are identical in both systems.

Third, some issues may be relevant in one political system but not another. As a result, the subtopics covering these issues will remain empty in the latter. As we will see in Chapter 4, this is the case for a number of specific health subtopics in the context of the EU. However, this is not a methodological problem but an empirical finding; it indicates that those issues receive little or no attention in a given political system. In fact, as mentioned previously, this is the way in which we can discover which issues do *not* receive a lot of attention in the EU, which is a very valuable outcome in the context of a study of agenda-setting.

Fourth, the static nature of the coding scheme makes it most useful in conjunction with other methods that are more sensitive to changes in definition and framing. In Chapter 4, the quantitative data from the coding exercise will be used to analyse the development of the EU agendas in health and environmental issues over time, as well as in comparison with the US. In Chapters 5 to 7, a number of specific issues will be analysed more in-depth in order to unravel the dynamics underlying agenda change. This allows a study of the subtleties of issue definition and issue framing in the EU, which form a useful complement to the overall picture obtained in the quantitative analysis.

3.3 Case studies: Selection and design

The case studies focus on different types of agenda dynamics in the fields of health and environmental policy. In health policy, which was included in this study as a novel and upcoming area of EU policy activity, the main question is how issues first come onto the EU agenda. In environmental policy, the central question is how issues that are already part of EU policymaking become the focus of (renewed) attention.

Let us begin with the health policy cases. Both issues that made it onto the EU agenda and those that did not were selected in these cases. Studying cases that made it onto the agenda serves a clear purpose, since it allows us to study both the factors that facilitated agenda access and the strategies employed by political actors to get the issue onto the agenda. In addition, it makes sense to study the issues that did not make it onto the EU agenda, for two reasons. First, studying instances of 'nonagenda-setting' is worthwhile in its own right, because agenda-setting is both about getting issues onto the agenda and about keeping them off that agenda. Second, cases in which issues did not make it onto the agenda form a useful contrast with cases that did make it onto the agenda. They allow us to compare cases of successful agenda-setting with cases of unsuccessful agenda-setting. This in turn will lead to firmer conclusions about the factors and processes that determine agenda success (cf. King, Keohane and Verba 1994: 129).

Mahoney and Goertz (2004) have formulated a number of criteria for selecting 'negative cases', that is, cases in which a phenomenon of interest did not occur. Stated succinctly, their 'possibility principle' dictates that one should select cases only in which the phenomenon of interest did not occur, but in which it could have occurred in principle. If the occurrence of the phenomenon was impossible from the outset, there is little use studying a negative case because it will not yield any insights beyond the trivial. In operational terms, and in terms of this study, this implies that cases should only be selected if: (1) there are no factors that make agenda access for the issue impossible; and (2) at least one factor that theoretically facilitates agenda access is present (cf. Mahoney and Goertz 2004: 657–8).

Since agenda access is not simply a matter of being 'on' or 'off' the agenda but a matter of receiving relatively much or little attention, three health issues have been selected for study which have attained different degrees of agenda status at the EU level. The first is EU smoking policy, which first came onto the EU agenda in the mid-1980s and has come to occupy a firm position in EU health policymaking: therefore, it is a good example of successful agenda-setting in EU health policy. The second, as a contrasting case, is EU alcoholism policy. This is an issue which arrived on the EU agenda much more recently (in the late 1990s and early 2000s), and whose agenda status has been much more tenuous. At the same time, smoking policy and alcoholism policy offer a number of interesting similarities. Both concern addictive substances which may have negative effects on their users and those around them, but which also can be legally marketed and have been part of European consumption patterns for centuries. Moreover, in both cases, certain member states as well as NGOs have sought actively to include the issue in the EU's policy agenda, but with different results. As a result, the cases of smoking and alcoholism policy allow us to analyse more in-depth the agenda dynamics and political strategies underlying the introduction of novel issues in EU health policy.

The third concerns the organization and financing of health care systems. As we will see in the quantitative analysis of Chapter 4, this is an issue area to which the EU has devoted relatively little attention. Until the late 1990s, there was little (theoretical) reason to expect the EU to deal with this issue, as no political actor actively pushed for its inclusion on the EU agenda and the EU treaties offered very little scope for EU institutions to take it up. However, since then a number of developments have combined to put pressure on this part of the EU health agenda. This has led to a number of initiatives related to the organization and financing of health systems, but arguably the agenda status of the issue has remained quite low. All in all, this case offers the opportunity to study agenda dynamics and strategies in an area that is rather different to the smoking and alcoholism issues.

In environmental policy, where the role of the EU is established much more firmly, the case study is used to analyse the dynamics of agenda-setting around recurring policy issues. One of the best examples of this is fisheries policy, which revolves around an annual policy cycle aimed at producing Total Allowable Catches ('TACs') and quotas for EU fishermen. Despite this regularity, EU fisheries policy has known periods of more fundamental policy debate and reform. This issue area is well-suited for analysing the agenda dynamics around issues that are firmly established at EU level, but which are still subject to debates about the content of policies. Rather than contrasting fisheries with an issue that did not make it onto the agenda, the waxing and waning of attention within one issue area are studied here. Because fisheries policy has seen periods of greater and more fundamental reform as well as periods of routine policymaking and policy stability, it offers the opportunity to analyse processes of rising and falling agenda status over time.

Each of the case studies builds on three sources. First, the relevant policy documents were studied for all four cases, including: Commission proposals, discussion papers and reports, European Parliament debates, Council conclusions and decisions, as well as reports and position papers prepared by interest groups and member state governments involved in the debate. In addition, documents were studied from other international organizations which have been active on these issues, since policy debates and agenda processes often involve a number of international organizations beyond the EU.

Second, the existing literature on these policy issues was examined. Much has been written on the two policy areas of environment and health in the EU (although more so on the environment). This literature offers a rich source of information, insights and analysis that are relevant to the research questions in this book. Older studies offer insights into the policy processes that preceded current policy debates and which are important for understanding those current debates. Moreover, general studies on these issues and issue areas offer an important background to what is happening at EU level.

Finally, a range of interviews was conducted with people who have been involved in each of the issue areas discussed in the case studies. These interviews were held mainly with officials of the European Commission and representatives of interest groups, but also with officials working at the permanent representations of relevant member states and members of European Parliament. In total, 24 people were interviewed (a list of interviews is in Annex 1). The interviews were held between March 2005 and October 2007. Some organizations and people were interviewed twice to review developments in their issue area after the first interview. The interviews were structured via a list of questions that covered recent agenda developments and the roles of various actors in them. They yielded valuable information about the processes and developments 'behind' the official documents, and about the way in which the participants in EU policymaking perceive the factors that determine the access of issues to the EU's political agenda. Where possible, the claims made in interviews were backed up by consulting relevant documentary evidence. Moreover, since the case study analyses stretch back for decades, the interviews could be used only to understand and reconstruct recent developments. Therefore, in the overall research design, the role of the interviews was complementary to, and supportive of, documentary evidence and insights from the secondary literature.

3.4   From methods to empirics

Agenda-setting is a multifaceted subject that raises both quantitative questions (about levels of attention) and qualitative questions (about the terms of debate and agenda processes). This study seeks to capture this range of questions by employing a combination of quantitative and qualitative methods. Having outlined the background, we can proceed with the empirics of agenda-setting in the EU. The next chapter will begin with a quantitative analysis of EU policy agendas over time and in comparison with the US. This will yield a number of preliminary conclusions that will be explored further in the case studies of Chapters 5, 6 and 7. Together, then, these methods will yield a variegated and better grounded understanding of agenda dynamics in the EU.

4
The Evolution of EU Policy Agendas in Comparative Perspective

4.1   Charting the development of EU agendas

The previous chapter introduced Baumgartner and Jones' policy agendas coding scheme as a way to assess attention for issues in the EU. This method allows us to reconstruct EU policy agendas in health and environmental policy over the past decades and to compare them with policy agendas in other political systems. This chapter charts the attention for health and environmental issues in the EU over the past 30 years and compares the EU agendas with those in the US.

The US offers a good comparison with the EU for a number of reasons. First, the US is roughly similar to the EU in terms of population and geographical size. Second, the US federal government operates in a multilevel system that gives an important role to the states in many fields. Third, the way in which policy is made at federal level in the US is very different from that in the EU, which offers an opportunity to explore the consequences of institutional and political differences on the content of policy agendas. State governments in the US are not involved directly in federal decision-making (apart from processes of constitutional amendment, which are outside the scope of this chapter); the US federal government has a wider policymaking remit than the EU (in practice even more so than on paper), and it has both extensive budgetary powers and all the law enforcement capabilities that a government could want. Moreover, within the US system of separation of powers, the locus of policymaking lies predominantly in the White House–Congress nexus, with broad equality of powers between the two chambers of Congress, and a much greater role for either compared to the European Parliament. Both the president and members of Congress are elected directly and fall under the continuous scrutiny of public opinion. Hence, in terms of actors and decision-making procedures, the US presents quite a different picture from the EU. These differences relate directly to the factors that were discussed in Chapter 2, and which (we may assume) affect the content as well as the process of agenda-setting. A comparison between the EU and US agendas allows us to assess to what extent such differences in agenda content actually exist, and how agenda-setting in the EU differs from what we know about other political systems.

A comparison of EU and US agendas is made possible by applying the same coding scheme in both contexts. For the areas of health and environmental policy, the coding scheme consists of 32 subtopics (listed in Annex 2). For health policy, groups of subtopics have been combined into five broader issue categories in order to compare the overall structure of the EU and US health agendas. An important next question is: which documents will be used to compare the two? After all, the types of policy documents produced in the EU differ from those produced in the US. This problem can be solved by looking at more than one type of document in each system, and by choosing documents that perform different roles in the policymaking process in each system. In this way, it is possible to be more confident that we are actually measuring the attention for issues, as opposed to just the idiosyncrasies of a particular type of document. Moreover, using different types of document makes it possible to compare differences in receptiveness to certain issues between venues in the EU and the US.

In the EU, the policy agendas coding scheme has been applied to two types of documents: preparatory documents from the European Commission ('COM' documents), and written questions in the European Parliament (European Parliament questions). It is important to note that the choice of these documents does not imply a statement about their importance in actually setting the agenda in the EU. For COM documents, it is quite reasonable to assume that they play an important role in agenda-setting, since the Commission has the exclusive right of initiative for both health and environmental policies. However, it would be quite implausible to any observer of EU politics to ascribe strong agenda-setting powers to written questions in the European Parliament. The point about including European Parliament questions is that they reflect the broad concerns of members of the European Parliament, even if they do not form the primary tool for getting those concerns on the agenda of other institutions. As a consequence, European Parliament written questions form a useful indicator for the scope of the European Parliament's agenda, even if they do not set that agenda.

COM documents were coded for each year from 1975 to 2005. Given the large number of European Parliament questions, they were not coded for each year but for one in every five years, beginning in 1978 and ending in 2003. This led to a total of 1240 coded COM documents and 2754 coded European Parliament questions in the two fields of health and environmental policy. These two types of EU document are compared with three types of documents in the US: bills in the House of Representatives, hearings in Congress and statutes. House bills can be seen as the rough equivalent to European Parliament questions, since both are expressions of interest in a given issue on the part of individual parliamentarians or representatives, and both are relatively easy to introduce in their respective political systems.[1] Congressional hearings play a somewhat different role, in that they reflect the agenda of the majority leadership in the two houses of Congress (Green-Pedersen and Wilkerson 2006: 1044). Statutes form the end-product of the legislative cycle in the US.

The US data for hearings and statutes were compiled from the US policy agendas dataset. This dataset is available online (see www.policyagendas.org), but the analysis in this chapter was carried out using the original databases kept at the University of Washington, Seattle. The data for House bills were compiled from the website of the Congressional Bills Project, which forms part of the larger US policy agendas project (see www.congressionalbills.org). For the 106th and 107th Congress (1999–2002), the bills data were not yet available online, and were compiled from the most recent data files kept by John Wilkerson at the University of Washington. Hearings and statutes were analysed for the period 1975–2004 (the 94th to 108th Congress). For bills, data were only available to the 107th Congress, so for those documents the period is 1975–2002. For health and environmental topics alone, the US datasets in this period consist of 12,667 bills, 6225 hearings and 878 statutes.

The next sections will present the empirical results of the comparison. They will begin by comparing the overall attention for health and environmental issues in the EU and the US. Then they will take a closer look at each of the two policy areas. For each area, they will note the similarities and differences between the EU and the US, based on a comparison that includes the ranking of specific topics in the time period under study as a whole, the spread of attention across subtopics, differences within specific topics (where appropriate) and developments in specific topics over time. In this way, we can obtain a clearer empirical picture of how the EU agenda in the two policy areas has evolved, and what sets it apart from the agenda of the US federal government.

4.2 Overall attention for health and environmental issues

Let us begin by looking at the percentage of documents devoted to health and environmental issues. Figures 4.1 and 4.2 show the development of the overall attention given to health and environmental issues in the EU and the US, respectively, beginning in the second half of the 1970s and ending in the first half of the 2000s. Comparing the EU and US documents reveals a consistent pattern: environment received more attention than health in the EU, while health received more attention than environment in the US.

In the EU, the pattern is fairly straightforward: health issues receive consistently less attention than environmental issues in European Parliament questions and COM documents, while issues in both areas receive more attention in European Parliament questions than in COM documents. The gap in attention for the two policy areas has even increased over time, with attention for environmental issues in European Parliament questions showing a steep increase between 1978

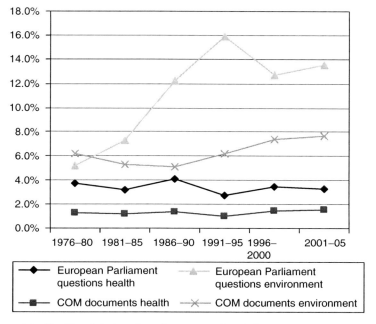

Figure 4.1 Health-related and environment-related documents as a percentage of all documents in the EU

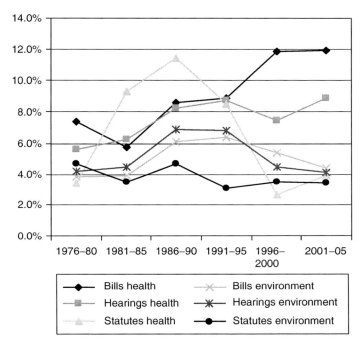

Figure 4.2 Health-related and environment-related documents as a percentage of all documents in the US

and 1993, and COM documents showing a gradual increase in environmental issues after the period 1986–90.

In House bills and congressional hearings, health issues receive more attention than environmental issues for all time periods. The gap has widened in recent years, with attention for environmental issues diminishing somewhat after the first half of the 1990s, and the attention for health issues either rising (bills) or remaining more or less constant (hearings). US statutes show greater variability, but generally the percentage of health-related statutes is also higher than the percentage of environment-related statutes.

These differences are as could be expected, given the EU's tasks and powers in the two fields. However, it is possible to take a closer look by analysing the specific issues that received attention within these policy areas: this will be done for each of the two policy areas separately.

4.3   Environmental issues in the EU and the US

Table 4.1 shows the ranking among 12 environmental subtopics in the EU and US documents over the whole period under study. This table reveals a strong overlap between all types of document, both within and between the EU and the US.

'Species and forest protection' ranks first for all five types of documents, indicating the importance of this issue area both in the EU and the US. However, it should be noted that this category consists of three types of issues: the protection and conservation of wildlife and habitats, animal welfare and fisheries conservation. Figure 4.3 disaggregates the attention for species and forest protection in the EU into these three types of issue.

As Figure 4.3 indicates, attention between the three types of issues differs greatly between European Parliament questions and COM documents. More than 50 per cent of European Parliament questions that deal with species and forest protection relate to the protection of habitats. This partly may be the result of the role that questions play in the European Parliament. A closer look at the actual questions asked reveals that many questions in this topic category are concerned with developments in specific natural areas, such as the protection of wild birds in a particular member state, or the construction of a road through a protected area. Questions are a way for European Parliament members to get attention to these problems and to show their constituency that they actually have taken the initiative to do something.

COM documents are dominated by fisheries issues, which make up almost 80 per cent of all documents on species and forest protection; this shows the large and recurring regulatory activity in this issue area. Each year, the Commission has to propose catch quotas for a range of species in several oceanic areas and it subsequently reports on developments in fish stocks. For the European Parliament, this is a much less salient issue area, because it has no formal role in the decision-making process around quotas. By contrast, COM documents lend themselves less well to addressing the kind of individual problems in specific natural areas that make up such a large part of European Parliament questions in this topic category. Since similar data are not available for the US documents, we cannot compare the EU and the US in this regard. However, what the EU data do show is that different EU institutions are receptive to different aspects of species and forest protection, reflecting the different roles that they play in the EU policymaking process.

Table 4.1   Ranking of environmental subtopics in the five types of document over the whole period studied

European Parliament questions	COM documents	House bills	US hearings	US statutes
Species and forest protection (32.7%)	Species and forest protection (39.1%)	Species and forest protection (23.2%)	Species and forest protection (20.3%)	Species and forest protection (44.1%)
Chemicals (14.9%)	Air and noise (15.9%)	Chemicals (13.8%)	Chemicals (18.8%)	Coastal waters (16.3%)
General (12.6%)	Chemicals (14.4%)	Coastal waters (12.8%)	Air and noise (14.0%)	Chemicals (9.7%)
Coastal waters (11.4%)	General (11.0%)	Air and noise (10.8%)	Coastal waters (13.4%)	Drinking water (6.9%)
Air and noise (10.1%)	Coastal waters (7.5%)	Drinking water (8.1%)	Drinking water (8.3%)	Air and noise (4.4%)
Waste (6.5%)	Waste (4.0%)	General (7.9%)	General (8.1%)	Land and water conservation (4.1%)
Land and water conservation (2.7%)	Research (3.9%)	Waste (7.4%)	Land and water conservation (4.4%)	General (3.4%)
Drinking water (2.6%)	Drinking water (2.0%)	Land and water conservation (7.0%)	Indoor (3.7%)	Indoor (3.1%)
Other (2.4%)	Other (1.0%)	Recycling (3.6%)	Waste (3.2%)	Waste (2.5%)
Indoor (1.9%)	Land and water conservation (0.5%)	Research (2.2%)	Research (3.2%)	Other (2.2%)
Recycling (1.3%)	Recycling (0.4%)	Indoor (2.1%)	Recycling (1.4%)	Recycling (1.9%)
Research (0.9%)	Indoor (0.3%)	Other (1.2%)	Other (1.0%)	Research (1.6%)

Note: The figures between brackets give the percentage relative to all environmental documents.

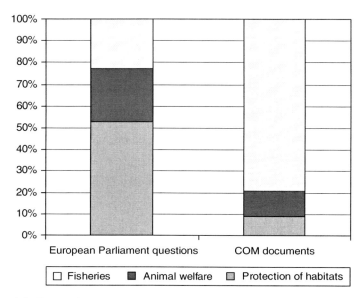

Figure 4.3   Types of issues under 'species and forest protection' in the EU

Going back to the EU–US comparison: even if we allow for the diversity of issues under the 'species and forest protection' category, the rest of the top five also show remarkable overlap: 'regulation of chemicals and toxic waste' ranks second for European Parliament questions, House bills and congressional hearings, while it comes in third for COM documents and US statutes. Other topics that appear in the top five of each source are 'protection of coastal waters' and 'air and noise pollution', which means that all five types of document share at least four of their five highest-ranking topics. The same is true for the bottom of the list, where three topics are among the bottom five for all types of document: 'indoor environmental hazards', 'recycling' and 'other environmental issues' (although the substantive meaning of the the latter category remains ambiguous). Moreover, 'environmental research and development' is among the bottom five for four of the types of document, while it ranks sixth lowest for COM documents. The most substantial differences appear in the 'drinking water' topic category, which ranks considerably higher in the US documents than in the EU documents. Still, the overall overlap between the rankings is striking. Moreover, it is even higher between European Parliament questions and House bills (which, apart from the substantively indeterminate 'general' category, have an identical ranking of their top four topics) than between European Parliament questions and COM documents, which suggests that variation within the EU is higher than that between more or less comparable documents in the EU and the US.

This is not to say that the EU and US agendas in environmental policy have been completely identical. Apart from the higher rank of 'drinking water' in the US and smaller differences in other specific topic categories, the spread among topics is more even in the US than it is in the EU, at least for bills and hearings. In the EU, the top three topics account for 60.2 per cent and 69.4 per cent of all European Parliament questions and COM documents, respectively, while they account for 49.8 per cent, 53.1 per cent and 70.1 per cent of bills, hearings and statutes in the US.

We can look at this more systematically by calculating the normalized entropy score for each type of document. Entropy is a measure of the spread among categories. A value of 0 denotes complete concentration in one category, while higher values indicate greater spread. When the entropy score is divided by its theoretical maximum, a value is obtained between 0 and 1, where 0 denotes complete concentration and 1 a perfectly even spread among topics (McCombs and Zhu 1995: 502–3).[2] When this is done for the figures in Table 4.1, we find the normalized entropy scores summarized in Figure 4.4.

Normalized entropy for European Parliament questions (0.81) is lower than that for either House bills (0.90) or congressional hearings (0.88), while COM documents (0.73) score much lower than either, and slightly lower than US statutes (0.75). These figures confirm the impression that

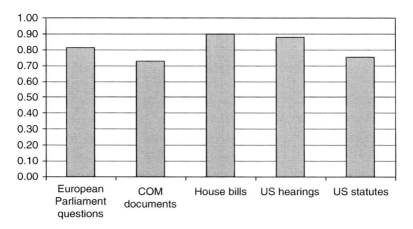

Figure 4.4 Normalized entropy scores for environmental issues in the five types of documents over the whole period studied

attention in the EU is focused on a relatively narrower set of topics than in the US. In addition, they show that entropy tends to be smaller for documents that are more 'downstream' in the policymaking process in both political systems. European Parliament questions show a wider spread of topics than COM documents, and the same is true for bills and hearings when compared to US statutes. Apparently, policymaking activity becomes more focused on a smaller set of issues as it proceeds, or a wider range of issues are brought up when no concrete decisions need to be made. This holds true both in the EU and the US. In terms of the conceptual distinction introduced in Chapter 2, this implies that the spread of topics is more even on governmental agendas than on decision agendas in both political systems.

Although entropy scores differ widely between the EU and the US over the whole period, they seem to converge somewhat over time. Figure 4.5 plots these developments for the five types of document, using the same periods as in Figures 4.1 and 4.2. As Figure 4.5 shows, entropy for bills and hearings peaked in the period 1991–5, and gradually decreased afterwards. Entropy for European Parliament questions also decreased

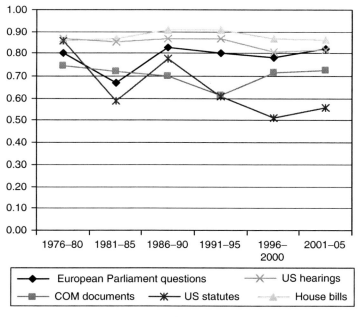

Figure 4.5   Normalized entropy scores for environmental issues in the five types of document over time

between 1988 and 1998, but at a slower rate than the entropy scores for bills and hearings. Moreover, between 1998 and 2003, entropy for European Parliament questions rebounded somewhat to reach the same level as the entropy for hearings. Entropy for COM documents shows very little variation, with the exception of a low in the period 1991–5. All in all, the differences in entropy were greatest in the period 1991–5, but have become smaller since then.

Comparison of developments in attention for specific topics over time reveals no consistent pattern. For some issues, attention in both the EU and US documents shows a similar long-term pattern. This is exemplified by the topic category 'regulation of chemicals and toxic waste': the development of attention for this topic category is shown in Figure 4.6.

For all five types of document, attention for this topic shows a peak in the early or late 1980s and subsequently falls to lower levels. This may be a coincidence, but also it may reflect an underlying common rise in interest for this type of issue during the 1980s. The peaks themselves differ

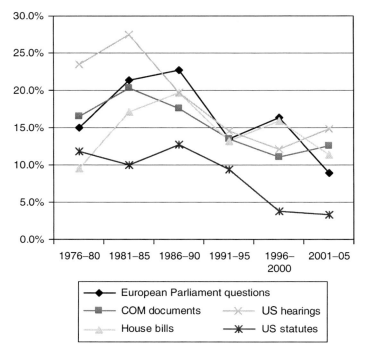

Figure 4.6 Documents relating to chemicals and toxic waste as a percentage of all environment-related documents over time

between documents, with US hearings and COM documents reaching their highest percentage in the period 1981–5 and US bills and European Parliament questions in the second half of the 1980s. This does not point to systematic differences between the US and the EU in this regard.

Other topic categories have a much less clear trend. This is shown in Figure 4.7 for the topic category 'species and forest protection', the highest-ranking topic for all five documents.

Attention for 'species and forest protection' shows rises and falls over time for all types of document, with no apparent consistency between documents from the same political system. As a result, the developments in specific topics tell us little about the differences and similarities between the US and the EU. In general, moreover, the differences between documents from the same political system (EU or US) are no less pronounced than those between documents from different political systems, again without any systematic link between two specific types of documents. As a consequence, attention for specific issues seems to reflect specific developments in attention in different institutions in the US and the EU, rather than differences between the EU and the US per se.

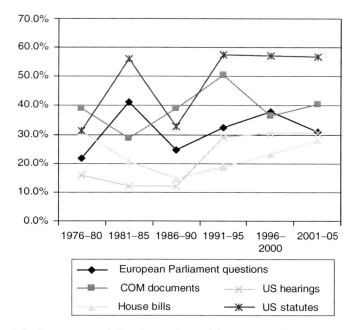

Figure 4.7 Documents relating to species and forest protection as a percentage of all environment-related documents over time

4.4 Health issues in the EU and the US

The comparison between health topics in the EU and the US results in a much more predictable pattern, with larger differences between the two political systems. We have seen above that the overall percentage of documents dealing with health-related issues is much higher in the US than in the EU. In addition to this, there are three other indicators for the lesser attention devoted to health-related issues in the EU than in the US. First, the ranking of issues shows large differences. Table 4.2 shows the attention given to five broad categories of health issues in the EU and the US. These five categories are combinations of the 20 subtopics that are defined in the policy agendas coding scheme. They are used for ease of interpretation, and because the number of EU documents in many of the 20 specific subtopics tends to be quite small.[3]

Table 4.2 shows a clear divide between the EU documents on the one hand, and the US documents on the other. House bills, congressional hearings and US statutes predominantly concern three broad categories that each account for between 20 and 30 per cent of health-related documents: 'diseases and medicines', 'facilities and professionals', and 'organization and financing'. By contrast, European Parliament questions and COM documents are dominated by one single category, 'diseases and medicines', which accounts for almost half of all documents. The category of addictive substances, which relates to issues of tobacco, alcohol and drugs, is also much more prevalent in EU than in US documents. However, 'facilities and professionals' is much less important in the EU, particularly in COM documents, while issues of the organization and financing of health systems, which are central to the US debate, are almost absent in EU documents.

These differences are brought out even more clearly when we take the original 20 health subtopics, the top three of which are reproduced in Table 4.3. Specific diseases and medicines are the two most important issues in both European Parliament questions and COM documents (although in reverse order), while they do not appear in the top three for US bills and hearings. In fact, none of the top three issues in the EU documents appear in the top three for bills and hearings. Health insurance is the most important issue in all three US documents, while long-term care also commands a lot of attention in bills and hearings. The differences are smaller among US statutes and the EU documents, which show overlap for specific diseases (in second place for US statutes) and health manpower issues (in third place for both European Parliament questions and US statutes).

Table 4.2   Ranking of five broad health issue categories in the five types of document over the whole period studied

European Parliament questions	COM documents	House bills	US hearings	US statutes
Diseases and medicines (46.9%)	Diseases and medicines (47.9%)	Diseases and medicines (28.5%)	Organization and financing (29.9%)	Diseases and medicines (30.8%)
Addictive substances (18.8%)	Addictive substances (29.6%)	Organization and financing (28.2%)	Diseases and medicines (26.4%)	Organization and financing (25.4%)
Facilities and professionals (16.5%)	General (14.1%)	Facilities and professionals (26.7%)	Facilities and professionals (22.3%)	Facilities and professionals (23.6%)
General (10.2%)	Facilities and professionals (5.6%)	General (10.0%)	General (12.2%)	Addictive substances (10.6.)
Organization and financing (7.6%)	Organization and financing (2.8%)	Addictive substances (6.6%)	Addictive substances (9.3%)	General (9.7%)

Note: The figures between brackets give the percentage relative to all health documents.

Table 4.3 Top three specific health subtopics in the five types of document over the whole period studied

European Parliament questions	COM documents	House bills	US hearings	US statutes
Medicines and medical devices (22.2%)	Specific diseases (23.5%)	Health insurance (12.4%)	Health insurance (15.3%)	Health insurance (12.4%)
Specific diseases (16.3%)	Medicines and medical devices (18.8%)	Long-term care (9.7%)	Comprehensive reform (10.8%)	Specific diseases (11.5%)
Health manpower (11.4%)	Tobacco (13.6%)	Facilities construction and regulation (9.4%)	Long-term care (8.6%)	Health manpower (10.9%)

Note: The figures between brackets give the percentage relative to all health documents.

Therefore, in general, attention for health in the EU focuses on issues that are normally referred to as 'public health' (diseases, medicines and addiction), while issues of 'health care' (organization, financing, facilities and professionals) receive much less attention than in the US. The difference is most pronounced for bills and hearings, but as Table 4.2 revealed, health 'care' issues also accounted for about 50 per cent of health-related statutes in the US.

The second indicator of differences between the EU and US is formed by the spread of attention among health-related topics, which is more uneven for health than for environmental issues. The top three topics, using the 20 specific subtopics, account for 49.9 per cent and 55.9 per cent of the total in European Parliament questions and COM documents respectively, whereas this figure is only 31.5 per cent, 34.7 per cent and 34.8 per cent for bills, hearings and statutes – a relatively much larger gap than in environmental policy.

Figure 4.8 shows the normalized entropy scores for the recoded and original subtopics. Because the number of health categories and subtopics is not identical to the number of environmental subtopics in Figure 4.4, the scores cannot be compared directly between the two policy areas. However, what is clear from Figure 4.8 is that the entropy in EU documents is considerably lower than in US documents. For bills, hearings and statutes, normalized entropy is between 0.92 and 0.95 for the five broad categories. For hearings and bills, this is also true for the

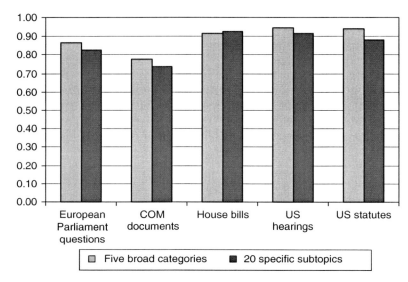

Figure 4.8 Normalized entropy scores for health issues in the five types of document

20 specific subtopics, while the normalized entropy score for statutes is slightly lower at 0.88. For the EU documents, the scores are well below 0.90 (for European Parliament questions) or even 0.80 (COM documents).

Moreover, moving from the five broad categories to the 20 specific categories leads to a greater drop in entropy for European Parliament questions and COM documents than for bills and hearings. This indicates that within the five broad categories, attention in the EU documents is focused on a smaller number of more specific topics than in US bills and hearings. For example, almost all attention for 'facilities and professionals' in the EU is concentrated in one specific subtopic: health manpower and training. Similarly, insofar as the EU devotes attention to issues of organization and financing, it is mostly in relation to issues of provider payments. Health insurance, overall the specific topic covered most often in US bills and hearings, does not appear even once in COM documents over all these years, and makes up only 1.5 per cent of all health-related European Parliament questions.

As a third indicator of differences between the EU and the US, we can disaggregate the specific topics even further by (qualitatively) looking at the documents which have been coded under them. For public health topics, such as 'regulation of medicines' and 'specific diseases', the EU documents cover a fairly wide spectrum of possible issues. However, for health care issues the EU consistently focuses on specific cross-border aspects. For example, the subtopic 'health manpower and training', which in the US contains documents relating to such issues as the training and supply of medical professionals, is used in the EU almost exclusively for documents that deal with the mutual recognition of professional medical qualifications between member states. Similarly, the topic of 'provider and insurer payment and regulation', which covers a wide range of issues in US documents, is limited in an EU context to basically one question: how to regulate payments for cross-border patient treatment. Again, EU involvement in this 'care' issue is limited to the cross-border movement of people – in this case, patients.

For a balanced assessment, it is important also to look at the similarities between the EU and the US health agendas. These similarities are a matter of developments over time, as the EU agenda has evolved gradually to encompass a wider range of issues. Two types of development can be noted here. First, for some issues, attention in the EU and the US has tended to converge somewhat: for example, the EU has devoted slightly more attention to issues of health care organization and financing over the years. Figure 4.9 tracks attention for these issues in the five types of document over time.

As Figure 4.9 shows, the peak in attention for these issues in the US stems mainly from the 1990s, when President Clinton's plans for comprehensive health insurance triggered massive activity from the lawmakers on Capitol Hill. Even without these highly salient and controversial proposals, the issues appear more often in US than in EU documents. Still, issues of health care organization and financing gradually have received more attention in European Parliament questions since 1988, and have made an (admittedly limited) appearance in COM documents since 2000, although the levels of attention are still very low compared to the US and other issues in the EU. (The developments around this issue area will be analysed further in Chapter 6.)

Similarly, attention for issues of diseases and medicines shows a convergence between the EU and US documents. As Figure 4.10 demonstrates, the percentage of European Parliament questions relating to diseases and medicines has risen gradually to more than 50 per cent of all health-related questions. However, for COM documents the percentage has fallen back to around 40 per cent, after a peak of more than 60 per cent in the first half of the 1990s. At the same time, attention for these issues increased in all three US documents, almost reaching the level of COM documents after 2000. As a result, this has now

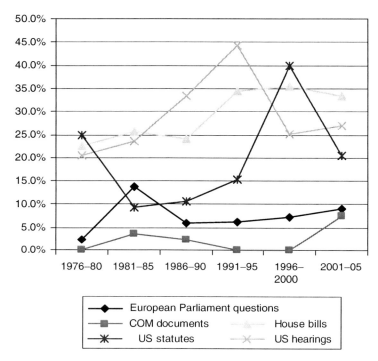

Figure 4.9 Documents relating to health organization and financing as a percentage of all health-related documents over time

become the largest health-related category in US statutes and hearings. However, it is difficult to say whether this is a structural change or simply a temporary shift in attention in the EU and the US.

A second, qualitative indicator of changes in the EU's attention to health issues is formed by the angle taken in documents. Within the broader category of 'diseases and medicines', for example, there is a marked shift from issues relating to the regulation of medicines to those relating to specific diseases. In the late 1970s, the regulation of medicines was the single most important specific health topic both in European Parliament questions and COM documents, but in the 1990s this was overtaken by specific diseases in both types of document. This reflects a shift from an approach focusing on market integration (i.e. creating a single market in medicines) to an approach focusing on the improvement of health as its primary objective. This shift can be seen also in the documents relating to addictive substances. The development of attention for these issues is reproduced in Figure 4.11.

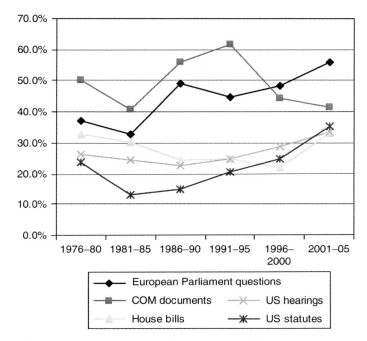

Figure 4.10 Documents relating to diseases and medicines as a percentage of all health-related documents over time

The graph shows a first peak in European Parliament questions in 1978 and in COM documents in the first half of the 1980s, then a second peak towards the present. However, the character of documents in the two peaks is very different. In the period up to 1985, European Parliament questions and COM documents on tobacco and alcohol were focused almost exclusively on the harmonization of taxes and excise duties as part of the creation of a single European market in these products. From the second half of the 1990s onwards, the vast majority of European Parliament questions and COM documents relate to the negative health impact of tobacco and alcohol consumption. In addition, combating the negative health effects of illegal drugs is an issue that gained more attention in the late 1990s.[4] Again, this reflects a shift from market integration concerns to health concerns, a development similar to what happened in EU environmental policy in the 1970s and 1980s (Hildebrand 2002: 19–23; McCormick 2001: 45–55). (The dynamics underlying this shift are the subject of the case studies on smoking and alcoholism policy in Chapter 5.)

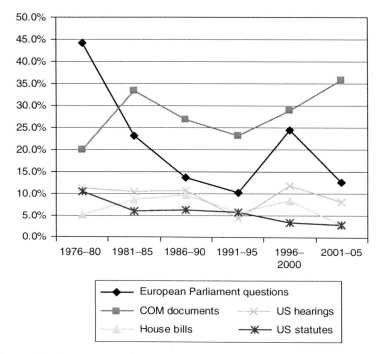

Figure 4.11   Documents relating to addictive substances as a percentage of all health-related documents over time

These developments over time have led to a broader, more health-oriented EU agenda. Still, attention in EU documents remains focused overwhelmingly on a more limited range of issues than in the US, with the EU focusing almost exclusively on issues of public health: diseases, medicines and unhealthy lifestyles. Issues of health care delivery remain firmly out of reach for the EU, even when issues of cross-border mobility have captured some attention over the past years.

4.5   Explaining EU receptiveness to health and environmental issues

Reviewing the evidence of the previous sections, a number of conclusions stand out. First, the EU has narrower policy agendas in health and environmental policy than the US federal government (which was to be expected on the basis of the theoretical framework presented in Chapter 2). Also, relative to health policies, environmental policies are more important in the EU than in the US, while within the field of health the EU focuses mainly on issues of public health and much less on health care. This also was to be expected, given the EU's limited remit in health in general, and its even more limited remit and resources in issues of (re)distributive policymaking.

Second, we found that policy agendas become narrower as we look at documents that are produced further 'downstream' in the policy process. This is not exclusive to the EU, but can be observed for both the EU and the US documents, suggesting that the various documents differ in terms of the 'ease' with which a diversity of issues can be brought to the fore. As issues move from the governmental agenda to the decision agenda some issues are 'filtered out', leading to a more limited subset of issues than those originally brought up.

These outcomes suggest that there are indeed important institutional and political differences between the EU and the US which affect the receptiveness of the two political systems to certain types of issues. However, what is more surprising is the extent to which the EU's environmental agenda is actually similar to that of the US federal government in terms of the categories of issues which have commanded most attention over the past three decades. This outcome is far from self-evident. For example, one could have assumed that the EU would have paid relatively more attention to research issues, because this is one of the few areas in which it has some budgetary capabilities. Alternatively, one could have expected that the EU agenda would be topped by issues of air and water pollution, since these are the quintessential cross-border environmental issues. As shown previously, these issues are indeed high on the EU's agenda, but this is also the case in the US, and even the shares of these two issue categories among all environmental topics are fairly similar. Moreover, the differences between documents from the same political system are often greater than those between a specific EU document and a specific US document.

Certainly, the timing of attention for specific issues sometimes differs between the two (although sometimes it is similar). However, this need not be crucial for a comparison between the two political systems. The important point in terms of receptiveness is that at some point in time these issues gained access to the political system; when exactly that was depends on a host of other factors, including the activities of political actors in each system. Moreover, when we compare different types of documents within either the EU or the US, we can observe differences in timing without any systematic order between documents. This again suggests that the differences within the EU and the US are often as important as the differences between them.

In the field of health, the differences between the EU and US agendas are much more pronounced, with the EU focusing almost exclusively on issues of public health, and the US government dividing its attention more evenly between public health and health care issues. Although this is not surprising, it makes the strong similarities in the field of environmental policy even more striking. Apparently, institutional and political differences between the EU and the US are highly consequential in the area of health, so this raises the question as to why they appear to be much less consequential when it comes to environmental issues.

Apparently, agenda formation in EU environmental policy is closer to the US than a comparison of both systems' institutional frameworks would suggest. There are three ways in which this may be the case. First, although the actors involved in policymaking processes differ between the EU and the US, they may play similar roles. In the EU, for example, several observers have pointed to the role of member states with stringent environmental policies in pushing for more ambitious EU policies (Héritier 1996; Liefferink and Andersen 1998). The role played by these 'green' member states may be equivalent to the role played by environmentally conscious members of Congress, or green states (such as California) in the US (cf. Vogel 1995: 6). In this way, different types of actors may push for similar agendas.

Second, agendas – in particular the more specific agendas within policy areas – are set in relatively closed circles of policy experts. Much of the literature on both the EU and the US has pointed at these 'policy subsystems' (Baumgartner and Jones 1993: 5ff.), 'policy networks' (Peterson 1995), 'advocacy coalitions' (Sabatier and Weible 2007), and 'epistemic communities' (Haas 1989) as driving forces behind policymaking in distinct issue areas. The similarities between the US and the EU may be greater at the level of policy experts than at the level of formal decision-making processes. As a result, specific differences in participants and procedures may be less relevant than the fact that the two systems develop environmental policy in roughly the same way. Put differently: under specific conditions, different processes may lead to fairly similar agenda outcomes.

Third, environmental policymaking in the US and the EU may be linked, and this link can take several forms. Policy experts from the US and the EU may interact in shared networks that form around specific issues and in broader policy areas. These networks facilitate the transfer of information and expertise, as well as the formation of consensus on what the important issues are to address. The existence of these types of networks has been documented widely in the literature: the concept of 'epistemic community', for example, was coined in the context of international policymaking, while Anne-Marie Slaughter (2004) highlighted the wide variety, and far-reaching roles, of government networks in many policy areas. Moreover, policy experts routinely meet during conferences and in committees organized by international organizations, such as the UN and its specialized agencies. In addition, developments in parts of environmental policy may be pushed forward by transnational events, or at least events with transnational exposure. Examples that come to mind are the Chernobyl disaster, which put the risks of nuclear energy on agendas worldwide, and the recent rise in interest in global warming. These types of transnational events may reinforce the efforts of transnational policy networks as well as raise public interest for issues across a range of countries.

The field of health shows that institutional characteristics can make a difference, but on a more general level. By exempting domestic health care systems from EU intervention, EU member states have made it much more difficult to develop major initiatives in this field. This is a clear difference in terms of the receptiveness of the two political systems, but it is also a fairly 'rough' one: some areas are taken off the EU agenda wholesale, but within the areas that do fall under the EU's competence (diseases, medicines, addictive substances), a gradual expansion of the EU's agenda can be witnessed, despite the EC Treaty's explicit ban on health-based harmonization. (How exactly these institutional and political limits operate in the practice of agenda-setting will be analysed further in the case study on health systems in Chapter 6.)

On the basis of the data presented in this chapter, these potential explanations are merely hypotheses that may be more or less plausible, but whose validity we cannot infer directly from the EU and US agendas. The case studies that will be discussed in the next three chapters offer an opportunity to explore further the relevance of these explanations because, in the end, they are based on claims about how agendas are set in the EU. Therefore, it is to a closer examination of these agenda-setting processes that we turn next.

5
Starting from Scratch: Moving New Issues onto the EU Agenda

5.1 The rise of public health issues on the EU agenda

Most health issues have come onto the EU agenda through the back door. For much of the EU's existence, health issues have been addressed as a part of efforts to improve the free movement of goods and workers among EU member states. As a result, at least until the early 1990s, 'health' was hardly recognized as a distinct policy area in the EU. Rather, bits and pieces of what we may call health policy were developed in the context of other policy areas and ambitions.

Nevertheless, one of the EU's first legislative initiatives in this field, Directive 65/65 from 1965, was aimed directly at protecting health in response to the thalidomide tragedy (European Community (EC) 1965; Permanand and Mossialos 2005: 50). From the mid-1950s onwards thalidomide, sold under several brand names such as Softenon and Contergan, was marketed as a pharmaceutical against morning sickness and nausea in pregnant women. However, it turned out that thalidomide could cause serious defects and deformities in newborns, something the medicine had not been properly tested for before it was placed on the market (Silverman 2002). The thalidomide tragedy gave a strong impetus to more stringent controls on medicines in Europe and the US. As part of this regulatory drive, Directive 65/65 provided for the compulsory authorization and labelling of pharmaceuticals, and spelled out the criteria to be used in granting and revoking authorizations. In the absence of a direct competence to protect health, the directive was adopted on the basis of the EU's authority to harmonize national legislation in order to create a common market, arguing that different authorization systems would hinder trade in pharmaceuticals. In fact, trade concerns were an important additional consideration, since each of the (then six) EU member states had begun to develop their own national authorization systems in the wake of the thalidomide disaster.

The history of Directive 65/65 shows that even in its early years, health concerns could make it onto the EU agenda in principle. At the same time, the thalidomide issue was a peculiar one in the sense that it constituted a widely publicized health crisis in all EU member states (and beyond), and that national responses to the disaster potentially affected the free movement of pharmaceuticals. This type of crisis-driven agenda expansion occurred a number of times in later decades, for example in response to the AIDS epidemic in the 1980s (Steffen 2004) and around the Bovine Spungiform Encephalitis (BSE, 'mad cow disease') crisis in the mid-1990s (Clergeau 2005; Moon 1999: 151).

Important as they have been for pushing health up the EU agenda, these crises only form incidental punctuations within a more sustained market orientation. In the case of food safety, for example, Clergeau (2005: 114) argued that '[f]ood safety was seen as a potential obstacle to the free movement of goods, both within Europe and internationally, before becoming a real public health issue'. Similarly, pharmaceuticals regulation after Directive 65/65 was aimed at facilitating trade in medicinal products by streamlining approval procedures further. As a result, Permanand and Mossialos (2005: 51) noted: 'Although all the directives stressed that health matters were of primary concern, they were mainly aimed at progress towards a unified medicinal market.' Moon (1999: 148) concluded in a more general fashion that '[l]egislation relating to public health has thus largely arisen as a response to economic imperatives and from a particular concern to support health-related industry'.

As shown in Chapter 4, the EU health agenda differs quite strongly from the health agenda of the US federal government. This is partly the result of the fact that generally, the EU has devoted most attention to health issues in the context of market integration. At the same time, the EU health agenda became more health-oriented during the 1990s in the sense that health concerns, rather than market integration concerns, became more central in COM documents and European Parliament questions. There is a move towards more 'purely' health issues, and within specific topic categories the documents in recent years focus more on health aspects than on market integration in comparison to the 1980s and early 1990s.

It is against this background that we can ask a number of questions about agenda-setting in EU health policy. How can health issues be placed on the EU agenda in the absence of direct EU competencies in this field? What strategies do actors employ to place an entirely new issue onto the EU agenda? When do they succeed, and when do they fail? Finally, what does this tell us about the possibilities for, and limitations of, agenda expansion in the field of EU health policies?

This chapter will study these questions for two public health issues in the EU: both have been subject to attempts at putting them on the agenda, but with differing results. As explained more extensively in Chapter 3, the first issue is anti-smoking policy, which is quite a successful issue in terms of agenda access in the EU. Anti-smoking policy will be contrasted with alcoholism policy, an issue which has had a much more difficult time in achieving agenda access (and which arguably has not reached the same level of policy attention as smoking). The next chapter will turn to the issue of the organization and financing of health care systems, a potentially vast issue area which has been subject to limited attention at the EU level, and then only in recent years.

In analysing these cases, this study is not just interested in the field of health policy per se. Rather, what it attempts to uncover are the dynamics and strategies in processes of agenda expansion in the EU, or the inclusion of novel policy issues on the EU agenda. Health is but one issue area among many that face more or less similar starting positions in terms of obtaining access to the EU agenda. By analysing the agenda processes around new health issues, we may shed more light on similar processes in these other areas.

5.2   Anti-smoking policy in the EU

5.2.1   The rise of smoking as a political issue

Although smoking only appeared on the EU agenda in the mid-1980s, the story of this issue begins some two or three decades earlier. At the beginning of the 1950s, evidence began to accumulate that smoking could cause diseases, in particular lung cancer. The tentative consensus on this became stronger with the publication of authoritative reports by the Royal College of Physicians in the UK in 1962, and the US Surgeon General in 1964 (Bayer and Colgrove 2004: 9–10). Nevertheless, responses to the issue varied widely between countries. In the US, some initial restrictions on advertising for tobacco products were adopted during the 1960s (Ibid.: 10ff.), and the US has remained a front-runner in anti-smoking policies ever since. Some European countries responded by adopting stringent legislation, whereas others adopted a relatively liberal stance towards smoking, and these differences persist to this day. Joossens and Raw's (2006) 'tobacco control scale', which scored the stringency of anti-smoking policies in 30 European countries in

2005, indicated vast differences, with certain countries in northwestern Europe (Iceland, Ireland, Norway and the UK) having adopted far-reaching anti-smoking policies, while others (such as Austria, Latvia, Luxembourg, Romania and Spain) have been much less active. The different policy responses reflect cultural differences in risk perception (Brandt 2004) as well as the political strength of the tobacco manufacturing industry in a country. An important issue in this regard has been the balance between (paternalistic) restrictions on smoking for the sake of health and (liberal) notions of free choice for individuals.

Whatever the policy approach taken, the consensus about smoking among health professionals has grown steadily stronger since the 1960s. There is no longer any serious doubt about the detrimental effects of smoking on the health of smokers. In addition, a degree of consensus has developed around the issue of 'passive smoking': that is, the effects of smoking on non-smokers who inhale smoke fumes. In the US, the first restrictions on smoking in public date from the 1970s. The evidence for the negative health effects of passive smoking (or 'environmental tobacco smoke' (ETS) as it is known in policy circles) have increased gradually since then, fuelled among others by reports from the US Surgeon General in 1986 and the Environmental Protection Agency in 1992 (Brownson et al. 1997). Even though the health effects of passive smoking are much smaller than the direct health effects of smoking on smokers themselves, the issue gained wide popularity among anti-smoking activists for a number of reasons. First, passive smoking was the perfect way to evade debates about paternalism and individual choice, because passive smokers did not choose to smoke or to inhale someone else's smoke. Therefore, the link with some public good that needed to be protected could be made much more easily. Second, for many anti-smoking activists, the resulting restrictions on smoking offered a good opportunity to 'delegitimate' smoking and induce smokers to give up their habit.

Alongside taxation and advertisement bans, restrictions on smoking in public places became a key policy priority among anti-smoking activists during the 1980s. These restrictions could take several forms, from designating specific smoking or non-smoking areas to completely banning smoking. Complete bans could cover a limited or wider range of public places, including public transport, workplaces and bars and restaurants. As a result, in the US, almost 400 local governments had adopted restrictions on smoking in public places in 1988, and smoking on domestic flights was banned completely in 1989. More restrictions, both as a result of legal measures and private initiatives, were adopted in subsequent years (Brownson et al. 1997: 171ff.).

5.2.2   Early international policy initiatives in anti-smoking policy

The issue of smoking rose on domestic political agendas in the 1960s and 1970s. From the early 1970s onwards, it also became the subject of international policy debates at the global level and within the EU. From the early days of the issue, the international dissemination of research results had been an important driver behind the rise of smoking as an issue on domestic agendas. From 1967 onwards, international contact between researchers and health authorities obtained a clearer focal point through the 'World Conferences on Smoking and Health', which were organized every four years, and which brought together tobacco control specialists from various countries. Beginning with the Third World Conference on Smoking and Health in 1975, these conferences were co-sponsored by the WHO, which had gained an interest in the health aspects of smoking (Phillip Morris 1978: 45 and 10). As a result, anti-smoking activism became firmly internationalized, with groups and regulators in one country learning from the experiences in other countries. An industry report from 1978 listed seven WHO resolutions on smoking to that date, beginning with a (still rather tentative) WHO Executive Committee Resolution in 1970. Moreover, WHO had set up an expert committee on smoking control, which met in 1974 and 1978 (Phillip Morris 1978). As a result, WHO interest in the issue gradually grew during the 1970s, even if smoking remained a low priority compared to other health issues. During that period, WHO's activities in this field remained limited to gathering and disseminating information on smoking issues and (domestic) smoking policies, and advising member governments when they sought information or assistance. No regulatory initiatives were taken and no budget was made available specifically for anti-smoking policies.

Not long after WHO became involved, the issue also popped up within the European Union. The health ministers of EU member states met during the 1970s to exchange information on, and coordinate policy responses towards, smoking – in particular advertisement bans, which were the main instrument in anti-smoking policies of the day. Further, the issue was picked up by officials within the European Commission, who prepared a pre-draft of a directive banning tobacco advertisements in the EU. This pre-draft became the subject of the first serious agenda battle around anti-smoking policy in the EU, and never made it to a 'real' proposal or a public Commission discussion paper.[1] Industry lobbyists and their allies raised two arguments against

EU level advertisement legislation. To begin with, they challenged the link between advertisement and overall tobacco consumption (as well as the link between smoking and health) in an attempt to undermine the substantive rationale for an advertising ban and increased tobacco taxes. In addition, they claimed that the EU did not have the competence to legislate on health-related matters, citing studies by legal experts to this effect. In the end, EU health ministers decided in their meeting of November 1979 not to pursue EU-level legislation on smoking issues but only to seek common approaches and coordinate activities. For the head of the industry association's EEC Task Force, '[t]hese perfunctory commitments prove[d] that the main political impact ha[d] been removed from the EC anti-smoking initiative for the time being' (British American Tobacco (BAT) 1979: 6). Indeed, EU activity in this field was stalled for a number of years. However, it was to experience a fresh start in the mid-1980s – and this time, it was there to stay.

5.2.3   EU anti-smoking policy gains a foothold

The rise of smoking as a policy issue at EU level began with the adoption of the Europe Against Cancer programme in 1987. The political push for this programme was provided by two European political heavyweights of the moment, President François Mitterand of France and Prime Minister Bettino Craxi of Italy, who had been convinced to take action by close acquaintances from the medical community (Nathanson 2004; Gilmore and McKee 2004). In addition, the European Commission became involved in cancer issues following the Chernobyl accident in 1986 (Gilmore and McKee 2004), while the medical consensus around the health effects of smoking (both active and passive) had solidified during the 1980s.

When the first action plan under the Europe Against Cancer programme was published, smoking was included as one of the key priorities. Building on this action plan, a wide range of policy measures was taken between 1989 and 1992 (cf. Gilmore and McKee 2004: 226–7; Hervey 2001: 102 ff.). These included seven directives which, among other things, banned tobacco advertising on television (as part of the 'Television without Frontiers Directive'), set maximum tar levels for cigarettes, mandated product labelling and health warnings, and-specified minimum excise duties for tobacco products. Moreover, the Council of Ministers adopted a (non-binding) recommendation that called upon member states to introduce restrictions on smoking in public places (EC 1989).

In addition to the legislation adopted during this 'wave' of tobacco-related policy activity, the Commission put forward a proposal for a complete ban on all forms of tobacco advertisements and sponsoring in 1989. In contrast to the late 1970s, this time a formal proposal actually was published but, similar to the fate of the earlier initiative, it ran into massive opposition from industry and some member state governments. Attempts to secure adoption failed in the late 1980s and early 1990s because a coalition of five member states (Denmark, Germany, Greece, the Netherlands and the UK) was able to form a blocking minority in the Council of Ministers (see Duina and Kurzer 2004 for a detailed analysis of member state positions and their underlying reasons). The stalemate around the advertisement directive continued until the mid-1990s, reflecting a more general slowdown in tobacco-related policy activity in the EU. Gilmore and McKee (2004: 227) attributed this to concerns over subsidiarity (which had been included in the Treaty of Maastricht of 1992 as a general principle of EU law), the rise of new health programmes on the EU's agenda (thus 'crowding out' the older cancer programme), and bureaucratic struggles within the European Commission to gain control over the unit that dealt with anti-smoking policy. As a result, in the years after 1992, no new anti-smoking initiatives were launched.

The advertising directive gained new impetus in the mid-1990s, when three of the member state governments in the blocking minority (Denmark, the Netherlands and the UK) began to shift position. According to Duina and Kurzer (2004), these shifts resulted from growing scientific evidence about the costs of tobacco use, the ascendancy of left-wing political parties to power in these countries and developments in international tobacco control policies (which will be discussed in more detail below). In 1998, the advertising directive was finally adopted (EC 1998). Not only did it ban 'direct' advertisements, such as advertisements in newspapers and sponsorship of events, but it also covered 'indirect' advertisements, for example, attaching brand names to objects such as parasols and ashtrays. By including indirect advertisements, the directive stretched the limits of the formal legal basis on which it was adopted. Because the EU did not have the authority to legislate directly for health purposes, the advertising directive had been adopted on the basis of the EC Treaty's internal market provisions, which provided for EU-level legislation in order to assure the proper functioning of the internal market. After an appeal by Germany, the member state which was most reluctant to adopt restrictive measures against smoking and which had voted against the directive, the ECJ annulled it because it was not clear how standards for advertising on static objects would contribute to this objective (ECJ 2000). Subsequently, a weaker version of the directive was adopted (EC 2003) and the ban on indirect advertisements was adopted as a recommendation rather than a binding directive (EC 2002c).

This meant a serious setback for EU anti-smoking activists, since potential further legislative measures (such as a ban on smoking in public places) would be very likely to run into the same legal limitations. Notwithstanding these, a number of developments in the 1990s and early 2000s served to strengthen the position of tobacco control policies on the EU agenda. These developments are the subject of the final part of our story on EU tobacco policy.

5.2.4 Tobacco control as a permanent feature of the EU agenda

During the 1990s, several developments in other international organizations gave new impetus to international anti-smoking policies. In 1992, the International Civil Aviation Organization (ICAO) adopted a resolution calling upon its member states to ban smoking on all international flights by 1 July 1996 (ICAO 1992). This became a widely observed standard that was quickly acted upon by a range of ICAO member states. It was picked up also by a number of major airlines which adopted smoking bans for their flights, contributing to the creation of a generally accepted practice in international aviation (Holm and Davis 2004: 34–5).

Although WHO had remained the focal point for anti-smoking policies on a global level, until the 1990s its activities remained limited to providing information and highlighting the dangers of smoking (for example, through the dedication of an annual 'World No Tobacco Day', which was first 'celebrated' in 1988). This changed when, in 1995, WHO began work on the Framework Convention on Tobacco Control (FCTC), which was meant to lay down a set of standards and practices to reduce smoking. This was a remarkable development, since it was the first public health treaty to be negotiated under the auspices of WHO since its creation in 1948. Work on the FCTC gained a boost when Gro Harlem Brundtland, the new WHO director-general, made tobacco control one of her two priorities (alongside malaria) on taking office in 1998 (Roemer et al. 2005: 938). In May 2003, the 192 countries in the WHO's World Health Assembly unanimously adopted the FCTC (WHO 2003). As of mid-May 2008, 168 countries had signed the FCTC and 154 had ratified it (WHO 2008).

The FCTC's wording left much room in terms of concrete implementing measures. Nevertheless, it was seen as an important agreement in political terms, since it signalled a consensus among a wide variety of states. It mandated the adoption of a range of tobacco control measures, and WHO provided practical support in implementing it through its Tobacco Free Initiative programme. This programme contained a special section on Europe, which was administered through WHO's Regional Office for Europe. Regular conferences of the parties to the FCTC were to be held in order to update the Convention and adopt additional guidelines on specific issues.

The debate on tobacco control policies also changed in favour of anti-smoking activists because of developments in the US. The number of local and private sector restrictions on smoking had continued to rise in the 1990s, stimulated in part by a 1992 report on passive smoking from the US Environmental Protection Agency (EPA) which declared smoke fumes to be a known ('Class A') carcinogen (Brownson et al. 1997: 171–2). In political terms, the debate took a dramatic turn when tobacco firms had to release a vast amount of previously internal and confidential documents following a series of lawsuits against them. As part of a 1998 settlement with US state governments, seven tobacco firms and two affiliated organizations had to release some six million documents, amounting to more than 35 million pages of internal reports, memos, bills and the like (WHO 2004a). The documents proved to be a treasure trove for tobacco control activists. The documents, and the trials leading to their release, showed among other things that the tobacco industry had known for a long time about the negative health effects of tobacco, but had sought deliberately to stir controversy about the scientific validity of these results. Also, tobacco firms had tried to increase the addictiveness of cigarettes and had targeted teenagers specifically in an attempt to hook them into smoking before they were adults – all in violation of their public statements at the time. Finally, the documents revealed in detail how the tobacco industry had sought to influence policymakers, the strategies they had employed and the 'tricks' they had used (for the international level, see e.g. Farquharson 2003; McDaniel et al. 2008; WHO 2000a; Yach and Bettcher 2000). For an industry which had sought always to operate discreetly, this type of exposure was devastating. The industry lost most of its credibility as a partner or even participant in policymaking, something that was reflected in the FCTC provision that explicitly called upon governments to exclude industry from tobacco control policies (Article 5(3) FCTC).

As a result of these developments, political support for tobacco control policies increased in Europe. In terms of policy initiatives, the most salient efforts from the mid-2000s onwards focused on passive smoking. The first European country to adopt a ban on smoking in bars and restaurants was Ireland in March 2004. In the next two years, Ireland was followed by Norway, Italy, Malta, Sweden and Scotland, with more countries planning to introduce a similar ban in later years (European Commission 2007a: 9–10; Joossens and Raw 2006: 248).

Building on this new 'wave' in European tobacco control initiatives, in January 2007 the European Commission released a Green Paper, 'A Europe Free from Tobacco Smoke'. The initiative for the Green Paper had come from DG Sanco's Unit on Health Measures, which had suggested the issue for adoption in the European Commission's annual workplan. In doing so, the unit was encouraged by member state governments which had adopted smoke-free legislation already and were now pushing for initiatives at EU level, most prominently among them the Irish government. The initiative was encouraged by the FCTC, which included a provision calling for the adoption of smoking bans in indoor areas (Article 8 of the FCTC; see the reference in European Commission 2007a: 8). The Green Paper reviewed the available scientific evidence on the health effects of tobacco smoke, and then presented two questions to stakeholders. First, they were asked whether they preferred a complete smoking ban, or a ban with exemptions. Second, they were asked to choose among five policy options which could be pursued at EU level:

(1) initiating no new EU initiatives;
(2) stimulating the adoption of voluntary measures by stakeholders;
(3) using the open method of coordination to facilitate a policy dialogue between member states;
(4) adopting a Commission or Council recommendation on smoke-free environments; or
(5) adopting binding EU legislation.

Adopting binding legislation was a difficult endeavour, both in terms of political support and legal basis. In order to overcome the legal limitations on adopting health-related measures, an option would be to adopt such a ban on the basis of the EU's authority in the field of occupational health and safety, premised on the idea that it would protect workers in the hospitality industry. Because of these potential problems, several public health groups decided on the fourth option, adopting a recommendation rather than binding EU legislation.

This made sense in the multi-level context of anti-smoking policy. Anti-smoking advocates felt that there was momentum for stronger regulations at the domestic level: an EU recommendation could push that momentum a bit further, whereas prolonged battles around legislation potentially could disrupt it.

At the time of writing, it is not yet clear which approach the European Commission will take in regard to smoking bans. However, all in all, anti-smoking policy has acquired a firm status on the EU agenda. It is widely debated, with a continuing drive towards further restrictions on tobacco products and tobacco use. At the same time, the abilities and competences of the EU relative to its member states and WHO have given it a specific position in the debate. Compared to WHO, the EU is able to adopt forms of binding legislation and link the smoking issue to other policy fields (such as agriculture, trade and occupational health and safety). This offers greater possibilities for anti-smoking advocates to further their cause on the international level. At the same time, the EU is constrained by its legal remit, most prominently the explicit prohibition to legislate on public health grounds alone. As a result, it often works as a catalyst vis-à-vis its member states and a 'conduit' through which developments in some member states are channelled to other member states. The main focus of legislative action and enforcement remains with the member state governments themselves.

5.3   Alcoholism policy in the EU

5.3.1   The alcohol and tobacco issues: Similar but different

The issue of alcoholism has several parallels with that of smoking. Both alcohol and tobacco are legal substances that have been used and sold in Western countries for several centuries and have become part of many people's lifestyles. Moreover, both alcohol and tobacco are addictive, and using them may have negative side-effects on other people who do not. As a result, both have become subject to attempts to discourage their use.

At the same time, there are differences which have had an impact on agenda-setting processes. In public health terms, the negative health effects of alcohol are more ambiguous than those of tobacco. For tobacco, the story is straightforward: any tobacco use is bad for health and the greater the use, the worse the health effects become. For alcohol, the negative effects appear only if people drink more than a moderate amount. In fact, drinking moderately (one or two glasses of alcoholic drinks a day) can be beneficial for health, as it has been linked to a reduced risk of heart disease. Therefore, the health message for alcohol is much less unequivocal than it is for tobacco. Another difference which has been referred to often concerns the vast differences in the cultural appreciation of alcohol. Such differences also exist for tobacco, but for alcohol they are argued to be ingrained much more deeply in cultural understandings, consumption patterns and policy practices. In Europe, the Nordic countries are (in)famous for their restrictive policies towards alcohol, which include high taxes and restrictive sales (sometimes through a government monopoly, as in Sweden). In the southern countries alcoholic drinks, in particular wine, are seen as an integral part of life, which is epitomized in the phrase that 'wine is not alcohol'.

Patterns of alcohol consumption in Western Europe have shown a gradual convergence over the past decades (Gual and Colom 1997; Simpura 1997; Tigerstedt et al. 2006: 118–19). In the southern countries, which traditionally have been the largest alcohol consumers in Europe, overall consumption has decreased since 1980, while it has increased somewhat in northern countries (Gual and Colom 2001: 1094). Also, the mix of beer, wine and spirits has converged across Europe, with northerners drinking more wine and southerners drinking less wine and more beer. Furthermore, 'binge drinking' (consuming large quantities of alcohol in a short time with a view to getting drunk), which traditionally was seen as a typical 'northern style' of alcohol consumption, has become more prevalent in southern countries, while issues such as underage drinking and drink-driving have received more attention across the continent.

The fate of alcohol and alcoholism as a policy issue in the EU has oscillated between various aspects of the issue: alcohol as a tradable good that is subject to the EU's free trade regime; alcohol as an established part of lifestyles that people care about; and alcohol as a health issue that has gained greater attention in a range of member states. As a result, alcohol has not experienced the type of 'attention boom' that smoking has at certain points in the past decades. Nevertheless, alcohol has been subjected to sustained attempts to bring its health effects onto the EU agenda, often using similar strategies and arguments as were used in the case of anti-smoking policy, even if the results have been more mixed for alcohol than for tobacco.

5.3.2 Early international initiatives in the field of alcoholism

Domestic policies to control alcohol consumption have a long historical pedigree. In his study of alcohol prohibition and the international temperance movement, Schrad (2007a; see also Schrad 2007b) showed that the creation of temperance movements and measures to curb alcohol use date back as far as the early 1800s, and even some centuries before. From the mid-1800s onwards, these movements formed international ties focused around a series of international temperance conferences (Schrad 2007a: 114ff.).

In that sense, alcoholism is far from a 'new' issue on the international agenda, although the international activities before the Second World War centred on private groups and initiatives. The issue only began to appear on the policy agendas of formal international organizations with WHO's activities after the Second World War. These activities began in 1950, almost immediately after the organization's creation, when an expert committee on mental health put forward alcohol as one of the priority areas for action. This was followed by the activities of specialized expert committees in the early 1950s and a number of regional seminars to disseminate their work. In all of these activities a central role was played by the WHO's regional offices, including the Regional Office for Europe (Moser 1970).

WHO's work in this period focused on developing common definitions and understandings of alcohol addiction and alcohol dependence. From the late 1960s onwards, WHO shifted its focus to alcoholism as a public health issue, broadening the scope from the previous focus on the pharmacological aspects of alcohol use (Edwards 2002: 759). In terms of its activities, WHO continued to work on developing definitions and strengthening the scientific basis behind alcohol control policies, but it also charted relevant policy approaches to alcoholism in WHO member countries and sought to raise attention among policymakers for alcoholism as a health issue (Edwards 2002; 2007). A landmark publication in this respect was the 1975 book *Alcohol Control Policies in Public Health Perspective*, which was written by a group of scientists in collaboration with the WHO Regional Office for Europe. Widely regarded as a key text in driving forward the international debate on alcoholism policy, the book 'was the first to place the public health significance of alcohol on the international scientific and policy agenda' (Stockwell 2003: 1173; see also WHO 1993: 12). Its most significant conclusion was that the problems related to alcohol were associated closely with the overall level of alcohol consumption in a society. As a result, so the authors concluded: 'Alcohol control measures can be used to limit consumption: thus, control of alcohol availability becomes a public health issue' (cited in Stockwell 2003: 1173).

In drawing this conclusion, the study defined one of the two approaches which have dominated the debate on alcoholism to this date. One side of the debate, supported by the alcohol industry, argues that the problem lies not with alcohol use in general, but with alcohol abuse. Hence, anti-alcoholism policies should focus on instances of abuse, not on the relatively harmless consumption patterns of 'normal' drinkers. The other side of the debate, exemplified by the 1975 study and dominant among anti-alcohol activists, argues that alcohol problems are related intimately to the general availability and consumption of alcohol. Even if they do not support prohibition or complete abstention, the supporters of this approach call for measures to reduce alcohol consumption in general, not only in a (relatively) small group of heavy drinkers.

Since the mid-1970s, WHO has supported the latter position consistently. Moving forward from its activities in the 1970s, the WHO Regional Office for Europe included a specific target for alcohol consumption in its 1980 action plan, Health for All in Europe. According to this target, WHO's European members should strive to reduce alcohol consumption by 25 per cent between 1980 and 2000. This general objective was specified in, and supported by, a series of more concrete initiatives, including the 1993 and 2000 European Alcohol Action Plans (WHO 1993; 2000b) and a 'European Charter on Alcohol' (WHO 1995).

Therefore WHO, and in particular its Regional Office for Europe, has played quite an active role in the international debate on alcohol and alcoholism over the past decades, and it continues to do so at present. By contrast, in the EU, the health aspects of alcohol and alcoholism have had a much more difficult time coming onto the agenda. Nevertheless, from the mid-1990s onwards, attention for the issue has increased and some tentative steps have been taken. It is to this gradual but limited rise of alcoholism as an agenda issue in the EU that we now turn.

5.3.3 Placing alcoholism on the EU agenda

Before the 1990s, EU policies regarding alcohol focused almost exclusively on it as an economic and trade issue. The production of wine was subsidized under the Common Agricultural Policy. Moreover, the EU and the World Trade Organization (WTO) sought to liberalize trade in alcoholic products by reducing national barriers to trade. These efforts affected national policies aimed at reducing alcohol consumption for social or health reasons, because restrictions on alcohol imports and sales often formed an integral part of those policies. As a result, many observers from the public health community felt that international trade liberalization undermined domestic attempts to control alcohol use and abuse (Gould and Schacter 2002; Hellebø 2003; Sulkunen 1981: 98–9; Tigerstedt 1990).

Despite the focus on the trade and agricultural aspects of alcoholic drinks, the health aspects of alcohol use received some scattered attention at EU level during the 1980s. In 1981, alcohol was included in the EU's second programme for consumer protection and information, and alcohol use was discussed as part of the Europe Against Cancer programme, which played such an important role in the development of EU anti-smoking policy. In neither cases did this lead to further policy initiatives. In addition, the European Parliament raised the issue of drink-driving in two resolutions in 1981 and 1984 (Österberg and Karlsson 1998: 66). The European Commission subsequently introduced a proposal for standardized alcohol limits for drink-driving throughout the EU (European Commission 1988), but this proposal never made it to a directive. Finally, the health aspects of alcohol consumption appeared in a 1986 Council Resolution on alcohol abuse, albeit in a rather tentative form (EC 1986). In addressing the issue, the Resolution 'invite[d] the Commission to weigh carefully the interests involved in the production, distribution and promotion of alcoholic beverages, and public health interests and to conduct a balanced policy to this end' – hardly a battlecry for an EU policy against alcoholism.

Although the issue popped up here and there during the 1980s, it never acquired much of an agenda status, and the various initiatives remained detached from each other. This changed in 1995, when two developments worked together to provide a new push to the debate on alcohol and alcoholism in the EU. The first was the accession to the EU of Sweden and Finland in 1995. The EU's rules on free trade of goods (which applied to alcoholic drinks, as they did to other tradable products) made it much easier for the citizens of these countries to bring large quantities of alcoholic drinks from abroad, and thus to exploit the large price differentials with neighbouring countries. In response, Denmark, Finland and Sweden cut excise duties on alcoholic drinks (Tigerstedt et al. 2006: 116ff.). Moreover, EU rules posed a threat to the Finnish and Swedish government monopolies on the sale of alcoholics. Although in 1997 the European Court of Justice upheld the Swedish alcohol retail monopoly, monopolies on imports, exports and wholesale were abolished during the 1990s (Tigerstedt et al. 2006: 114). As a result, the Finnish and Swedish governments sought to bring alcohol onto the EU agenda as a health issue rather than an economic or free trade issue. The Swedish government was particularly active in this regard (cf. Government of Sweden 2002: 13ff.). It pushed for statements on alcoholism policy in the Council, seconded a national expert to the Commission to develop an EU strategy on the issue, and actively used its EU presidency in the first half of 2001 to push forward debate on the issue.

These initiatives were aided by the second development, which began in 1995. In that year a new type of sweet alcoholic drink, 'alcopops', appeared on the European market. Since these drinks particularly appealed to (and were aimed at) young teenagers, they elicited an immediate response from concerned politicians. Two British Members of European Parliament introduced an declaration calling for action against alcopops, and the issue was raised in the Council of Ministers (Tigerstedt et al. 2006: 122–3). As a result, the issue of youth and drinking arose as a common worry in EU member states. Another area of potential convergence was the issue of drink-driving, which had been tentatively raised in the 1980s but still commanded a high death toll on European roads. Therefore, 'youth and alcohol' and 'drink driving' offered good opportunities to push the issue of alcoholism forward without squarely addressing alcohol consumption in general.

In June 2001, at the end of the Swedish presidency of the EU, the Council of Ministers adopted a Recommendation 'on the Drinking of Alcohol by Young People, in Particular Children and Adolescents' (EC 2001a). The recommendation called on member states to address the issue of drinking among youths, also in relation to drink-driving by young people. Although non-binding, the recommendation urged member states to take a number of measures to combat drinking among youths and stimulate research. Moreover, it called upon the Commission to facilitate the implementation of the recommendation and to continue to work on policies to address the issue, stating in its preamble that '[t]he present recommendation represents a first step towards the development of a more comprehensive approach across the Community' (EC 2001a: recital 6). This call was restated in the Council conclusions of that same date, which explicitly 'invit[ed] the Commission to put forward proposals for a comprehensive Community strategy' (EC 2001b: point 21).

These initiatives within the EU converged with activities within WHO. In February 2001 WHO's Regional Office for Europe, together with the Swedish government, organized a ministerial conference on young people and alcohol in Stockholm. The resulting declaration urged the Regional Office's member states to take a number of actions to prevent alcohol-related harm among youths (WHO 2001). For the advocates of EU policies on alcoholism, the WHO conference offered useful ammunition, and the conference declaration was referenced in the Council Conclusions of June 2001 (EC 2001b: point 6). In 2002, alcohol was included as a 'health determinant' in the EU action programme in the field of health (EC 2002b). This opened the door to EU funding of initiatives related to alcohol – not only research but also information campaigns and the formation of policy networks. Additionally, NGOs working on alcoholism issues could receive funding for proposals under the action programme.

Groups pushing for EU alcoholism policies tried to reinforce momentum by gathering and disseminating information on the negative effects of alcoholism in European countries and building networks of policy officials dealing with the issue (EuroCare 2005). In framing alcoholism as an issue, these groups focused not only on health effects but also loss of productivity, crime and domestic violence as a result of alcohol consumption. In an attempt to parallel the debate on smoking, some introduced the term 'passive drinking' to denote the negative effects of alcohol consumption on the people in the drinker's environment (EU Reporter 2005). Citing the title of a 2003 WHO report, a distant follow-up to the influential 1975 report on alcoholism, advocates argued that alcohol was 'no ordinary commodity', thus attempting to shift the focus away from alcohol as 'any' tradable good to alcohol as the potential source of health and social risks. The main focus of these attempts to create momentum for alcoholism issues was the strategy on alcohol and alcoholism, for which the 2001 Council Conclusions and Council Recommendation had called. This strategy offered the potential for a more comprehensive EU approach to alcohol and alcoholism issues. For this reason, it became the central battlefield for alcoholism issues in the mid-2000s.

5.3.4   The struggle around an EU alcoholism strategy

Central to the debate on an EU alcoholism strategy was the definition of the scope of the problem. Paralleling the divide which had arisen in the 1970s, the alcohol industry argued that alcohol abuse, rather than alcohol consumption as such, was the problem that needed to be tackled. However, anti-alcohol activists were afraid that this way of framing the problem would direct attention to individual drinkers and divert it away from the way in which alcohol production and consumption were organized. They insisted that alcohol consumption should be the issue, and that alcohol production needed to be dealt with in order to tackle it.

Following the WHO Ministerial Conference and the Council Conclusions, the European Commission established a working group on alcohol and health with a view to developing an EU anti-alcoholism strategy. In early 2005, the working group presented a discussion paper that would serve as the basis for an EU strategy (European Commission

2005a). The paper addressed the by-now familiar issues of drink-driving and underage drinking. In addition, its coverage included the advertisement of alcoholic drinks (with special reference to young people), the availability and price of alcoholic drinks, and early interventions in problem drinking by adults. Most of the measures proposed still related to 'soft instruments' (such as information dissemination and self-regulation) and stressed member-state initiatives. Even then, the discussion paper pushed the scope of debate on alcoholism in the EU one step forward by tentatively including elements of a more comprehensive approach to alcohol control. This was reflected in the draft version of the Communication on Alcohol-Related Harm which was circulated within the Commission by DG Sanco in 2006. The communication incited fierce lobbying on the part of the alcohol industry, which sought to redirect the focus to alcohol abuse and ensure industry participation in the policymaking process. The industry did so primarily by mobilizing other Directorates-General such as DG Enterprise, which were more sympathetic to the economic aspects of the issue and less so to the health effects which DG Sanco tried to bring to the fore.

The end result was a Communication that was much more modest in its ambitions and scope (European Commission 2006d). The focus was again on the (uncontroversial) issues of underage drinking and drink-driving. Self-regulation and cooperation with industry were the central elements of the proposed approach, with the EU assuming a supportive rather than a leading role in developing policies. Moreover, the Communication foresaw the creation of a European Alcohol and Health Forum, which would bring together the various stakeholders from industry and the health community with a view to developing common approaches to combating alcohol-related problems.

Anti-alcoholism advocates offered different assessments of the consequences of the Communication for their cause. Some argued that, even though the Communication was weaker than earlier drafts, at least 'the fact that there is an alcohol strategy at all is a victory for public health, and it cements alcohol's place in the EU agenda' (Baumberg and Anderson 2007: 1) Others saw the Communication and the creation of the Alcohol and Health Forum as a serious loss of momentum. Although the Communication recognized the EU's role in the field, at the same time it restricted that role to coordination and support rather than direct EU intervention in alcohol control. As a result, compared to EU anti-smoking policy, the EU's role is likely to remain limited. Moreover, the Alcohol and Health Forum gave formal status in the policy process to industry groups, in contrast to their formal exclusion from tobacco policies. This made a huge difference for future initiatives and attempts to set the agenda.

Assessment of the agenda success of the Communication depends crucially on the benchmark used. In a comparative perspective, it is fair to say that the status of alcohol on the EU agenda is much weaker than that of tobacco control and anti-smoking policy, and that it is likely to remain so in the near future. So far, the debates preceding the 2006 Communication offered the best opportunity for anti-alcoholism advocates to push for a more comprehensive approach to alcoholism issues in the EU, but the opponents of such an approach have been able to fend off this challenge, at least for now. As a result, alcohol is an example of an issue which has secured a position on the EU agenda, but a relatively weak position.

5.4   The dynamics of agenda expansion in EU health policy

The two cases of anti-smoking and anti-alcoholism policy highlight a number of important dynamics in agenda-setting processes around new issues in the EU. As shown above, the issue of smoking has gained a much firmer position on the EU agenda than alcoholism. In terms of the distinction introduced by John Kingdon (see Chapter 2), both smoking and alcoholism issues have come onto the EU's governmental agenda: that is, the set of broader issues that are discussed among policymakers. However, alcoholism issues have hardly appeared on the EU's decision agenda (the set of issues that are up for active decision-making), while smoking issues have established themselves firmly on that agenda. Therefore, the cases offer an opportunity to study both the way in which issues come onto the EU's governmental agenda, and the reasons why some issues 'move on' to the decision agenda.

In both cases, the key role in moving issues onto the EU's governmental agenda has been the creation of cross-border debates on those issues among policy experts in different countries. Issues only came onto the EU agenda after a convergence had taken place in the perspectives (and often policies) in a range of EU member states. In the case of smoking, much of this convergence had taken place already during the 1970s and 1980s, fuelled by developments not only within Europe but also beyond, particularly in the US. Additionally, for specific issues within smoking policy, developments in member states preceded those at EU level. The same is true of alcoholism policy, where shared concerns about drinking among youths led to the entry of alcoholism issues onto the EU agenda.

Although to an extent these developments in the member states and among policy experts took place independently from political actors within the EU, they have been stimulated actively by those actors themselves. For example, the Swedish government and WHO have sought actively to create transnational networks of alcoholism policy experts in order to create shared understandings of the issue and policy approaches to tackle it. From an agenda-setting perspective, these activities have been crucial preconditions for the entry of the issue onto the EU's (governmental) agenda, as they cleared the way for joint initiatives at EU level. The dynamics behind this rise of issues to the EU level are captured well by a Commission official who worked in the unit responsible for the Green Paper on a smoke-free Europe. When asked how and why the unit decided to put forward this specific issue, the official explained:

> It's in the air. [...] At that time, we had got the tobacco file from another unit, so we didn't yet know what to do with it. [...] The first member states had also started to put in place smoke-free legislation. Ireland had already done it. Then we thought: we might push it at EU level to get more member states on board. Often, these ideas don't drop from heaven, but they are somewhere here. They are like a flower that grows and that gets a new blossom. It is organic, it develops from something that is in the air, that has been on the ground.

The 'something' that is in the air or on the ground consists of policy debates in professional networks of policy experts. People who are working on an issue in national governments, NGOs and international organizations read the same (professional) publications and meet regularly, exchanging information on the 'state of the art' in their field – not just in terms of technical knowledge and expertise, but also in terms of what is politically 'hot' and which new policy developments are taking place. In this environment, Commission officials develop a feeling for the issues that will be received favourably by member-state governments and interest groups, and the issues that will not go anywhere. In terms of 'who started the process', this makes it difficult to single out a clear initial source or driver of the process.

However, no matter whether the initiatives are taken by the Commission (as in the example above), by member-state governments (as in the example of Sweden and alcoholism policy) or by members of the European Parliament, in each case the preconditions for successfully placing the issue onto the EU's governmental agenda are the same: a convergence in policy perspectives among policy experts within the EU, and the existence of transnational professional networks that bring these experts together. Therefore, agenda-setting processes in the EU are seldom a matter of a member state (or other actor) simply using the EU for its own purposes, or the Commission squarely placing an issue on the agenda. Typically, agenda-setting is the outcome of an interplay between various actors in different venues who (happen to) strive for similar policies. Thus, alcoholism came onto the EU agenda through a combination of activism by the Swedish and Finnish governments, concerns about alcopops in the European Parliament and among public health groups in the EU, sustained advocacy by the WHO Regional Office for Europe, and the Commission's willingness to pursue the issue.

What, then, explains why smoking issues have come so much further on the EU's political agenda, moving to its decision agenda on a number of occasions, than alcoholism issues? The crucial determinant here is formed by the scope of participation in policy debates at EU level. In Chapter 2, it was noted that moving an issue from the domestic to EU level involves elements of both conflict expansion (more actors become involved) and conflict contraction (some actors are excluded from the debate). Both cases show attempts to control the struggle around these two dynamics. Conflict on both issues was expanded because actors from several countries became involved in debates that formerly were predominantly domestic in scope. At the same time, the actors in each case sought to contract (i.e. limit) conflict by excluding opponents from the EU policy process. In the anti-smoking case, tobacco control activists were most successful in this regard, since they were able to move the tobacco industry to the periphery of the policymaking process. In this way, they were able to build up a strong monopoly on the definition of the issues involved and the potential policies to be adopted. In the alcoholism case, anti-alcohol activists were unable to establish exclusive participation in the policymaking process, most importantly because the alcohol industry enjoyed much more credibility among policymakers than the tobacco industry. For the alcohol control community in Nordic EU member states, this meant being confronted at EU level with actors who effectively had been marginalized in the domestic policymaking process. As a result, they lost (part of their) grip on the policy agenda in their field, contrary to the fate of the tobacco control community in the other case.

As also argued in Chapter 2, agenda struggles in the EU involve a substantive component (what the issue is about) as well as a scale element (why the EU rather than the member states should be dealing with the issue). Opponents of EU activity in both cases have been able to use scale arguments to undermine attempts to place the issue on the EU agenda. In the tobacco case, this was done eventually through a legal challenge to the tobacco advertisement directive before the European Court of Justice. In the case of alcoholism, both issues of legal competence and the (broader) lack of an established basis for dealing with these issues at EU level have troubled the advocates of EU initiatives. In each of these cases, the opposition was based on problems with the substance of the policy initiatives. Arguments of subsidiarity and legal basis were invoked subsequently to defeat the proposals.

At the same time, the case of anti-smoking shows that at least part of this type of opposition can be overcome. After the creation of the Europe Against Cancer programme, and the prominent place accorded in it to tobacco, the European Commission was able to build up a body of law quickly as well as sufficient expertise in the area. This helped to cement the place of tobacco control on the EU's agenda, and made it much more self-evident that smoking-related issues would be dealt with at EU level. In the case of alcoholism, the Commission, advocacy groups and Nordic governments have aimed to develop a similar basis for EU debates and intervention, but so far they have not succeeded in doing so. As a result, debates on alcoholism policy in the EU have been affected to a much larger extent by the question of whether the EU should be involved in the issue at all, and if so, whether the EU's role should be more than a mere facilitator.

What we find, then, is a twofold dynamic that determines the fate of new issues on the EU agenda. On the one hand, issues that are 'hot' among (domestic) policy experts and are discussed in transnational professional networks tend to 'trickle up' to EU level. On the other hand, for issues to move onto the EU's decision agenda, a number of institutional and political barriers need to be overcome. The next chapter will turn to another issue area which has received attention at EU level recently, but which has had a difficult time moving from the governmental to the decision agenda: the organization and financing of health care. The (largely failed) attempts to move it onto the decision agenda offer valuable additional insights into what determines agenda access in the EU.

6
A Bridge Too Far? The Limits of EU Agenda Expansion

6.1 Health care issues on the EU agenda

The previous chapter analysed how public health issues may come onto the EU agenda. In terms of the broader long-term development of the EU's public health agenda, it was argued that a shift has taken place from a focus on issues related to the internal market to a focus that is informed more by health concerns per se (even if the EU's legal competence often required framing those concerns in terms of market integration).

However, the EU agenda has been much less open to issues that relate to health care, such as the regulation of health care facilities and professionals and the organization and financing of health care systems (see the figures in Chapter 4). Within the field of health care, most attention has been given to issues relating to the free movement of workers. For workers in medical professions, the key issue has been to establish systems of (mutual) recognition of qualifications that allow health professionals who are trained in one member state to practise in another. To that effect, the EU adopted a range of 'sectoral' directives on the mutual recognition of specific categories of health professionals in the second half of the 1970s and the first half of the 1980s. The directives covered doctors, nurses, dentists, midwives and pharmacists (cf. Hervey and McHale 2004: 204–5). In 1989 and 1992, these specific directives were complemented by two general directives on mutual recognition, which also applied to health professions not covered by the sectoral directives (Hervey and McHale 2004: 215–16).[1] As Hervey and McHale (2004: 215) observed, the directives on mutual recognition were 'limited by reference to Community competence, which is essentially confined to what is necessary for creating a "single market" in persons'. As a result, the training, regulation and organization of health professionals remained firmly in the hands of member states. Issues of facilities construction and regulation even remained completely outside of the EU's ambit, apart from occasional project subsidies for facilities in border regions that served more than one member state.

The link to the single market is even clearer for the health-related aspects of the free movement of workers in other sectors. The background to these initiatives is formed by the coordination problems (potentially) caused by people living in one member state and working, living or simply holidaying in another member state. The core issue here is: who will pay if that person makes use of health facilities in one member state, but is covered for health expenses in another? A coordination scheme for cross-border workers was created as early as 1971, when Regulation 1408/71 stipulated which national social security scheme would apply to workers and their families who moved through the EU (EC 1971).

Until the late 1990s, this was the only issue related to health care organization and financing that received any serious attention at EU level. The organization of health care systems and the way in which they were financed were issues that remained firmly off-limits for EU policymakers. Since the late 1990s, this situation has changed somewhat, with debates on health care systems arising on at least two fronts within the EU institutions. Yet, these debates have remained limited in scope, and attempts by the European Commission to give the EU a broader role have met consistently with fairly hostile responses from the member states and European Parliament.

The organization and financing of health care (or debates about 'health systems') offer a good opportunity to study the limits of agenda expansion in the EU. Why is it that these issues have had such a difficult time coming onto the EU agenda, and what does this tell us about agenda processes in the EU? These are the central questions in this chapter. The next section will sketch the complex policy arrangements governing health systems in the EU member states. Also, it will discuss the reforms which have taken place in them over the past decades, and the roles played in policy debates over the reforms by a number of international organizations. Section 6.3 will analyse the rise of issues related to health systems on the EU agenda, focusing in on two developments which have offered opportunities for the European Commission to push these debates. Both attempts have led to policy activity, but at the same time they have run up against clear limits in terms of agenda access. Finally, section 6.4 discusses the implications of the analysis for our understanding of processes of agenda expansion in the EU.

6.2   Health care systems and the reform debate in Europe

6.2.1   The complexity of European health care systems

Health care is a massive industry in almost all industrialized countries. The median member state of the OECD spent 8.5 per cent of GDP on health care in 2002. Among the (then 15) member states of the EU, this figure varied between 6.2 per cent for Luxembourg and 10.9 per cent for Germany, with seven member states spending more than 9 per cent of their GDP (Anderson et al. 2005: 905).

In terms of organization and financing, European health care systems can be divided into two distinct types (Freeman 1998: 395–6; Sieveking 2007: 29–30). The first type is exemplified by the British National Health Service (NHS): the 'NHS' or 'NHS-type' system. In NHS systems, health care is the exclusive responsibility of the state. It is financed primarily from tax revenue, while the provision of health care (in hospitals and by medical doctors) is organized and operated by the government. In principle, every citizen has access to health services without paying. Apart from the UK, this type of system is also in place in Ireland, the Nordic EU member states (Denmark, Finland and Sweden), and the EU's southernmost member states (Greece, Italy, Portugal and Spain).

The second type is the 'social insurance' system. Health care is financed from health insurance funds that rely on contributions from employers and employees. Coverage of the population by these insurance funds is (almost) universal and compulsory, and the minimum range of services to be covered by the insurance is stipulated by law. Health care services are delivered by providers that are paid according to service. This type of system is predominant in continental Western Europe (Austria, Belgium, France, Germany, Luxembourg and the Netherlands).

Within these broad categories, many differences exist between countries. For example, some social insurance systems operate on the basis of benefits in kind, where patients can go to health care providers that are paid directly by their insurance fund, whereas other systems rely on reimbursement of the costs incurred by patients. Similarly, the choice of insurance fund is free in some countries, but compulsory in others (according to region or occupation). All combinations are possible. Thus, Austrians are required to take insurance with a local sickness fund, which offers benefits in kind. In France, the choice of insurance fund is prescribed also, but these funds operate under a cost reimbursement system. Belgium shares the latter characteristic with France, but Belgians have a free choice of insurer. To complete the circle, Germany allows free choice of insurer, but these insurers operate according to benefits in kind (Sieveking 2007: 30).

In some countries, patients need a referral from a general practitioner to access specialist services (Denmark, the Netherlands), while in others they do not (France, Germany; Freeman 1998: 396). In almost all countries patients have to pay a direct contribution when they use certain services, but the extent and height of these co-payments vary, with elaborate exemptions for certain types of patients and/or treatments (Abel-Smith and Mossialos 1994: 127–9; Freeman and Moran 2000: 39–40). Also, countries differ as to which treatments and medicines are provided by their NHS or are covered by health insurance. Further, many countries have systems of reference prices for treatments and medicines according to which providers and/or patients are reimbursed, but these reference prices vary between countries (cf. Abel-Smith and Mossialos 1994: 132).

All in all, then, the development of European health systems has led to highly complex and country-specific arrangements in which the different elements are closely interlinked. In many ways, health care systems are closely tied to the states in which they developed. This is reinforced by the fact that European health care systems have been organized on a territorial basis (Martinsen and Vrangbæk 2008: 169; Sieveking 2007: 31–2; Vollaard 2004: 267). This means that all people in the territory of a certain country are covered by that country's health care system and obliged to participate in it (i.e. pay taxes or be insured). Moreover, in order to keep control over health care provision, in principle the health care system will pay only for providers that operate in that territory. As a result, the movement of patients across borders may occur incidentally or as a result of emergencies, but is ruled out generally.

The territoriality principle serves a dual purpose: on the one hand, it has been used to enforce a degree of equity or solidarity in European health systems; on the other, it has allowed governments to exert control over health care spending and quality. The principle of solidarity means that good-quality health care should be open to all citizens, regardless of income or health status. In practice, this implies that each person's contribution to health care revenues (through taxes or insurance premiums) is not related, or only within tight bands, to the use that a person makes of health care services. Moreover, taxes and health insurance premiums often are related to income, so the more affluent pay more for essentially the same services. In order to enforce this type of solidarity and prevent the healthy and rich from opting out of the system, territorial restrictions have been put in place.

In addition to enforcing solidarity, the territoriality principle allows governments to exert control over health care providers, and thereby over the costs and quality of health care provision. Cost containment in particular has been a central concern in debates on health care policy since the 1970s. In the decades after the Second World War, when European welfare states were being built up, the health care sector grew enormously both in absolute terms and relative to total GDP. Between 1960 and 1975, health care spending as a proportion of GDP doubled in France, Germany and Sweden, while it increased by two-thirds in the UK and 50 per cent in Italy (Freeman and Moran 2000: 37; see also Abel-Smith and Mossialos 1994: 90). Health costs continued to rise in most EU member states during the 1990s (Anderson et al. 2005: 905). Attempts to curb health costs have included elaborate regulation of health care providers, such as setting annual budgets, measures to discourage health care professionals from authorizing expensive treatments, and limits on the supply of health care facilities through a reduction in the numbers of medical professionals and hospital beds (Abel-Smith and Mossialos 1994: 125–30). These types of measures would be much more difficult to implement or enforce, if patients could move freely between countries in search of health care services for which their 'home country' subsequently would have to pay.

Despite the national variety in organizing and financing health care, common reform trends and a degree of convergence among European health systems can be observed over the past decades. These reforms, and the resulting convergence, were driven partly by a transnational policy debate that formed an important background to, and context for, later debates on health care systems in the EU.

6.2.2   The international health care reform debate

The degree of convergence that can be witnessed over the past 20 to 30 years is the result of shared attempts to introduce elements of competition into health care systems (Defever 1995: 3; Freeman 1998: 395; Freeman and Morgan 2000: 42; McPake 2002: 120; OECD 1994: 45ff.; Van de Ven 1996: 655–7). Competition in health systems can take two forms (Freeman 1998: 399). First, it can take place between insurers or providers for consumers and patients. Traditionally, the choice of insurance fund (in social insurance systems) and health providers (in NHS and social insurance systems) was heavily restricted in many countries. People had to be insured with a particular insurance fund (e.g. the fund for the region where they lived) and could go to only one or a limited number of providers (e.g. the hospital nearest to their place of residence). Increasingly, however, citizens have been given a greater choice among different insurers and providers, which now have to compete for customers. Second, it can take place among health care providers for contracts from those paying for health care. When insurers and health authorities have the choice to contract selectively with providers, they only need to pay for the services of those providers with whom they have contracts, so their customers will go only to those providers. In this approach to introducing competition in health care, a purchaser of health services (an insurer or health authority) is supposed to operate as 'a prudent buyer on behalf of its members' (Van de Ven 1996: 656). As a result, providers are forced to compete for customers by competing for contracts.

The idea behind these reforms was that competition would stimulate efficiency in health care. In most cases, greater efficiency was seen as a way to curb (the growth in) health care spending. In addition, the introduction of competition was a response to the perceived (and desired) greater role for consumers or patients in the health care system. Competition was thought to move power away from medical professionals, who traditionally have played a central role in decisions on health care, towards consumers and their representatives. These objectives were interlinked by the fact that the shift from medical professionals towards consumers could help to achieve greater cost-consciousness in health care delivery (Trappenburg 2008: 78ff.).

In terms of putting the issue on the agenda, the spread of ideas on competition in health care is a good example of an international 'epistemic community' that formed around a set of shared ideas among policy experts in different countries (Lee and Goodman 2002). Its roots can be traced to the US, where health economics developed as a branch of economics during the 1970s and 1980s. The economic analysis of health care issues, in particular in regard to the ever-increasing costs of health care in the US, led to the elaboration of a set of proposals to introduce elements of competition into the health care system. A key feature of these proposals was the separation of health care provision (i.e. the actual delivery of services by hospitals and medical professionals) from the purchase of health care (i.e. the decisions to spend money on various health care services). These ideas spread from the US to other parts of the world, beginning with the UK. In an influential book, US health economist Alain Enthoven (1985) applied the new thinking on competition in health care to the British NHS. This led to the introduction of 'internal markets' in the NHS in 1991, in which health care providers had to compete for contracts from regional health authorities.

These reforms were helped in no small part by the fact that competition and liberalization were the political orthodoxies of the time, and of the Thatcher government in particular (cf. Abel-Smith and Mossialos 1994: 132; Freeman 1998: 398).

Additionally, the idea of competition in health care was picked up by several international organizations. A key role in this regard was played by the OECD, whose work on health care reform reflected the new thinking in health economics (Freeman 1998: 398). Through analysis of health care issues and specific health care systems, as well as the formation of international networks of experts, the OECD became an important proponent of competition-oriented health care reform. Furthermore, ideas about competition in health care became an important part of World Bank policies towards developing countries (Lee and Goodman 2002: 100 and 104ff.), and of World Bank projects aimed at reforming health care in the former communist countries of Central and Eastern Europe (Moon 1999: 155–7). As a result of these reforms, health care systems across the Western world have converged on what the OECD has called the 'public contract model' of health care. This model is characterized by the public financing of health care (either through taxation or mandatory health insurance), coupled with contracts between health care providers and insurers or health authorities (Freeman and Moran 2000: 42; McPake 2002: 121; OECD 1994: 50; Van de Ven 1996: 656).

As some authors have pointed out, the observed trend towards more competition in health systems obscures important differences in national reform policies and their effects on health systems. Alan Jacobs (1998) has argued that convergence has taken place in the policy instruments that are used, but that these instruments serve different purposes in different countries. Moreover, he has pointed at the difference between the rhetoric of competition and market liberalization and the sometimes much less radical policy practice. These caveats are warranted. As shown in the previous section, vast differences remain in the way in which health care financing and service delivery are organized across Europe. Yet in terms of understanding agenda-setting processes, the rhetoric of policymaking is highly significant. It is precisely the fact that the international discourse on competition and liberalization offered a common rhetoric to introduce and justify different types of health care reform which has made it an important element of agenda-setting. For national supporters of reform, the international debate has offered both a set of new ideas that they could use and a welcome source of political support for their cause.

At the same time, opponents of competition and liberalization in health care have been able to draw on the work of other international organizations. In response to the wave of health care reform during the 1980s and 1990s, the WHO and the Council of Europe adopted statements that stressed the importance of quality and equity in health care systems. In the 1996 Ljubljana Charter on Reforming Health Care, the health ministers of WHO's European member states stated that 'health care should first and foremost lead to better health and quality of life for people', and declared as their first principle that '[h]ealth care reforms must be governed by principles of human dignity, equity, solidarity and professional ethics' (WHO 1996). Building on the Ljubljana Charter, the Council of Europe's Parliamentary Assembly adopted a recommendation in 2003 in which it declared that 'the main criterion for judging the success of health system reforms should be effective access to health care for all without discrimination, [which is] a basic human right' (Council of Europe 2003: point 4). These declarations clearly show the different approaches to health care which have come to characterize policy debates in this field: the economic angle taken by the OECD and World Bank, versus the public health or human rights approach espoused by WHO and the Council of Europe.

In this light, it is remarkable that the EU has not played a greater role in the debate. From a venue shopping perspective, the EU would seem to be a potentially attractive venue for supporters of health care reform, given its receptiveness to principles of market liberalization, and for those seeking a more balanced approach to health care issues at the international level, given the EU's wide remit compared to other international organizations. The European Commission has been ready to take up a role in debates on health care systems since the first half of the 1990s. As Ed Randall (2001: 159) noted about that period, '[t]he Commission [was] undoubtedly attracted by the idea of becoming an important player and a partner for member-state health-care systems [...] even if it [was] expressly forbidden, by Treaty, from seeking a direct role in managing or harmonizing health services', and it was supported in that ambition by a range of academic health policy experts. In his foreword to a 1995 study on health policy commissioned by the European Commission, Padraig Flynn, Commissioner for Employment and Social Affairs, stated his ambition for the EU to play a greater role in the coordination of health care systems (Abel-Smith et al. 1995: xi–xii). The study put forward a range of proposals for a more active role for the EU, and the European Commission in particular, in the field of health policy (Ibid.: 128ff.). Some of these proposals related to public health issues, but several others were related directly to the organization and delivery of health facilities and services. The study already identified five Directorates-General in the European Commission which were involved in projects related to 'health economics/systems research' in 1993 (Ibid.: 127).

However, member state governments did not share the Commission's enthusiasm about a greater role for the EU in this area (Randall 2001: 159–60). For the Commission to become an active participant in debates on health care systems, it had to wait for a suitable occasion to which it could link its ambitions in this field. Around the turn of the century, two such occasions presented themselves.

6.3   The EU and the reform of health systems

6.3.1   Health services and free movement

The first occasion arose when, in 1998, the ECJ challenged the territoriality principle inherent in European health care systems. In the decades before this ruling, the issue of health care financing had come onto the EU agenda exclusively in relation to the free movement of workers. The reasoning had been straightforward: if the free movement of workers across borders was to be facilitated, something had to be arranged for social security benefits such as old age and health benefits. Otherwise, workers coming from one member state to work in another would risk losing the benefits that they had built up in their state of origin, while not being entitled to similar benefits in the state in which they currently worked. This, in turn, would imply a serious discouragement of cross-border work and effectively undermine the concept of free movement of workers.

Therefore, in 1971, the EU adopted Regulation 1408/71 on the Coordination of Social Security Schemes, which covered, among other things, 'sickness and maternity benefits' (EC 1971: Article 4(1)(a)). Regulation 1408/71 established for member state nationals working in another member state, and their families, the right to receive health care in the country where they lived (EC 1971: Article 19): so, for example, a German working in the UK would have a right to NHS services, just as a British national would.[2] Apart from this, Regulation 1408/71 took care *not* to facilitate overly the cross-border movement of patients beyond their country of residence. To that end, it made a distinction between emergency treatment in another member state (for instance, a Dutchman falling ill during a holiday in France) and planned visits to another member state in order to receive treatment (for example, a Belgian citizen going to a hospital in France for surgery). In the case of emergency treatments, the Regulation provided that the patient had a right to treatment in the country they were staying in 'as though he were insured with it' (EC 1972: Article 22(1)(a)). For planned treatment, by contrast, prior authorization was required from the insurer or competent health authority in the country of residence (EC 1972: Article 22(1)(c)). Hence, the provisions in Regulation 1408/71 were drafted so as to facilitate the free movement of workers and cover emergency treatments abroad, but they were not meant to provide for the free movement of patients. In this way, the principle of territoriality upon which European health care systems were built remained intact.

After its adoption, Regulation 1408/71 was amended regularly to specify certain provisions and its scope was increased gradually over time. The initial Regulation had applied to workers, civil servants and refugees, and to those were subsequently added self-employed people, students, pensioners, and citizens of non-EU member states legally residing within the EU. These amendments and extensions were quite uncontroversial, and therefore did not lead to heated debate. The only challenge to the substance of the Regulation came with two cases before the ECJ in the late 1970s. Both cases dealt with a Dutch national, Mrs. Pierik, who had been refused authorization to go to Germany to receive hydrotherapy treatment for rheumatic ailments. This refusal was challenged on the basis of Article 22(2) of Regulation 1408/71, which stipulated that authorization should be granted 'where the treatment in question cannot be provided for the person concerned within the territory of the Member State in which he resides'. According to the Court, this implied that national authorities were obliged to grant authorization if the treatment provided abroad either was unavailable in their own country, or if it was more effective than treatments available in their own country (ECJ 1978; 1979).

In response, member states decided to specify Article 22(2) further, so as to make it clear that patients could not claim a right to treatment abroad. After the amendment, Article 22(2) provided that authorization should be granted only if the treatment was available in the patient's home country, if it was covered by that country's health system, and if it was not available within the time 'normally necessary' in that country (a formulation meant to exclude treatment abroad as a way to avoid waiting lists; Hervey and McHale 2004: 116). Therefore, in the end the closed regime of Regulation 1408/71 was salvaged. In practice, authorizations for planned treatments abroad were scarce, so that cross-border movements of patients remained limited (Martinsen 2005: 1047; Mossialos and Palm 2003: 6).

A more serious legal challenge to the regime of Regulation 1408/71 was launched in the late 1990s, when the ECJ began a series of rulings that effectively undermined the territorial restrictions sanctioned by the Regulation (cf. Hervey and McHale 2004: 124ff.; Martinsen 2005; Mossialos and Palm 2003; Rich and Merrick 2006; Sieveking 2007). The first two cases, which set the stage for the subsequent case law, concerned Luxembourg citizens. Raymond Kohll claimed reimbursement for dental treatment that his daughter had received in Germany, even though he had been refused authorization by his insurance fund in Luxembourg. Nicolas Decker had not even asked for authorization, but nonetheless claimed reimbursement for the pair of glasses that he had bought in Belgium on prescription from his Luxembourg doctor. On the basis of Regulation 1408/71, his insurance fund also had refused to pay. In the *Kohll* and *Decker* cases, which were decided on the same day in April 1998, the ECJ took a crucial step in comparison to the earlier *Pierik* cases. Rather than interpreting the provisions of Regulation 1408/71, the Court looked at the issue from the point of view of the free movement of goods and services. After all, glasses were a good that could be traded across borders, just as other goods such as cars or mobile phones. Similarly, dental treatment was a service that could be offered to compatriots and foreigners alike: therefore, the provisions in the EC Treaty guaranteeing the free movement of goods and services among EU member states also applied to glasses and dental treatment. From this perspective, the prior authorization requirement that was enshrined in Regulation 1408/71 constituted a barrier to trade that could be justified legally only if it served a legitimate objective, and if that objective could not be achieved through less trade-restrictive means.

In both cases, the ECJ ruled that such a justification could not be provided. The Luxembourg government, and with it eight other member state governments that submitted opinions in the cases, had argued that the authorization requirement was needed in order to safeguard the financial status of the health care system, ensure the quality of the goods and services provided, and (in the *Kohll* case) ensure the maintenance of balanced medical services available to all. Although the ECJ acknowledged that these were valid objectives, it denied that authorization for buying glasses or receiving dental treatment was required to achieve them. To begin with, the Luxembourg health insurance funds were obliged only to pay the rates that they had set themselves, so in financial terms it made no difference whether glasses and treatment were provided abroad or in Luxembourg itself (ECJ 1998a: paragraphs 37–40; 1998b: paragraphs 37–42). Moreover, so the Court stated, the framework for mutual recognition of qualifications between EU member states ensured a basic quality level in health care provision (ECJ 1998a: paragraphs 41–5; 1998b: paragraphs 43–9). Finally, the Court held that prior authorization for dental treatment was not 'indispensable for the maintenance of an essential treatment facility or medical service on national territory', thus dismissing the third line of defence brought up by the member states (ECJ 1998b: paragraphs 50–2).

The *Kohll* and *Decker* rulings presented much more serious challenges to the system of Regulation 1408/71 because they relied directly on Treaty provisions on the free movement of goods and services. As a result, the rulings could not be rectified by amending Regulation 1408/71 itself, as had been the response after the *Pierik* cases. Moreover, the ECJ introduced an important change in perspective regarding cross-border health issues. Whereas previously they had been treated as an appendix to the free movement of workers and other persons, the Court now presented them in terms of free movement of goods and services. At issue was no longer how to facilitate the free movement of persons, but how to facilitate the cross-border provision of medical products and services in their own right. The rulings were met in the member state governments by a combination of panic and denial. Panic stemmed from a fear of losing control over the cross-border movement of patients and the direct threat that the rulings presented to the territoriality principle. Denial was reflected in a tendency to interpret the rulings in a very narrow way, as pertaining only to the specific cases at hand: cases of non-hospital treatment in the context of Luxembourg's social insurance system with cost reimbursement. In this line of argument, systems in which insurers rather than patients paid health providers, and systems in which health care was offered by an NHS, would not fall under the Treaty provisions on the free movement of services (European Commission 2003c: 8; Greer 2008: 222; Martinsen and Vrangbæk 2008: 170).

This narrow interpretation became untenable after subsequent ECJ rulings. In the *Geraets-Smits/Peerbooms* and *Müller-Fauré/Van Riet* cases (ECJ 2001; 2003), the Court extended its argument from the *Kohll* and *Decker* cases to the Dutch social insurance system with benefits in kind. Moreover, it ruled that the Treaty provision on the free movement of services applied to both hospital and non-hospital treatment (ECJ 2001: paragraph 53). Similarly, in the *Watts* case (ECJ 2006), the ECJ concluded that health care in NHS systems also constituted a 'service' in terms of the EC Treaty, thus shattering any hope on the part of governments in charge of NHS-type systems that they would not be affected by the emerging case law. However, at the same time the Court did acknowledge that, in contrast to treatment outside of hospitals, prior authorization for hospital treatment could be justified in order to control costs and maintain a balanced provision of health care services in a country. It circumscribed room for manoeuvre in this regard by outlining a range of criteria to which systems of prior authorization had to conform. The aim of these criteria was to ensure that prior authorization would not be used to privilege national health providers over foreign health providers. Therefore, the Court laid down a number of procedural criteria for authorization systems that were meant to ensure impartial and objective treatment of authorization requests (ECJ 2001: paragraph 90). Also, the ECJ stressed that decisions should be based on international medical science and not just on what happened to be considered normal practice in a country (ECJ 2001: paragraph 94 and 108). Finally, it stated that authorization could be refused only 'if the same or equally effective treatment can be obtained without undue delay at an establishment having a contractual arrangement with the insured person's sickness insurance fund' (ECJ 2001: paragraph 108; see also ECJ 2003: paragraph 90). Hence, although the Court took care to balance the various interests involved in cross-border health care provision, it unequivocally ruled against the restrictive, territorially based approaches to cross-border treatments that dominated in almost all EU member states.

From the case proceedings, it was clear that the Court had taken on a cause which was not supported by member state governments. In the *Kohll* and *Decker* cases together, nine governments had submitted opinions, all to the effect that health care should not be covered by the Treaty's free movement provisions. In the *Geraets-Smits/Peerbooms* case, ten (out of the 15) EU member states submitted opinions. They were joined by the governments of Norway and Iceland, which would be affected by the ECJ ruling through the Agreement on the European Economic Area. Again, the governments were unified in their opposition to further extension of the Court's case law. At the same time, the ECJ rulings presented health policy communities in the member states with a *fait accompli* that they would have to deal with in one way or another.

In that same period, issues of health care organization and financing were taken up by member state governments out of free will. However, this was not an initiative of health policymakers, but of policymakers in the fields of economic and social policy, who had gained an interest in health care systems. This presented the second occasion for health care issues to come onto the EU agenda.

6.3.2 Health care and the Lisbon Strategy

Almost simultaneous with, but substantively completely apart from, the ECJ rulings on patient mobility, issues of health care organization and financing appeared at EU level in the context of the 'Lisbon Strategy'. Named after the city where it was adopted by the European Council, the Lisbon Strategy involved an ambitious plan to make the EU 'the most competitive and dynamic knowledge-based economy in the world, capable of sustainable economic growth with more and better jobs and greater social cohesion' within the next ten years (European Council 2000: point 5). The definition of this objective stemmed from observations that European economies were lagging behind in terms of economic growth and employment, and that processes of population ageing would place greater stress on European economies and social protection systems. To achieve the objective of becoming competitive and dynamic, the European Council stated that it would be necessary 'to undertake both economic and social reforms as part of a positive strategy which combines competitiveness and social cohesion' (Ibid.: point 4). European cooperation was thought to be indispensable to achieve those reforms; however, it was not to take place through binding EU legislation such as directives or regulations. Rather, it would be organized on the basis of mutual learning and best practice. To that end, the Strategy created the Open Method of Coordination (OMC), a framework within which member state representatives would define common objectives and indicators to measure them, submit country reports on the progress towards those objectives, and then formulate recommendations on the basis of a benchmarking exercise between countries.

Social protection schemes, such as pensions and health care systems, were integral to the ambitions of the Lisbon Strategy for two reasons. First, social protection schemes played an important part in the European economies, accounting for substantial proportions of GDP. Second, the process of ageing was particularly likely to impact on these schemes: disbursement of pension benefits would increase with a growing elderly population, while demand for health care and long-term care services was likely to rise. Therefore, the reform of social protection schemes was an important part of the Strategy. At the same time, the Strategy sought to combat poverty and social exclusion. This led to the establishment of an OMC for social protection and inclusion through the creation of a Social Protection Committee, consisting of member state representatives (EC 2000; European Council 2000: point 32).

Initially, most attention focused on pension schemes because they were most directly relevant to, and affected by, the issue of ageing.

In 2002, an additional OMC process was created for pensions, but a separate OMC for health care would be initiated only in 2005. Nonetheless, the reform of health care systems had been an issue in the early discussions following the adoption of the Strategy. The 'common challenges' to health care systems and the need to reform those systems were mentioned repeatedly in European Council meetings following Lisbon (e.g. European Council 2001a: points 7, 32 and 47; 2001b: point 43; 2001c: point 30). The issue was elaborated further in a 2001 Communication of the European Commission on 'the Future of Health Care and Care for the Elderly' (European Commission 2001c). Apart from identifying common threats to European health care systems, which formed the rationale for addressing the issue of health care reform at EU level, the Communication formulated three long-term objectives for European health care systems: accessibility, quality and financial viability. These objectives were endorsed subsequently by the Barcelona European Council (European Council 2002: point 25) and became the basis for further work on health systems and health reform.

The three objectives were neither new nor unique to the EU. In his classic study of agenda-setting in the US, based on interviews conducted in the late 1970s, John Kingdon (2003 [1984]: 120) had noted that as he 'asked people in health what the major problems were, respondent after respondent referred to what one of them called "the big three": cost, access, and quality'. Apparently, the 'magic triumvirate', as Kingdon called them, has formed a common frame of reference for health policy experts across the Atlantic and over the decades. However, what was specific about their use in the Communication was the balance sought between them. Apart from the (probably quite universal) ambitions that health care should be of good quality and financially sustainable, the Communication stated that 'access to health care is a fundamental right and an essential element of human dignity; it must therefore be guaranteed for all' (European Commission 2001c: 9).

Based on this early work, the scope for future cooperation in the field of health care (reform) was tested further in a questionnaire sent to all member state governments (Council 2003). The resulting report identified the challenges facing member state governments in relation to access to, and the quality and financial sustainability of, health care systems, and proposed to continue the 'process of mutual learning and co-operative exchange' which had developed gradually. In 2004, this led to the formal creation of an OMC for health care and long-term care (European Commission 2004b: 26; 2004d), which became operational in 2005.[3]

In terms of placing the organization and financing of health care on the EU agenda, the results of the Lisbon Strategy and the OMC have been mixed. On the one hand, the issue now is on the agenda in the sense that member state representatives and the Commission discuss it regularly and have accepted it as part of the ongoing debates at EU level: thereby, health care reform has become an issue at EU level. For example, this is demonstrated by the fact that the Commission stressed the need for health care reform in seven member states in its 2007 Proposal for a Council Recommendation on Employment Policies (European Commission 2007d). Also, the formulation of common objectives implies a step towards formulating a common, shared understanding of that to which health systems within the EU should aspire.

Significant as this move towards a common understanding may be, the high-pitched rhetoric of common principles, as well as the recommendations for reform, do not detract from the fact that the principal locus of health care debates remains in the member states. First, the common principles are sufficiently general and vague to allow for a wide range of health systems and types of reform. In themselves, they do not imply specific types of reform, not to mention the fact that often, the three objectives may lead to quite contradictory recommendations. As a result, the need for 'reform' has been repeated often in EU documents, but mostly what these reforms should entail is not specified. Second, the instrument through which policy coordination is to take place, the OMC, was set up deliberately to maximize member states's room for manoeuvre. Not only was the OMC based on self-reporting by member state governments, but also in the end the recommendations flowing from the process were for member state governments themselves to take up (or ignore, as the case may be).

Therefore, the Lisbon Strategy and OMC have led to an institutionalized 'talking-shop' around health care issues. This is not insignificant – after all, all agenda processes begin with talk, and the OMC has yielded a set of principles, objectives and problem definitions that will be difficult to ignore in any future debate on health care systems in Europe. Nevertheless, the OMC has been limited in the sense that there is little realistic chance of the issues 'expanding' from it to other, more binding venues. Given the political sensitivity and high stakes involved in the issues under debate, this is unlikely to change in the near future.

However, in parallel to the Lisbon Strategy and the OMC, issues of health care organization and financing were taken up in the second policy stream that appeared around health care in the EU after 2000. This stream was a direct response to the ECJ rulings on patient mobility and, because of its connection to the internal market, here the prospect of measures that went further than mere talk was much greater. Therefore, we need to return to the internal market debate if we are to understand more fully the role that health care systems have played – and currently play – on the EU agenda.

6.3.3   Health care and the internal market

The ECJ rulings produced quite an uproar in health policy circles, although the immediate impact of cross-border treatments on health systems was limited. Apart from possible legal restrictions, cultural and linguistic barriers prevented large flows of patients across borders; moreover, most patients preferred to be treated close to their home. As a result, cross-border treatments remained a rather small part of all health expenses – estimated at around 0.5 per cent of total health spending in the late 1990s (DG Sanco 2001: 13). In practice, cross-border patient mobility remained confined to certain border regions and to a very limited number of highly specialized treatments on offer in only a few European hospitals. Regular 'medical tourism', as it became somewhat pejoratively known, in which patients would go abroad to circumvent waiting lists, was an exception and is likely to remain so in the near future.

Still, the ECJ rulings opened the door to possible increases in patient flows in the future. In addition, the rulings had a number of more fundamental implications. First, by defining health care as a 'service' in terms of the EC Treaty, the ECJ made it clear that health care systems were not isolated from the general economic norms enshrined in EU law – not even when those systems were financed from taxes, as in NHS systems. Therefore, in principle they were subject to the same regime as commercial services, even if the Court had acknowledged a number of objectives that could justify restrictive policies. This opened the door to the application of a broad range of Treaty provisions that related to services, such as those for competition policy (the control of cartels and mergers), state aid to enterprises and public procurement. This could lead to considerable uncertainty and a loss of control over health care on the part of member state governments.

Second, the rulings touched upon the internal organization and financing arrangements for health care in the member states. Although the ECJ had begun its examination of the cases routinely with the assurance that 'Community law does not detract from the powers of the Member States to organise their social security systems' (e.g. ECJ 1998a: paragraph 21; 2001: paragraph 44), it had formulated subsequently a number of requirements flowing from EU law which had clear implications for the internal organization of those systems. So, even apart from the potential rise in cross-border treatments, the ECJ cases walked a fine line between the things that the EU had been tasked to do (i.e. create a common European market), and the things that it had been ordered explicitly to keep out of (i.e. determining the shape of health care systems).

Member state governments were all but unified in their dismissal of the rulings, as was shown in their submissions to the various ECJ cases. As a former German civil servant told Scott Greer (2008: 222), the German health minister Horst Seehofer 'instructed his officials to "destroy those decisions"' (for other hostile reactions by Seehofer, see Martinsen 2005: 1052–3).

By contrast, for the European Commission, the rulings offered an excellent opportunity to play a greater role in health care issues. In its June 2002 meeting, the Council of Health Ministers agreed to a Commission proposal to start a 'high-level process of reflection' with a view to 'developing timely conclusions for possible further action' (Council 2002). The high-level reflection group consisted of health ministers from 14 member states (all but Luxembourg), plus representatives from the European Parliament and a number of EU-level interest groups (DG Sanco 2003: 3). To some extent, the creation of the high-level group was a response to the ongoing work under the Lisbon Strategy, which had taken off by that time. As Scott Greer (2008: 224) noted on the basis of interviews with member state health care officials, health ministers had become aware of (and irritated by) the fact that 'the Court and colleagues in industry and trade ministries were "reshaping their systems while their health ministers discussed cancer research"'. As a result, health ministers were forced to act in order to reclaim some of the initiative. This was reflected in the June 2002 Council conclusions, where they stated that 'there would be value in the Commission pursuing in close cooperation with the Council and all the Member States – *particularly health ministers* and other key stakeholders – a high level process of reflection' (Ibid.: point 7 at page 11; emphasis added).

The substantive remit of the high-level group was slightly ambiguous. On the one hand, the Council conclusions took a defensive approach, noting the 'common principles of solidarity, equity and universality' underlying European health care systems, as well as 'the responsibilities of the Member States for the organisation and delivery of health services and medical care', and stressing that 'other developments, such as those relating to the single market [...] should be consistent with the Member States' health policy objectives'. These words clearly indicated health care ministers' desire to minimize the impact of EU policies on their national systems. On the other hand, the conclusions considered that 'there is a need to strengthen cooperation in order to promote the greatest opportunities for access to health care of high quality while maintaining the financial sustainability of healthcare systems in the European Union', and it mentioned a number of concrete issues for cooperation, including the 'need to exchange clinical and other information' and the establishment of European 'reference centres' for highly specialized treatments.

It was the message of stronger cooperation that would come to occupy a central place in subsequent Commission documents. In its 2004 Communication on the follow-up to the high-level reflection process, the Commission sought to broaden the agenda by stating that, apart from the issue of patient mobility, 'health systems across Europe also already face common challenges' and 'cooperation at European level has great potential to bring benefits both to individual patients and to health systems overall' (European Commission 2004c: 2). In addition to recommendations on patient mobility, the Communication set out 'a range of ways in which European collaboration can bring concrete benefits to the effectiveness and efficiency of health services across Europe' (Ibid.: 3). Moreover, the Commission established a high-level group on health services and medical care to continue the work of the high-level reflection process (European Commission 2004e).

Around the same time, the debate on health care and the internal market gained a boost, albeit a 'negative' one, when the Commission, through its DG Internal Market, presented a proposal for a Services Directive. The Services Directive was meant to clarify the legal framework for service provision across borders, and thereby give new impetus to the creation of European markets in a range of services. As part of this endeavour, the proposed directive sought to codify ECJ case law on patient mobility (European Commission 2004a: 14). Included in the proposal's definition of 'service' was health care (see e.g. recital 14); Article 23 of the proposal outlined the framework for the 'assumption of health care costs' made abroad, including the conditions under which authorization could be required. The proposed text closely followed, and basically did little more than to codify, the ECJ's case law in this field. Still, it incited a fierce response from national health care communities around the EU, who feared that the directive would be the first step towards the further liberalization of health care systems. The health care sector was joined in its criticism by numerous other interests that were opposed to greater cross-border competition in their sector. The opposition as a whole was led by trade unions, which mainly opposed the principle that service providers would be allowed to operate abroad under the rules of their home country. After massive protests, culminating in large-scale protest marches (an almost unique case of public mobilization around an EU policy issue), the European Parliament made a number of fundamental changes to the proposal. Among other things, it excluded health care from the scope of the directive and deleted the proposed Article 23 on cross-border treatments (European Parliament 2006).

The proponents of a greater EU role in health care policies received another blow when the proposed Constitutional Treaty was rejected in referenda in France and the Netherlands in 2005. Opposition to the EU's liberalizing policies (in France) or its increasing remit in general (in the Netherlands) had fuelled a substantial part of the 'no' vote. In the mandate for an alternative 'Reform Treaty', which was concluded at the June 2007 European Council, the Dutch government insisted on including an interpretive provision on 'services of general interest', such as health care. The provision, which was annexed as a protocol to the new Lisbon Treaty, underlined the role of national and local governments in providing and organizing those services, and the legitimacy of diversity among member states in the way that they organized these services. Moreover, it stressed that '[t]he provisions of the Treaties do not affect in any way the competence of Member States to provide, commission and organise noneconomic services of general interest' (European Council 2007: 21, footnote 12). This protocol certainly was not the final legal word on the EU's role in relation to health care systems, but it signalled once again the political sensitivity of taking up health care issues and the strong feelings of (at least part of) the member state governments in this regard.

Recognizing the vast political resistance to including health care in the Services Directive (not only in the European Parliament but also among member states), the Commission proposed to begin a separate legislative initiative on cross-border health care (European Commission 2006a: 3). In a broad consultation process among member states and stakeholders organized by DG Sanco, it invited answers to a set of quite general questions on what the role of the EU in the field of health care should be, again stressing the issue of patient mobility and 'the wider challenges facing health systems, beyond the specific case of cross-border health itself', such as rising costs and ageing populations (European Commission 2006c: 5). Later that year, the Council of Health Ministers adopted a Statement on 'Common Values and Principles in EU

Health Systems' (Council 2006: 33–7), which it urged the Commission
to respect when drafting any proposals. The statement identified
four common principles underlying European health care systems –
universality, access to good quality care, equity and solidarity – but also
emphasized the great diversity among member state systems and the
primacy of member states in putting these principles into practice. As
the statement said:

> In particular, decisions about the basket of healthcare to which citizens
> are entitled and the mechanisms used to finance and deliver
> that healthcare, such as the extent to which it is appropriate to rely
> on market mechanisms and competitive pressures to manage health
> systems must be taken in the national context (Ibid.: 34).

It acknowledged that 'there is immense value in work at a European
level on health care', but apart from clarifying the legal rights and obligations
of citizens when they receive treatment abroad, this work would
have to be limited to information exchange and mutual learning.

A similar message had been given by the European Parliament in a
2005 report and resolution, in which it stated that 'further cooperation
between the Member States, coordinated by the Commission where
appropriate, should concentrate on the specific issues related to cross-
border health care' (European Parliament 2005a; 2005b: point 3),
although it expressed the hope that 'the free movement of patients
constitutes an incentive also for national healthcare services to meet
the highest possible standards' (Ibid.: point 26). This position was
repeated in the European Parliament's response to the Commission's
consultation (European Parliament 2007).

In summer 2008, the Commission published its proposal for a Directive
on the Application of Patients' Rights in Cross-Border Healthcare, which
was based on the outcomes of the consultation (European Commission
2008a; 2008b). Compared to earlier Commission documents, its language
on mutual cooperation had been toned down considerably. The
main part of the proposal focused on clarifying the rules and procedures
to be followed in cases of cross-border patient mobility. In addition, it
included a number of specific initiatives for cooperation, such as the
establishment of European 'reference networks of health care providers'
to bring together expertise on highly specialized treatments (rather than
the designation of a limited number of centres of reference which had
been under debate before), the development of joint standards in order
to connect national health information systems, the establishment of

an EU network for medical health technology assessments, and the joint collection of statistical data. These were significant initiatives in terms of stimulating cooperation between member states. At the same time, they tied in with the existing focus of the EU on cross-border health issues and its specific focus on public health rather than health care issues. However, they fell far short of a strategy to address the 'common challenges' of rising costs and ageing, or to give the EU a role in comprehensive health care debates.

6.4   The limits of agenda expansion in EU health policy

The above analysis has shown that the status of health care issues on the EU agenda is mixed. Until the late 1990s, it was warranted to claim that health care hardly occupied any position on the EU agenda. Since then, several developments have led to greater attention for health care issues. As Scott Greer (2008: 220) noted, 'there are legal debates, policy debates, specialized publications (such as *Eurohealth*), interest groups, and all the other activities that come with a recognized policy issue'. In a way, then, even issues of health care organization and financing have made their entrance onto the EU agenda and are likely to remain there for the foreseeable future.

At the same time, agenda attention for health care issues remains limited in a number of ways. First, much of the debates on the organization and financing of health care take place in relatively inconsequential venues. If we apply John Kingdon's distinction between 'governmental agendas' and 'decision agendas', the debate on health care systems has been confined mainly to the (broader but less consequential) 'governmental agenda' of the EU. Only seldom has the issue come onto the EU's decision agenda, and when it has, generally it has met with fierce resistance from national politicians and the European Parliament.

Second, the debate on health systems has focused on a limited number of specific issues. In the tobacco case of Chapter 5, as in the fisheries case that will be discussed in the next chapter, the EU has been involved in all aspects of the issue, and EU policy debates have included the full range of policy options available at national level. By contrast, in the case of health systems, whole issue areas have been practically ignored in the debate. In all fairness, the area of health care organization and financing *is* much broader and more complex than tobacco control, and perhaps fisheries policy, but in terms of understanding the limits on agenda expansion in the EU, it is important to note which health care issues have and have not made it onto the EU's political agenda. What is striking about the agenda process sketched above is that the debate has concentrated on the cross-border aspects of health care provision and financing. Attempts to broaden the agenda to a more general consideration of the effectiveness and efficiency of health systems, which the Commission has consistently pushed for, have failed so far.

In terms of agenda status, then, the organization and financing of health care is comparable to the alcoholism policy discussed in the previous chapter. That issue also has reached the EU governmental agenda. As a consequence, the debate around it shows many of the same features that Greer identified for health care policy, such as specialized publications, ongoing legal and policy debates and active interest groups. Yet, both alcoholism and health care systems issues have found it more difficult to enter the EU's decision agenda. Hence, relative to other issues on the EU agenda and to domestic agendas, the agenda status of both alcoholism policy and health care systems policy has remained weak.

How then can we explain both the rise of issues of health care systems on the EU agenda and the limits on their agenda status? Over the past 15 years, the European Commission has been the most active proponent of a greater EU role in debates on health care systems. Starting with commissioner Padraig Flynn in the mid-1990s and continuing with the activities of several Directorates-General (Employment, Sanco, Internal Market) in the past few years, the Commission has sought to expand the reach of the EU in this field. In doing so, it has been helped by two factors. The first is the gradual rise of common debates on, and understandings of, health care problems in European states which led to the identification of shared challenges and approaches to tackling those problems. The main challenge, as health policymakers in most European countries have identified it, has been to contain the costs of health care systems while maintaining a fair degree of equal access for all citizens. In the last decade, this issue has gained an additional twist with the increased attention for the consequences of ageing populations. The common approach consists of the OECD's 'public contract' model: the introduction of elements of competition in health systems coupled with public funding of and universal access to health services. Even if actual health policies are still very different between European countries, these commonalities in policy debate have allowed the Commission to frame European debates in terms of 'common' challenges which, *because* they are common to all or most EU member states, may benefit from joint initiatives at EU level.

The second has been ECJ case law, which has defined health care service delivery firmly in terms of the EU internal market. This case law required some kind of response on the part of member state health ministers. Moreover, as internal market issues are central to the EU's tasks and remit, it gave the Commission a perfectly legitimate (and legal) basis to deal with health care systems issues.

These developments, coupled with Commission activism, have led to openings on the EU's political agenda in the sense that issues of health care systems have become topics of discussion and an exchange of views. However, the Commission has not been able to move issues of health care organization and financing from the EU's governmental to the decision agenda, except for a much narrower set of health care issues directly linked to cross-border service delivery. Any attempts to bring broader issues of health care systems and reform to the fore have run into the reluctance of member state governments to allow the EU, and the Commission in particular, to play an active role in this field. Because of this reluctance, subsidiarity issues have played a central role in EU debates on health care systems. The success of this agenda-limiting strategy has rested on two crucial factors. First, EU member states have been unanimous on the role of the EU in the field of health care systems. As a result, the Commission has not been able to exploit the differences between member states to push the issue further. This has been different in the alcoholism case, where some member state governments have pushed actively for the issue at EU level, while others have opposed it. Therefore, the key political struggle in the alcoholism debate was between different policy approaches to the issue, even if subsidiarity arguments were used often by opponents of EU activity in that field. By contrast, the debate on health systems has been dominated to a far greater extent by the question of whether the EU should play a role in it and, if so, how far that role should extend – quite apart from the substantive policy preferences of member state governments. Second, the position of member state governments has been strengthened by the unanimity, at least on this point, between their different units. Although issues of health care systems have been discussed in different venues within the EU – related to economic and financial policy, social policy and health policy – member state government representatives in each of these venues have shared reluctance to allow the EU to play a more active role. Among themselves, governmental departments have differed considerably on the course to take with regard to health care organization and financing, but at least they have shared an understanding that the role of the EU in this field should not go beyond facilitating the exchange of views and regulating some specific cross-border aspects of health care delivery. This, too, has made it difficult for the Commission (to be more precise, its various Directorates-General) to tap into differences between various parts of government in order to move the issue forward.

The result of all this is a fascinating agenda struggle at the European level in which the two sides have employed different strategies. On the one hand, the European Commission has sought to break up the issue area into small, specific pieces in the hope of building up the kind of impetus that may lay the ground for further initiatives. By creating specific groups dealing with issues such as quality standards for hospital treatment, or common formats for information exchange, the Commission has tried to keep the debate away from the larger and more principled arguments on subsidiarity and the role of the EU in health care. Instead, it has sought to appeal to the shared problems and understandings of issue specialists. On the other hand, member state governments have sought to reinforce the broad, formal limits on EU competence in the field of health care by adopting general statements of principle. These include, for example, the Statement on Services of General Interest which was included in the Treaty of Lisbon (2007) and the Statement on Common Values and Principles adopted by the Council of Health Ministers.

The fascinating thing about this clash of strategies is that the final result is unclear. As long as member state governments remain united in their opposition to a greater EU role in the field of health care systems, Commission attempts to keep the issue alive will lead only to limited agenda successes. At the same time, broad statements of principle cannot prevent the Commission from taking up specific health care issues that are related to other aspects of its remit. Eventually, this may lead to a greater EU role through a process of piecemeal agenda expansion. Therefore, the long-term fate of the issue of health care systems is still uncertain. However, the agenda process around this issue does show what the limits are in bringing a novel issue onto the EU (decision) agenda.

7
Changing the Tune: Agenda-Setting Dynamics around Recurring Policy Issues

7.1 EU fisheries policy as a recurring issue

The previous two chapters examined cases in which political actors sought to bring a new issue onto the EU agenda. This chapter will focus on agenda-setting processes around issues that are well-established already at EU level, and fisheries is such an issue. The EU has been engaged in fisheries issues since the early 1970s, and it adopted a fully fledged Common Fisheries Policy (CFP) in 1983. Since then, fisheries issues have become a recurring item on the EU agenda.

The recurring character of fisheries issues has been institutionalized in various ways. First, every year the Council of Fisheries Ministers sets total allowable catches (TACs) and quotas for fishermen. TACs specify how much of a specific fish stock can be caught in a certain year, and quotas divide up the TAC among the EU member states. Similarly, technical measures for fisheries, such as the minimum mesh sizes that fishermen are allowed to use, are updated regularly and therefore have appeared on the EU agenda repeatedly. Second, from the 1980s onwards, the European fishing industry was subjected to Multi-Annual Guidance Programmes, which contained detailed plans for the development and restructuring of fishing fleets in the EU.

In addition to these 'routine' recurring decision-making processes, the Regulation that established the CFP's fisheries conservation and management system in 1983 foresaw reviews of the existing policy in 1992 and 2002 (EC 1983). Although formally these reviews only pertained to some specific elements of the policy, in practice they were occasions to debate the future of EU fisheries policy in a more comprehensive manner. In a sense, then, the return of the issue to the political agenda has been built into the policy itself. This is brought out clearly by the numbers of

127

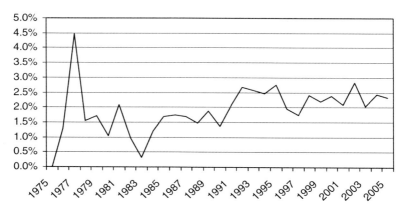

Figure 7.1   COM documents on fisheries as a percentage of all COM documents from 1975 to 2005

Commission documents about fisheries issues over time. Figure 7.1 shows the number of fisheries documents as a percentage of all COM documents in a given year. Apart from a few peaks and lows between 1975 and 1985, fisheries have appeared and reappeared consistently in Commission documents, reflecting the exclusive right of initiative that the Commission has in relation to fisheries policies and decisions taken under the CFP.

Given the recurring character of fisheries issues, the challenge for political actors is not to get the issue on the agenda: firm agenda status is virtually guaranteed by the way in which the policy is organized. However, within the broad field of fisheries, a further struggle takes place about the elements of fisheries policy that should receive attention.

From its inception, the CFP has sought to balance three distinct objectives: developing the fisheries industry as an economic and food-producing sector, supporting communities in coastal regions that are heavily dependent on fisheries, and protecting and conserving fish stocks and the broader marine environment. Related to these objectives is a range of specific issues which, at one time or another, have played an important role in the debates on fisheries, such as the access of fishing vessels to foreign waters, trade in fish and fish products, subsidies to the fishing industry, approaches to conserving fish stocks and the closure of certain sea areas to fisheries. Attention can vary between each of these issues and between the three broad objectives that underlie the CFP. Therefore, the agenda struggle around fisheries policy revolves around attempts to place certain issues or perspectives higher on the agenda, and to prevent others from reaching high agenda status.

The analysis in this chapter is structured as follows. Section 7.2 outlines the development of the EU's CFP. It shows which issues have played a role historically in international fisheries debates and highlights the extent to which certain issues are entrenched in the way that the fisheries policy community deals with fisheries. Furthermore, the historical development of the CFP shows how the EU relates to other international venues in terms of fisheries policy, how this has affected EU fisheries policy, and what specific angle the EU has taken in its approach to fisheries management.

Next, section 7.3 analyses the debate around the CFP in the past 20 years. In doing so, it focuses in on the struggle which arguably has been at the core of fisheries policy developments in the EU: the attempts to shift the CFP towards a more environmentally oriented approach, or the attempts to 'green the CFP'. It will show how political actors have succeeded in reframing fisheries issues and involving a different set of policy venues, and how this has affected the debate on fisheries in the EU. Finally, section 7.4 draws some more general conclusions about agenda-setting in EU fisheries policy, and discusses the relevance of this particular case study for understanding other issues of recurring agenda-setting.

7.2 The creation of a CFP

7.2.1 The internationalization of fisheries issues: Between access and conservation

Nowadays, fish are considered to be a textbook example of a common pool resource that requires international cooperation to prevent its depletion (literally so, in e.g. Eggertsson 1990: 84ff.; Molle 2003: 68–9). This is caused by the fact that, on the one hand, seas and oceans are open in principle to fishermen from various countries, and on the other, fish migrate, crossing the borders of state jurisdictions on the seas. In this situation of open access to a renewable resource, fishermen will tend to take more fish than are sustainable to maintain a viable stock. This results in the depletion of stock (i.e. the extinction of certain fish stocks), and the demise of the industry itself.

The interaction between fishery activities in different countries did not become apparent until the late 1800s. Before that time, the limited operating range of fishing vessels, combined with the relative abundance of the seas, had made fisheries a local activity carried out by vessels from different countries in their 'own' coastal waters. However, in the late 19th century, technological innovation led to substantial increases in the amount of fish that could be caught, as well as in the distances that vessels could travel and the area that they could work in (Farnell and Elles 1984: 2–3; Pauly et al. 2002: 689). Steam engines made it easier to travel to distant fishing areas, while on-board facilities made it possible to store fish for longer periods of time. As a result, fishermen began to operate in waters that traditionally had been the working grounds of fishermen from other countries. Within Europe, this led to a move towards the northwestern seas adjacent to Norway and Iceland, which were (and still are) the richest fishing areas in Europe (Wise 1984: 20ff.). In response to this move, and in order to protect both fish stocks and domestic fishing industries, governments began to claim certain coastal waters for the exclusive use of their own fishermen. The extent of these coastal waters was calculated from the coastline of a country. However, in some cases, such as the heavily indented Norwegian coast, what constituted 'the coastline' was defined quite liberally, thus enclosing vast areas of sea as 'inland waters' from which the territorial waters were subsequently determined (Wise 1984: 69).

The first attempt to regulate access to fishing grounds was made in 1882, when eight countries from north-west Europe agreed on the North Sea Fisheries Convention. This limited the area over which states could claim jurisdiction to three nautical miles from the coastline, and specified rules for defining the coastline (Wise 1984: 69). Even though Norway and Sweden refused to sign the convention, this signified the starting-point for international agreements on fisheries in Europe. The issue of access to fishing grounds which lay behind the 1882 Convention was by far the most important one in that period. However, issues of fisheries conservation also made an appearance, as scientists became aware of the interdependence of fish stocks in different waters. During the 1882 conference, the German delegation had sought to put the conservation of small fish on the agenda, but this attempt had failed. However, by the end of the century, it had become increasingly clear that overfishing represented a threat to fish stocks. In response to this, the International Council for the Exploration of the Sea (ICES) was set up in 1902. Rather than regulating fishing activities, its mandate was to collect information and to do scientific research with a view to increasing the knowledge base about fish stocks in the north-east Atlantic (Farnell and Elles 1984: 4; Wise 1984: 78–9).

Therefore, in the first half of the 20th century, access and conservation issues developed along different tracks, with formal authority over conservation issues left firmly in the hands of individual states. Issues of access remained controversial, with expanding fishing fleets and catch capacities intensifying the competition for fishing grounds. In the 1930s and 1950s, this led to a series of disputes between the UK and its northern neighbours (Norway and Iceland), after the latter had expanded unilaterally the coastal waters over which they claimed jurisdiction. In the case of *UK* v. *Norway*, the International Court of Justice ruled in favour of Norway, which subsequently declared a 12-mile fishing zone around its coastline. The UK–Icelandic conflict developed in a more dramatic way. During the three 'cod wars' from 1958 onwards, UK fishing vessels were escorted by marine ships to protect them from being arrested by the Icelandic coastguard, and shots were exchanged between British and Icelandic marine vessels (Leigh 1983: 64–7). In addition, attempts failed to arrive at uniform international norms for the determination of territorial waters at the first and second United Nations Conferences on the Law of the Sea (UNCLOS I and II) in 1958 and 1960 respectively (Wang 1992: 25–6).

Debates on conservation issues were revitalized after the Second World War when the International Conference on Overfishing was held in London, in which 12 Western European states participated. It led to a convention that laid down minimum mesh sizes for fishing nets (an often-used method to protect small, immature fish) and size limits for a number of species. However, the participants were unable to agree on limits to the quantity of fish caught, even though this was seen as essential to ensure the conservation of fish stocks (Nature 1946; Wise 1984: 79–80).

Around the same time, the UN began to set up international fisheries organizations, which brought together states in order to manage fish stocks in the sea areas where their fishermen were active. The first such organization was the International Convention for the North West Atlantic Fisheries (ICNAF), which was created in 1949 (Farnell and Elles 1984: 4). ICNAF had a permanent commission advised by a scientific committee. The commission could make recommendations for the regulation of fishing activities, including technical requirements (such as mesh sizes) and catch limitations. However, these recommendations had to be accepted by the government of a state in order to become binding on that state. As a result, ICNAF provided a framework for cooperation on fisheries management issues but could not impose any regulations on its members. Notwithstanding the variety in institutional specifics, this became the general model for regional fisheries management organizations (RFMOs), which currently cover a wide range of fisheries areas in the world (FAO 2008; McDorman 2005; Sydnes 2001).[1] Most directly relevant for European countries were the creation of the General Fisheries Council (since 2004, General Fisheries Commission) for the Mediterranean (GFCM) in 1952, and the North East Atlantic Fisheries Convention (NEAFC) in 1963. All these RFMOs operate under the auspices of the Food and Agriculture Organization (FAO), a specialized agency of the UN.

As a result, there was a web of international institutions and agreements in Europe in the field of fisheries already before the EEC was created, and before it began to work on a fisheries policy. At the same time, a number of issues remained unresolved. These included the access rights of fishing vessels to foreign waters and the effectiveness of conservation regimes. For some actors, the EU offered new opportunities to address these issues. Yet within the specific institutional context of the EU, they acquired some additional twists.

7.2.2   Towards an EU fisheries policy

The first attempt to place fisheries on the EU agenda was made when the UK began talks on becoming an EU member in the early 1960s. During those talks, the UK government indicated 'their interest in the settlement of common fishery problems on a European basis' (UK negotiator Edward Heath, as quoted in Wise 1984: 74). When French President Charles de Gaulle vetoed British entry into the EU, the UK government convened a separate fisheries conference in 1964 with a view to establishing European-wide norms for access of fishing vessels. The European Commission was present at this conference as an observer. The resulting convention provided for a six-mile zone within which the coastal state had exclusive rights, and a 6-to-12-mile zone in which fishermen from other countries could fish, if they had done so traditionally. The convention did not address the issue of conservation, thus falling short of a comprehensive approach to fisheries issues. Moreover, as in 1882, a number of Nordic states with rich fishing waters refused to sign the convention, so this still did not resolve the issue of access (Wise 1984: 75–7).

In the end, a CFP was created on a different basis: that of agricultural policy. An EU policy on fisheries had been foreseen in the Treaty of Rome, which established the European Economic Community in 1957. Article 38(1) of the Treaty stipulated that '[t]he common market shall extend to agriculture and trade in agricultural products', whereby 'agriculture' was defined to include fisheries. Moreover, Article 38(4) mandated the creation of a 'Common Agricultural Policy' for agricultural products, the broad objectives and outlines of which were specified in subsequent Treaty articles. Despite the inclusion of fisheries in agriculture, the EU's Common Agricultural Policy (CAP) focused exclusively on the products of soil and stock farming, which most people would consider to be 'agriculture' in a strict sense. The construction of the CAP took up so much effort that fisheries was left aside for the moment (Holden 1994: 17). As a result, by the mid-1960s trade in fish products was still a matter for the member states, with each state levying its own import tariffs both towards other member states and towards those outside the EU (Leigh 1983: 23).

The construction of a CFP was taken up finally as a result of efforts to liberalize the trade of fisheries products in global organizations. Activities under the General Agreement on Tariffs and Trade (GATT, the predecessor of the WTO) and the OECD had led to a lowering of tariffs on fisheries products in Europe, thus intensifying competition between fisheries industries both within and outside of the EU. In addition, tariffs on trade in fisheries products between EU member states were abolished gradually during the 1960s (Holden 1994: 18; Leigh 1983: 24; Wise 1984: 87). This posed a particular threat to French and Italian fishermen, who had been protected by high trade barriers and had difficulties competing with more efficient fisheries industries in other EU member states and the rest of the world. In response, in the early 1960s the French government began to push for a CFP along the lines of the Common Agricultural Policy. This implied that the liberalization of trade in fisheries products would be accompanied by EU policies to support the fisheries industry through subsidies and price guarantees (Holden 1994: 18; Lequesne 2004: 19; Leigh 1983: 24–6; Wise 1984: 87).

For the European Commission, this offered the opportunity to settle a number of fisheries issues at the same time. The Commission plans, which were presented first in 1966, included a number of elements that were to become central to the CFP. First, the plans sought to settle issues of access by introducing the principle of 'equal access', whereby fishermen from across the EU would have access to the fishing grounds of all member states. This was the fisheries equivalent of the free movement principles in the EEC Treaty, which governed trade in products and services, the activities of workers and the establishment of firms. Second, the CFP proposals provided for free trade in fisheries products among EU member states, an issue which had been discussed between European countries before but always had been given much less attention than access rights. As under the CAP, free trade under the CFP was to be accompanied by a system of price support that guaranteed minimum prices to EU fishermen, combined with protection from cheaper imports from outside the EU. Third, the CFP instituted subsidies for modernizing fishing fleets and aimed to harmonize national fisheries policies (e.g. regarding state aid to fishermen) with a view to creating equal competition conditions between all member states (Leigh 1983: 25ff.; Wise 1984: 88ff.).

In contrast to these three elements, the fourth potential element, conservation, received little attention in the original CFP. It hardly played a role in the Commission proposals and subsequent discussions among member states (Holden 1994: 18; Wise 1984: 106). The regulations that established the CFP in 1970 did provide for EU conservation measures in the 12-mile territorial waters of the member states, but it excluded any role of EU institutions outside that area. Since most fish stocks dwelled on the high seas, this provision had little practical effect, although it did establish the kernel of a more extensive future EU role in this area (Leigh 1983: 31).

The CFP was established finally in 1970 after prolonged debates between member states on the specifics of the access and common market provisions. The final boost to consensus was given by the impending talks with the UK, Ireland, Denmark and Norway about their accession to the EU. These were all important fisheries nations with, even more importantly, some rich fishing grounds. It was in the interest of the existing six members to codify the principle of equal access before the accession talks started, so that it could be presented as part of the EU package (the *acquis communautaire*) that the new member states had to adopt in order to become members. To that end, the two regulations that founded the CFP were hammered through on the very day that talks with the four applicants would begin.

7.2.3   Developing a conservation policy within the CFP

Understandably, the four aspiring members were not too happy about the *fait accompli* with which they had been presented. As a concession, the Accession Treaty of 1972 contained two provisions that modified the original CFP package. First, as a modification to the equal access principle, the access regime of the 1964 Convention was adopted as a transitional regime until the end of 1982 (EC 1972: Article 100(1)). Second, the Accession Treaty stipulated that the EU would have to come up with a conservation policy within six years after the accession of the new member states (EC 1972: Article 102). For Norwegian fishermen, these concessions still fell short of what they found acceptable, and fisheries issues were decisive for the defeat of EU membership in the Norwegian referendum on accession (Leigh 1983: 6). The other three countries did join the EU, thus integrating the provisions of the Accession Treaty into the future operation of the CFP.

Quite apart from these intra-European debates, global developments in the field of fisheries policy had been on the move as well. The most important development in this regard was the declaration of 200-mile Exclusive Economic Zones (EEZs) by a number of states, beginning in Latin America. In these EEZs, states claimed the exclusive right to regulate economic activity, including fisheries. Although controversial at first, this state practice attracted growing consensus during the third UN Conference on the Law of the Sea (UNCLOS III), which had begun in 1973. UNCLOS would lead to a formal agreement only in 1982, but around the mid-1970s the principle of EEZs had been established as a matter of unwritten but generally accepted international law. The advent of EEZs changed the context of fisheries policy dramatically because vast areas of what was formerly the 'high seas' would come under the jurisdiction of a particular state. For the European Commission, this provided an additional argument to move to an EU conservation regime and to argue for a common EU presence in RFMOs. Because of its close link with the external relations of the EU, the issue was taken up first by the Commissioner for External Relations, Sir Christopher Soames, whose Directorate-General prepared a Communication to the Council on the implications of the establishment of EEZs in February 1976 (European Commission 1976a; Farnell and Elles 1984: 16–17). In April of that year, a separate Directorate-General for fisheries was created, building on the group of officials that had worked within DG Agriculture thus far (Wise 1984: 157).

In September 1976, the Commission presented its proposals for a revamped CFP (Wise 1984: 149ff.). The three elements of the 1970 CFP were to be maintained; in addition, the Commission proposed to introduce an EU-wide conservation policy. In order to do so effectively, so the Commission argued, it would be necessary to establish a 'Community Zone' for fisheries that would cover all the EEZs to be established by the member states. Moreover, the Commission proposed to transfer the conduct of external fisheries relations (i.e. agreements with other states and participation in RFMOs) to EU level (European Commission 1976b). The external elements of the proposal were quickly agreed. In a meeting in October 1976, the member states agreed to establish collectively EEZs on 1 January 1977 and to allow the Commission to represent the entire EU in its dealings with states outside the EU (Wise 1984: 157–8). However, EEZs were not established in the Mediterranean; as a result it was decided later that the new conservation regime would not cover that area (Holden 1994: 40; Lequesne 2004: 59).

By contrast, the internal aspects of the proposed policy gave rise to prolonged debate and stalemate. To begin with, the perennial issue of access became a bone of contention again, particularly in view of the end of the temporary arrangements contained in the Accession Treaty. In the end, this was settled by retaining the 1972 arrangement, albeit with more opportunities for member states to restrict fishing access to their 12-mile territorial waters and by establishing a special zone off the northern coast of Great Britain where Scottish fishermen had preferential access, the 'Shetland Box' (EC 1983: Articles 6 and 7; Wise 1984: 228–30).

The conservation measures led to long debates. In keeping with the consensus on fisheries management which had developed within UNCLOS, the Commission proposed to introduce a system of limited catches. To that end, for each species every year a TAC would be calculated: this TAC would be divided between the EU and third countries which had access to those fishing areas. Subsequently, the EU part of the TAC would be divided among its member states in quotas. The fishermen from a given member state would be allowed to catch no more than their country's quota for that year. In order to avoid recurring debates about the division of quotas, the shares of each member state in a particular TAC would be fixed once and for all (the principle of 'relative stability'). This meant that the definition of relative shares became crucial for future fishing opportunities in each member state, necessitating long negotiations to arrive at an outcome to which all member state governments could agree. Eventually, this occurred on 25 January 1983, when the EU member states adopted a Regulation on the Conservation and Management of Fisheries Resources (EC 1983).

The CFP was finally complete and included a fully fledged fisheries management policy, the central elements of which are still in place today. However, this was by no means the end of debates on the CFP. On the contrary: the debate about fisheries conservation would become more intense as the results of the CFP's conservation system became apparent. The 1983 Regulation foresaw evaluations of, and revisions to, the access arrangements within 10 and 20 years after its adoption. However, even apart from those formalized feedback points, fisheries management issues were to come back onto the EU agenda in the 1990s and 2000s.

7.3   'Greening' the CFP

7.3.1   The mixed blessings of the CFP

Assessing the first ten years of the CFP's conservation policy, the former head of the DG Fisheries' Conservation Unit, Mike Holden, noted that: 'On the basis of whether the conservation policy has achieved its political objectives, the conservation policy can only be adjudged a total success. [...] In contrast, it has been an almost total practical failure' (Holden 1994: 167). This judgement, in particular in regard to the CFP's conservation objectives, is mirrored in almost all assessments of the CFP (see e.g. Daw and Gray 2005: 190; Karagiannakos 1996; Payne 2000: 306; Symes 1997: 139).

Politically, the CFP has been a success in the sense that many of the thorniest political issues have been pacified. The issue of access, which had led to sustained controversy among European countries from the late 19th century onwards, has been effectively settled under the CFP. Also, decision-making on TACs and quotas has become a routine political process. The setting of TACs and quotas has been subject to recurring bickering over their size, but in the end consensus has been reached every year, and the principle of relative stability has been maintained, even after the accession to the EU of the major fishing nations, Portugal and Spain.

However, in terms of conservation the results have been more mixed. Although the state of fish stocks has not deteriorated uniformly for all species (Holden 1994: 156ff.), experts generally agree that the state of European fisheries has worsened over the years. Several reasons have been cited for the apparent ineffectiveness of the CFP in conserving fish stocks. First, the EU's decision-making process has led routinely to higher TACs and quotas than those recommended by scientists (Daw and Gray 2005: 190; Holden 1994: 56ff. and 106ff.; Karagiannakos 1996; Symes 1997: 147). In the Council of Ministers, which ultimately sets TACs and quotas, the balancing act between conservation concerns, the economic interests of the fisheries industry and the social needs of fisheries-dependent regions has led fisheries ministers to increase the sizes of TACs and quotas compared to those proposed by the Commission on the basis of ICES recommendations. Similarly, the setting of more stringent technical measures, such as larger mesh sizes to protect small fish, has been held up for years due to controversies in the Council (Daw and Gray 2005: 190; Holden 1994: 91ff.; Symes 1997: 148), while efforts to reduce the capacity of the EU's fishing fleet have been both limited and ineffective (Hatcher 2000).

Second, enforcement of the adopted policies is notoriously difficult and compliance has been low. The activities of fishermen at sea are difficult to monitor and intensive inspections are often prohibitively expensive. Hence, the fisheries sector has been haunted by what is generally known as 'IUU' (illegal, unreported and unregulated) fishing (Bray 2000). As a result, the difference between officially registered catches of fish and actual catches has been estimated to be as large as 60 per cent (Karagiannakos 1996: 245).

Third, a related problem is that of by-catch and associated discards. TACs and quotas are set for individual species, but as different fish stocks do not swim in isolation from each other, fishermen tend to catch fish from several species at the same time. This means that, apart from the species that they are authorized to fish for, the catch also includes species that they are not, or for which they have already exhausted their quotas. Since fishermen are not allowed to sell this by-catch, they throw it back into the sea ('discards'), even though most of the fish are dead by then. These discards can amount to up to 60 per cent of a vessel's total catch (Gray 1997: 154; Todd and Ritchie 2000: 142). Thus by-catch contributes to stock depletion, even though it does not fall under official TACs and quotas.

These conservation problems are not unique to Europe or the EU. Similar problems of stock depletion have occurred in other parts of the world (Carr and Scheiber 2004; Daw and Gray 2005: 189; Pauly et al. 2002). On some occasions this has led even to stock collapses and the complete disappearance of stocks. In the 1990s, such stock collapses led to the closure of formerly rich fishing grounds off the coast of New England in the US, and on the Grand Banks off Newfoundland in Canada (Government of Canada 2008; Pauly et al. 2002: 690). These collapses and the subsequent closures of complete sea areas for fisheries generated much publicity, sending shockwaves through fisheries policy communities worldwide. In addition, they helped to fuel rising consumer awareness of fisheries conservation problems as well as greater involvement of environmental groups in fisheries issues. Until the 1990s, such issues were discussed in a relatively closed circle of fisheries management experts and representatives of the industry. During the 1990s this began to change, as environmental NGOs took an increasing interest in fisheries issues and established campaigns against fishing practices that threatened fish stocks and the marine environment more generally (Gray et al. 1999; Richards and Heard 2005; Todd and Ritchie 2000). In response to these NGO activities and the general rise of public concern over fish depletion, in 1997 Unilever (the world's largest buyer of fish) and the WWF initiated the Marine Stewardship Council(MSC), a certification scheme for fish caught in a sustainable way. Fish that was caught in compliance with the MSC criteria was awarded a label similar to the label for sustainable wood products established by the Forest Stewardship Council (FSC).

It is against this background that the conservation of fish stocks has risen on the agenda again during the 1990s and 2000s. Much of this agenda struggle, in the EU and beyond, has focused on efforts to give environmental concerns a more central role in fisheries policies. As a result, it has pitted so-called ecosystems approaches against traditional fisheries management approaches.

7.3.2 The rise of ecosystem approaches to fisheries management

Traditional fisheries management focuses on single stocks. For each individual stock, a maximum allowable catch is calculated based on an assessment of the state of the stock and projections of its future development. This approach is used widely and can rely on well-established methodologies for assessing fish stocks and establishing 'reference points' for setting TACs (Holden 1994: 176ff.; Link 2002). However, what this fails to do is to take into account the interactions that exist in the marine environment. For example, larger fish eat smaller fish, therefore fishing for a certain stock not only affects that particular stock but also predator stocks (which lose part of their food base), and species that are eaten by the stock that is being fished. This web of interactions extends beyond fish species to other living organisms in the marine environment, which are part of that environment's food web (Morishita 2008: 22; Parsons 2005: 383 and 384). In addition, fishing activities (such as the use of certain types of fishing nets) may affect the marine environment apart from catching fish, for example, when they damage coral reefs. Therefore, it can be argued that fisheries management should focus not on single species, as is the common practice, but on the entire ecosystems to which those fish belong. By taking into account the complex interactions between elements of the marine ecosystem, a much more comprehensive assessment can be made of the effects of fishing activities and hence of the proper management measures to be taken. This can lead to substantially different outcomes. Just taking into account the interrelations among fish stocks may lead to vastly different levels of optimal catches for each single species – often, levels which may seem counterintuitive.

In fisheries circles, this alternative approach to fisheries management has become known as the 'ecosystem approach' (Barnes and McFadden 2008; Link 2002; Morishita 2008; Parsons 2005). Although appealing in theory, its main drawback is that it is much more difficult to operationalize into concrete proposals for fisheries management, because it is newer and because of the complexities raised by assessing dynamic interlinkages within ecosystems. Among fisheries scientists, attempts have been made to develop methods and concrete management tools that would fit an ecosystem approach. However, in policy circles, the term has been used as a shorthand for a more holistic approach to fisheries management that seeks to integrate the effects of fisheries on other aspects of the marine environment, as well as the effects of other human activities on fish stocks. As a result, as US fisheries experts Cassandra Barnes and Katherine McFadden (2008: 387) noted: 'The practical applications of this strategy are not yet completely defined, but the philosophical shift towards EAM ["Ecosystem Approaches to Management"] has begun.' It is this philosophical shift which has been at the forefront of political debates on fisheries in the recent decade.

The term 'ecosystem management' already existed when the CFP's conservation policy was adopted in 1983. A contemporary observer, Michael Leigh, mentioned the ecosystem approach as an alternative to the CFP's focus on single species management in his 1983 book on the CFP (Leigh 1983: 89). However, his passing reference testifies to the rather ephemeral status of the concept at the time. This was also reflected in the UN Conference on the Law of the Sea (UNCLOS III), which finally led to the Convention on the Law of the Sea of 1982 (LOS Convention; UN 1982). The LOS Convention stipulated the obligation of coastal states to maintain living resources in their EEZs by fixing TACs and quotas (Articles 61–2). In addition, it required cooperation between states and the creation of RFMOs to protect species migrating between EEZs or roaming the high seas (Articles 63–4 and 117–18). However, the ecosystem approach was not implied in the UNCLOS regime. Although reference was made to 'effects on species associated with or dependent upon harvested species' (Articles 61(4) and 119(1)(b)), the instruments foreseen by the LOS Convention conformed to traditional fisheries management approaches (cf. Morishita 2008: 20). These approaches were enshrined also in the CFP's conservation policy, which had borrowed much from the general principles on fisheries management developed during the talks leading up to the LOS Convention (Leigh 1983: 8).

The credentials of ecosystem approaches received an important boost with the 1992 UN Conference on Environment and Development in Rio de Janeiro (Rio Summit). One of the results of the Rio Summit was the UN Convention on Biological Diversity (CBD) of 1992 (UN 1992b), which had as its objective the promotion of the maintenance of biodiversity, defined as 'the variability among living organisms from all sources' (Article 2). Inherent in the concept of biodiversity and the Convention's approach to safeguarding it was a focus on ecosystems, defined as the 'dynamic complex of plant, animal and micro-organism communities and their non-living environment interacting as a functional unit' (Article 2).

On the basis of the CBD, its secretariat began to develop a specific Programme of Work on Marine and Coastal Biological Diversity, which was adopted at the 1998 meeting of the Conference of the Parties to the CBD (CBD 1998). Under its basic principles, the Programme squarely stated that '[t]he ecosystem approach should be promoted at global, regional, national and local levels', signifying a move towards a more comprehensive and environmentally oriented approach to managing the seas.

The Rio Summit also had produced a commitment to establish a separate agreement to implement the UNCLOS provisions on the protection of fish stocks on the high seas (see Agenda 21, paragraph 17.49(e); UN 1992a). This led to the adoption of the UN Agreement on the Conservation and Management of Straddling Fish Stocks and Highly Migratory Fish Stocks (UN Fish Stocks Agreement; UNFSA; UN 1995). Although formally an implementing agreement to the LOS Convention, its wording and approach were influenced heavily by the biodiversity focus of the Rio Summit and the CBD. Among the Agreement's general principles, the protection of biodiversity was accorded a separate provision (Article 5(g)), while reference to ecosystems and/or interdependencies of species was made in four additional principles (Article 5(b), (d), (e) and (f)). Moreover, Article 5(c) and Article 6 of the Agreement laid down the precautionary principle, which requires action to be taken even in the absence of full scientific evidence. As a result, the concept and 'philosophy' of the ecosystem approach had gained a firm foothold in the Agreement.

The Agreement was not the only international instrument to promote a more ecosystem-based approach in fisheries management. Parallel to the Agreement, the FAO developed a Code of Conduct for Responsible Fisheries (FAO 1995; cf. De Fontaubert 1995). This Code also included ample references to ecosystem approaches: as its first general principle, it stipulates that '[s]tates and users of living aquatic resources should conserve aquatic ecosystems' (FAO 1995: Article 6.1). The text of the Code refers to 'biodiversity' five times and to 'ecosystem(s)' no fewer than 24 times. Although non-binding, the Code became a standard document for 'best practice' in fisheries management, thereby contributing to the legitimacy of biodiversity and ecosystem arguments in fisheries management debates. This was made even more explicit in 2001, when the FAO organized a Conference on Responsible Fisheries in the Marine Ecosystem. In the declaration coming out of that conference, the participating states included, as their principal objective, that 'in an effort to reinforce responsible and sustainable fisheries in the marine ecosystem, we will individually and collectively work on incorporating ecosystem considerations into that management to that aim' (FAO 2001).

Moving to ecosystem approaches is easier said than done, and the adoption of principles to this effect does not mean that practical policies will follow. However, the move to ecosystem-based language had two important effects on fisheries policymaking: it legitimated the use of biodiversity arguments in fisheries policy debates, and led to the participation of environmental policymakers in fisheries policymaking.

7.3.3 'Greening' international and EU fisheries policies

Within the EU, DG Environment became more active in fisheries issues from the mid-1990s onwards. This interest was fuelled by the depletion of stocks (tying in with the EU's role in species protection) and the effects of fishing on ecosystems and biodiversity. In its efforts to become involved in fisheries issues, DG Environment could draw on a body of established principles and policy programmes. First, integrating environmental protection in other policy areas had become a general principle in the EC Treaty following the Amsterdam Treaty of 1997 (Article 6 of the EC Treaty). This commitment was confirmed at the highest political level in the European Councils of Luxembourg in December 1997 and Cardiff in May 1998 (European Council 1997; 1998; see also European Commission 1998b). Based on the Treaty's integration provision, DG Environment could promote actively an environmental angle to hitherto separate policy fields such as fisheries (see European Commission 2002b).

On a more concrete level, the protection of biodiversity was part of the EU's environmental policy through the Birds Directive (EC 1979) and the Habitats Directive (EC 1992a). Both directives foresaw the establishment of nature areas that would receive special protection because of their significance for sustaining certain species. Under the Birds Directive these are called Special Protection Areas (SPAs), and under the Habitats Directive, Special Areas of Conservation (SACs) or Sites of Community Importance (SCIs). Together, they form the 'Natura 2000' network of protected nature areas. As of June 2008, this network included more than 5,000 SPAs totalling some 518,000 square kilometres (DG Environment 2008a), and more than 21,000 SACs/SCIs accounting for almost 656,000 square kilometres (DG Environment 2008b).

Under the Birds and the Habitats Directives, nature protection sites could be established not only on land but also in the seas. This opened the door to protecting particularly sensitive and ecologically significant parts of the sea. Since fishing is one (although by no means the only) human activity that affects those areas, creating this type of

Marine Protected Areas (MPAs) could interfere directly with fisheries management measures. Depending on the status of the Area, fisheries could be restricted to certain periods or stocks, certain types of fishing equipment could be banned, or fishing could be prohibited altogether. At the global level, the creation of MPAs as an instrument of comprehensive environmental control of sea areas was promoted by the Conference of the Parties to the CBD in 2004, which set the objective to establish effective networks of MPAs by 2012 (CBD 2004a; 2004b). Following the adoption of the Convention itself, the EU developed a Biodiversity Strategy in 1998 (European Commission 1998a). Building on this strategy, a number of more concrete biodiversity action plans were adopted, including a Biodiversity Action Plan for fisheries (European Commission 2001b). Commitments to integrate environmental concerns into fisheries policy and to promote the wider establishment of Natura 2000 sites in marine environments were confirmed in a series of subsequent documents (EC 2002a; European Commission 1999; 2002a; 2002b; 2004f; 2006b; DG Environment 2007).

The attention given to biodiversity and habitat protection did not translate automatically into more restrictive fishing policies. After all, these policies had to be decided by the EU's fisheries policy community, therefore any potential conflict between the imperatives of habitat protection and fisheries policy would not necessarily be decided in favour of the former (see also European Commission 2008c). However, what all the activity did do was to involve a different set of policymakers in fisheries debates that were receptive to different issues and arguments than the ones traditionally dominant in fisheries policy circles. A concrete example of an issue where this made a difference is the debate on 'bottom trawling'. Bottom trawling is a fishing technique whereby fishing nets are towed on, or very close to, the sea floor in order to 'scrape' the fish out. According to environmental NGOs, bottom trawling represents a particularly unsustainable technique because it leads to increasingly rapid depletion of fish stocks, and the sea floor may be damaged in the process. As a result, a coalition of NGOs, the Deep Sea Conservation Coalition (DSCC), started a campaign for a moratorium on bottom trawling (DSCC 2004; 2007). Rather than directly targeting organizations that were responsible for fisheries management, the coalition sought to include a ban on bottom trawling in a UN General Assembly Resolution, similar to the earlier resolutions banning the use of large-sized driftnets (Lequesne 2004: 113ff.; Todd and Ritchie 2000: 142–3). In so doing, they could tie in with the issue of biodiversity which had become an accepted part of the international environmental agenda.

As a result, in 2004 the Conference of the Parties to the CBD called on the General Assembly to eliminate 'destructive practices' in fisheries (CBD 2004a: point 61). In an interview, a Greenpeace representative explained the strategy:

> The technical bottom trawling moratorium [...] was presented by NGOs as a biodiversity issue. The problem is that it damages highly sensitive habitats in the deep seas. It is also a problem of fisheries management, because a lot of these fisheries stocks [...] are under threat. It is an important point, but it is a secondary point if you see what biodiversity damage is caused. So there the environmental ministries woke up and realized they needed to take part in the discussion.

The issue of bottom trawling was included in a 2004 General Assembly Resolution, urging for interim bans in anticipation of more comprehensive decisions in the future (UN 2004: point 66). In the end, the General Assembly did not adopt such a full ban (UN 2006: point 83); however, by that time, the debate had had repercussions elsewhere. In the EU, it resulted in proposals to limit the use of bottom trawling in sensitive areas (European Commission 2007c). The campaign on bottom trawling, and the positive reception that it had received from many political actors, also served to alert parts of the fisheries policy community to the fact that their playing field had changed. In an interview, a WWF representative pointed to the effects that the campaign had on NEAFC, the RFMO which covers the north-east Atlantic:

> They have changed the way they are working a lot, mainly due to the lobby on bottom trawling. Because, we were saying that high-seas fisheries is not managed, RFMOs are not doing their job, things need to be changed and we need a UN resolution to do that. Then NEAFC [North East Atlantic Fisheries Convention] said: OK, we are going to step up to the plate and we are going to do more than we are doing now.

All in all, the biodiversity or ecosystem angle has opened up new opportunities for political actors to influence fisheries policy. In addition, the greater recognition of interactions in the marine environment has led a number of countries to formulate oceans policies that seek to integrate the various activities on and in the seas within one policy framework. Based on the examples set by Australia, Canada and the US, the European Commission launched its own initiative for a 'maritime policy' in 2007. Led by DG Fisheries (renamed DG Maritime Affairs and Fisheries to mark the occasion), the maritime policy attempted to formulate a framework for comprehensive policymaking in coastal and sea areas (European Commission 2007b). So far, the maritime policy has remained a rather abstract concept, and although most of the interviewees shared the idea that the initiative is useful to highlight the broader context of fisheries issues, they were all quite sceptical about its practical implications for fisheries policy. Greater importance was attached to the marine strategy, an initiative by DG Environment that is to become the environmental 'pillar' of the maritime policy (European Commission 2005b). In contrast with the maritime policy, the marine strategy has resulted in an actual directive that lays down a framework for developing integrated marine policies in different European sea areas (EC 2008). Even if this has not led to concrete changes in fisheries management for now, it has institutionalized further the role of environmental concerns and environmental policymakers in EU fisheries policies.

Against the background of these broader changes in the context of fisheries policy, the CFP itself underwent reforms in the 1990s, and particularly in 2002. It is with the debates on the CFP in a strict sense that we complete the analysis of the agenda struggles around fisheries policy.

7.3.4   Reforming the CFP, 1992–2002

When the CFP's conservation policy was adopted in 1983, it provided for reviews of the Regulation's access provisions after 10 and 20 years (EC 1983: Article 8). These provisions concerned the limited access of foreign vessels to the 6-to-12-mile zone and restricted access to the Shetland Box. However, in practice, these reviews became the occasion for much more comprehensive debates on the CFP.

The 1992 review remained limited in scope (EC 1992b; see also Symes 1997: 144–5). Although the new Regulation briefly referred to the implications of fisheries for the marine ecosystem, essentially the mix of objectives and instruments remained the same. The greatest political challenge to the CFP in that period was the accession of Portugal and Spain to the EU in 1986. The total fishing capacity of the two entrants amounted to some 75 per cent of that of all the old ten member states combined. Applying the principle of equal access to this modern-day armada was not an attractive prospect to the other member states, but in the end the issue was resolved with a ten-year transition period, in which vessels from the two new member states had restricted access to other fishing grounds in the EU (Symes 1997: 144). Portugal and Spain challenged the existing division of quotas under the principle of relative stability, but this system was not altered.

During the 1990s, pressure to reform the CFP began to mount. For the Commission, the planned review of the CFP in 2002 offered the perfect occasion to take up that endeavour, even though in formal terms the review only concerned access provisions. As the Commission said in the Green Paper launching the 2002 reforms: 'Today's situation calls for a thorough and urgent reform of the CFP independent from the legal requirements linked to the 2002 deadline' (European Commission 2001a: 5). The irony of the matter is that in the end, almost every element of the CFP was brought up for reform except the access arrangements. These were maintained exactly as they had been in the 1983 Regulation, and the Commission had had no interest in changing them in the first place.

Thinking about the reforms had begun several years before the review deadline. The 2002 reform was already on the EU's fisheries agenda in the mid-1990s (see e.g. Gray 1997: 151), and the Commission began to consult NGOs about reforming the CFP in 1998 (Gray et al. 1999: 137). Elements of what was later to become the 2002 reform package were pioneered in discussion documents published in 2000 (European Commission 2000a; 2000b). The 2001 Green Paper that officially set off the reform process painted a bleak picture of the CFP's achievements. It pointed out the failure to protect fish stocks effectively, warned of the imminent collapse of fish stocks, and attributed this situation to the multiple objectives that the policy was supposed to achieve: environmental, economic and social. Instead, the Commission urged for clearer priorities aimed foremost at conserving fish stocks, integrating environmental concerns into the CFP, involving stakeholders more closely, strengthening supervision and enforcement, and reducing the (over-)capacity in the European fisheries industry.

For the purpose of this chapter, five proposals are most relevant.[2] First, the Commission sought to introduce longer-term plans. Rather than having annual TACs and quotas (which tended to be inflated in the Council), the Commission wanted to move towards decisions for multiple years. Moreover, these plans would have to be based on an 'ecosystem-oriented management' approach (European Commission 2001a: 21). Second, stakeholders would be involved more closely by creating Regional Advisory Councils (RACs). These councils would be composed of stakeholders from the fisheries industry and NGOs, with a view to giving advice on issues pertaining to a specific region in the EU, such as the Mediterranean, North Sea and Baltic Sea. Third, subsidies for the construction of new vessels would be phased out completely in an attempt to reduce the size of the EU's fisheries fleet. Fourth, the Commission proposed the creation of a 'Community Joint Inspection

Structure' (European Commission 2001a: 30), which would help to achieve greater harmonization of, and coordination between, enforcement agencies in the member states. Finally, the Commission sought to integrate the Mediterranean fully into the CFP, ending the region's exemption from the CFP's conservation policy.

In the end, the adoption of multi-annual recovery and management plans, the creation of RACs, and the phasing out of construction subsidies were included in the new CFP adopted in December 2002 (EC 2002d; European Commission 2002e). Separate initiatives were launched to apply the CFP's conservation regime to the Mediterranean (European Commission 2002c), reduce discards (European Commission 2002d), and establish a joint inspection structure (European Commission 2003a). The latter included the creation of the Community Fisheries Control Agency, which was set up in 2005.

Admittedly, the reform of the CFP is more radical on paper than in reality. TACs remain set at higher levels than those recommended by scientific advisers (Daw and Gray 2005: 190), and several elements (such as the strengthened enforcement system) still need to be developed further. As a result, almost all the interviewees for this study expressed their dissatisfaction with the speed and extent of the changes in the CFP. Nonetheless, as was acknowledged by the interviewees, some changes have been made. Most importantly perhaps in terms of studying agenda-setting processes, the CFP has been set on a course towards the greater inclusion of environmental concerns and greater participation of environmental NGOs and policymakers. Insofar as the CFP has changed and is likely to change, it has been in the direction of stricter controls on fishing activity, reduced fishing capacity and a more comprehensive approach to protecting the marine environment. By contrast, there is no longer a move towards expanding the other two traditional concerns of the CFP (economic development of the fisheries sector and support for fisheries-dependent coastal communities). The actors advocating these causes are effectively fighting a rearguard battle: they may slow down or soften impending reforms, but they no longer set the agenda for EU fisheries policy.

7.4   Agenda change in EU fisheries policy

Agenda-setting around fisheries issues has taken place in two different types of policy venues. The first type includes the 'traditional' fisheries management venues such as DG Fisheries and the Fisheries Council of Ministers, as well as the FAO and the RFMOs that operate under its aegis. Agenda processes in these venues have focused on refining existing approaches to fisheries management: strengthening enforcement and control of regulations, improving decision-making on single-stock TACs and quotas and reducing the negative side-effects of fisheries policies, such as by-catch and discards.

The second type involves venues that, until the early 1990s, were hardly involved (and not very much interested) in fisheries issues. Within the EU, they include DG Environment and the Environmental Council of Ministers, while on a global level they are exemplified by the CBD and the UN General Assembly. The agenda debates in these venues have revolved around much more fundamental challenges to existing fisheries management approaches, aimed at the introduction of more comprehensive ecosystem management approaches and connecting fisheries issues to other environmental issues.

The debates in these two types of venues have not evolved in isolation from each other, neither do they exclude each other. For example, initiatives to combat illegal, unreported and unregulated (IUU) fishing, which have been developed mainly in 'traditional' fisheries management venues, are important for the proponents of ecosystem approaches. After all, what is the use of protecting habitats and working with multi-species TACs if enforcement is lacking? Conversely, initiatives in the newer, environmentally oriented venues have trickled through to traditional fisheries management venues, as exemplified by the FAO Code of Conduct on Responsible Fisheries, or NEAFC's response to the debate on bottom trawling. Therefore, the greater involvement of environmentally oriented venues represents a classic venue shopping strategy: by framing fisheries issues in environmental (in this case, biodiversity) terms, environmental NGOs have been able to raise attention on the part of environmental policymakers, who subsequently have sought to gain a foothold in fisheries policy debates. This type of venue shopping has included both horizontal and vertical elements. The horizontal element consists of the inclusion within the EU of DG Environment as a participant in fisheries policies alongside DG Fisheries. The vertical element can be found in attempts to involve UN agencies and the UN General Assembly in global debates on fisheries policy.

Apart from the substantive positions taken, the debates in the two types of venue have developed at markedly different degrees of abstraction. Within traditional fisheries venues, the focus has been on building up technical expertise and consensus around specific policy options. In the new venues, the debate has been much more abstract, trying to define general principles and approaches whose practical implications often have remained vague. As a consequence, the dynamics of the policy debates and the requirements for successful participation have differed considerably between the two types of venue. The participants in traditional fisheries venues have had to rely more on specific technical expertise, while the newer venues have required greater skill in appealing to broader principles and politicizing the issue. This has meant that fishermen have ignored largely the policy debates in the newer venues and tended to downplay their relevance to fisheries management issues, while some environmental groups consciously have decided to focus their energies on venues outside the traditional fisheries policy community.

How, then, do the agenda processes studied in this chapter relate to those on health policy analysed in Chapters 5 and 6? As explained above, the fisheries issue differs from health issues in the sense that it involves agenda-setting around a recurring policy issue rather than an issue that is new to the EU agenda. Nevertheless, clear similarities in agenda dynamics can be observed between agenda-setting around new issues, and processes of agenda-setting around recurring issues that are aimed at introducing a new approach to those issues. Both cases involve attempts to involve a new set of policymakers in an issue and thereby shift policy debates on that issue away from an existing venue towards a new venue. Also, the strategies employed are similar in both cases. For example, both types of venue shift involve the building up of political impetus around a new approach, attempts to circumvent established policy venues and, more generally, the development of sufficient credibility for the new venues to take initiatives in relation to the issue. For issues that are new to the EU agenda, these attempts focus on the involvement of EU policymakers vis-à-vis national policymakers, while for issues that are already on the EU agenda, they are meant to legitimate a role for a different set of EU policymakers than formerly had been involved. In that sense, a considerable overlap can be observed between the agenda processes described in Chapters 5 and 6, and the processes analysed in this chapter. The most important difference between the two types of processes is that, for recurring policy issues, it is no longer necessary to justify a role for the EU as such. This was already settled before, when the issue first came onto the EU agenda, and now it is taken for granted.

This also implies that agenda processes around recurring issues resemble the type of agenda processes which have been described in domestic political systems. Of course, the specific actors, venues and some of the arguments will differ, as they will when we compare two different countries. However, the dynamic of the process, with its attempts to change issue frames and the associated policy venues, is almost identical. The main difference between the debates around EU fisheries policy and, for example, the cases in the US that Baumgartner and Jones (1993) describe, is that in EU fisheries policy vertical venue shopping (towards other international organizations) has played a greater role. Partly, this may be a result of the issue at stake: after all, fisheries issues involve all kinds of international interdependencies that necessitate international cooperation. However, on closer examination, often the instances of vertical venue shopping in fisheries policy are not related to international interdependencies, but to the development of shared understandings which can be 'imported back' subsequently into domestic (including EU) policy debates. Therefore, overcoming domestic political constraints is an equally important consideration, even in fisheries policy. It may well be that it is the EU's peculiar characteristics as a polity – being more developed than other international organizations, yet competing with those other international organizations for policy niches – that make it more amenable to vertical venue shopping strategies.

8
Reflections on EU Agenda-Setting

8.1 Understanding the rise of issues on the EU agenda

Having analysed the quantitative data in Chapter 4 and the case studies in Chapters 5 to 7, we can make a more general analysis of what drives the formation of policy agendas in the EU. In so doing, we need to make a distinction between the EU's 'governmental agenda' and its 'decision agenda' (cf. Kingdon 2003 [1984]: 4). The governmental agenda consists of issues that are discussed by policymakers in a given period, while the decision agenda concerns issues that are up for active decision-making. As we saw in the previous chapters, issues that come onto the governmental agenda do not necessarily move on to the decision agenda, and the factors that drive the two types of agenda are not identical.

Drawing together the findings of the previous chapters, we can discern three steps in the formation of EU policy agendas, with issues proceeding through each of these steps before they reach the EU's decision agenda. The first step consists of the development of transnational European policy debates. At this stage, an issue is not yet on the agenda of the EU proper, but it can be said to be on the agenda of a transnational policy network. The second step occurs when EU policymakers pick up the issue and develop a debate on it within EU institutions; then the issue enters the EU's governmental agenda. In the third step, the issue moves on to the EU's decision agenda if supportive EU policymakers are able to overcome (potential) blockades by adversaries, either within the EU institutions themselves or among member states. Let us take a look at each step in greater detail.

At its origin, the rise of issues on the EU's governmental agenda is a consequence of their rise in transnational policy networks. These networks consist of policy experts in a given domain who read the same publications, go to the same conferences and meetings, and in these ways develop shared understandings of policy problems and the available policy options to deal with them. The members of these networks may include not only politicians and civil servants operating in a given policy area, but also representatives of interest groups, academics and (specialized) journalists. Often they are rooted in domestic policy networks, but they also include policy experts from international organizations and international interest groups. For transnational policy debates to develop, there has to be a relatively broad consensus among policy experts in that network on what the important issues are in their field. This in turn implies that first, there has to be a degree of convergence among the perspectives of policy experts across EU member states; second, that these experts need to be connected through a transnational network. These two factors mutually reinforce each other, since the convergence of perspectives may give rise to the formation of transnational networks to exchange ideas, while the existence of a transnational network may foster a convergence of perspectives on policy issues.

This type of transnational policy debate can be seen in each of the cases discussed in Chapters 5 to 7. In the tobacco, alcoholism and fisheries cases, international debates on the issues (or in the fisheries case the ecological approach to the issue) had been going on among (domestic) policy experts for quite some time before the EU became active. In the health systems case, a transnational policy debate had developed among health policy experts about the key problems in organizing health care (mainly cost containment, fuelled further by an ageing population) and the most useful approaches to deal with them (reform of health systems to introduce greater elements of competition). In the 1980s, this debate was centred on the OECD, and formed an important prerequisite to the subsequent access of the issue to the EU agenda.

Although at this stage the transnational policy debate may be a European debate, it is not yet an EU debate. For this to happen, policymakers within the EU need not only to be receptive to the issue, but also willing and able to pick it up. As members of a transnational policy network, EU policymakers may contribute to the transnational policy debate that developed in the first stage. However, they may also use the EU itself as a venue for discussing the issue, sponsoring research, exchanging views and developing shared ideas. Then, the issue enters the EU's governmental agenda. The flow of issues from transnational policy debates to the EU governmental agenda can take place through three pathways, which may operate in conjunction with each other. The first pathway occurs when domestic groups, officials or politicians take an issue to EU level. This happened, for example, when the Swedish government tried to bring alcoholism onto the EU agenda. This pathway is the clearest example of a direct link between domestic agendas and the EU agenda.

A second pathway is for one of the EU institutions to take up an issue. In most cases this is the European Commission, which is particularly well placed to take initiatives in relation to the EU agenda. Among the cases discussed in this book, an example of the Commission placing an issue onto the EU agenda is the Green Book on smoke-free environments, which was initiated by the competent unit within DG Sanco. Although this pathway seems to be initiated exclusively at the EU level, nevertheless the rise of issues remains closely tied to developments at the domestic level. Because the Commission tends to take up issues that it believes have a chance of succeeding, it will push them if it sees sufficient support among the policy experts that subsequently have to decide on them. Thus, the Commission came up with the issue of smoke-free environments after observing the rise of smoking bans in the member states, and published its Green Paper after consulting NGOs and member state officials. Here too, the EU agenda reflects the (broader) agendas of policy experts in an issue area.

The third pathway goes via international organizations. Here, the issue first rises in an international organization, then comes onto the EU agenda. For example, this happened in the fisheries case, where the CBD played an important front-running role among international organizations, and in the alcoholism case, where the WHO Regional Office for Europe became active on the issue before the EU.

More often than not, these pathways will combine in a specific agenda process. For example, certain issues or policy options may be developed by policy experts in domestic contexts, they discuss it among each other, attention is given to them in other international organizations, the Commission picks up what is 'in the air', and tries to place it onto the EU agenda. In fact, many of the cases of agenda-setting in this book more or less conform to this model, albeit with differences in the specific sequence and timing.

The move from international policy debates to the EU governmental agenda implies a first filter of issues, because EU institutions are not equally receptive to all issues. Thus, as we saw in Chapter 4, the EU agenda in the field of environmental policy is much more comprehensive than that in the field of health policy, where the EU tends to focus more on issues of public health than on issues of health care. An important reason for this is that environmental and public health issues tie in much more easily with the EU's remit, and the EU institutions have built up a much greater capacity (in terms of both manpower and expertise) to deal with them. Even then, the EU governmental agenda includes a wider range of issues than its decision agenda. For an issue to move from the governmental to the decision agenda, a number of additional hurdles need to overcome. This was brought out, among other things, in the quantitative data of Chapter 4, which showed that written questions in the European Parliament tend to cover a wider variety of issues than the Commission's preparatory (COM) documents. When no concrete decision is at stake (as in European Parliament written questions), it is relatively easy to take up and discuss issues, but when preparations are being made for actual decision-making (as in COM documents), this becomes increasingly difficult.

The same can be seen in the qualitative case studies. In each of the four cases (smoking, alcoholism, health systems and fisheries) the issues came onto the EU's governmental agenda. Of these four issues, only smoking and fisheries made it through to the EU decision agenda, whereas the debates on alcoholism and health systems remained confined largely to the governmental agenda. In each case, the key lay in the dynamics of participation in debates on the issue. The issue of alcoholism had come onto the EU's governmental agenda through the activities of public health experts in the member states, DG Sanco and WHO. However, the passage from this agenda to the EU decision agenda was blocked by the opponents of taking up the issue (primarily in the alcoholic drinks industry), who were able to mobilize other Directorates-General within the European Commission which had a greater interest in the economic and trade aspects of alcoholic beverages. This we can call a 'horizontal blockade' of access to the decision agenda, because it relies on the mobilization of actors that favour a substantively different approach to an issue than the proponents of agenda access. The health systems case shows a different type of dynamic, which we can describe as a 'vertical blockade' to entry onto the EU's decision agenda. Here, the opposition was not primarily to the substance of policy initiatives, but to the fact that the European Commission was assuming a more active role in the first place. Access to the decision agenda was blocked because (nearly) all of the member state governments were reluctant to allow the EU to play a role in this area beyond that of a platform for exchanging views.

The difference between horizontal and vertical blockades has important implications for the conditions under which issues may come onto the EU's decision agenda, and the strategy to be followed by prospective agenda-setters. Horizontal blockades can be overcome by limiting the scope of participation to policymakers that favour entry onto the decision agenda. Anti-smoking policy is a case in point. Because of its loss of credibility during the 1980s and 1990s, the tobacco industry and its potential allies within the European Commission effectively could be excluded from the policymaking process on anti-smoking policy. As a result, public health policymakers found it much easier to translate general policy debates into concrete policy proposals, thus carrying the issue over from the governmental agenda to the decision agenda. Therefore, the key to overcoming horizontal blockades is to exclude those actors and policymaking venues that oppose policy initiatives on the issue.

In the case of vertical blockades, this will not make a difference. After all, as we saw in the health systems case, despite their differences in the substantive approach to the organization and financing of health care, economic, financial, social and health policymakers from the EU member states shared the view that the EU's role in the field should remain limited. This was reinforced by the near-unanimity among the different member states in this respect. Hence, limiting the scope of participation would still leave the opposition intact. If this type of blockade is to be overcome, the only chance for the proponents of agenda access is to widen the scope of participation, in the hope of including policymakers that are willing to consider a greater role for the EU in this field. To take a hypothetical example, if for some reason financial policymakers should be more receptive to a greater EU role than health policymakers, then shifting the debate to financial policymakers would be a way to bypass the blockade put up by health policymakers. In the case of health systems, this has not yet happened, but some of the initiatives taken by the Commission can be interpreted as attempts to find the venue most receptive to issues of health care organization and financing.

Horizontal and vertical blockades are particularly relevant when an issue first comes onto the EU agenda (as in the novel issues of Chapters 5 and 6). When an issue is already on the agenda (as was the case with fisheries in Chapter 7), agenda dynamics follow a much more 'classic' pattern of venue shopping that closely resembles Baumgartner and Jones' (1993) analysis of venue shopping among parts of the US federal government, and which was found by Sheingate (2000) in his analysis of the reform of EU agricultural policy. By constructing a different image of an issue (in this case, fisheries conservation as an issue of biodiversity rather than stock management), the proponents of policy change have been able to mobilize a new set of policymakers (environmental

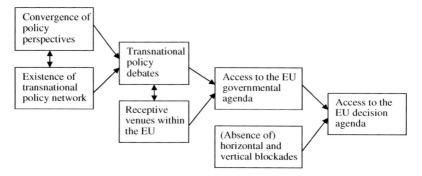

Figure 8.1   Three steps in the formation of the EU political agenda

policymakers) that have a different type of interest in the issue than traditional policymakers (in this case, fisheries management experts). This, in turn, has led to the rise of new approaches to the issue in policy debates and eventually policy proposals.

The three steps discussed above are summarized schematically in Figure 8.1.

The analysis presented here has a number of implications for our understanding of the EU. In Chapter 1, three debates were discerned to which this study may contribute: our understanding of policymaking in the EU; debates on European integration; and normative debates on the EU as a polity. The remainder of this chapter will discuss the implications of this study for each of these debates.

8.2   Agenda-setting and policymaking in the EU

Studying agenda-setting teaches us something about policymaking in the EU. In a narrow sense, it helps us to understand how issues come to the attention of EU policymakers and why some issues and policy options are taken into consideration, while others are ignored. In addition, the analysis in this book contains at least three more general lessons for our understanding of policymaking in the EU.

The first lesson is that EU policymaking processes can be understood properly only by analysing them within the context of policymaking processes at the domestic level and in other international organizations. In each of the cases studied in this book, institutions at several levels (national, European and global) were working on the same issues simultaneously. Moreover, many of the same actors were active at different levels at the same time. Therefore, the case studies show that policymaking at EU level can be understood properly only if one takes the developments at other levels into account. The rise of smoking bans in order to prevent passive smoking is a perfect example of these multi-level policy dynamics. As we saw in Chapter 5, the issue arose in parallel in several EU member states, WHO's FCTC and the EU itself. Often, the key players at each of these levels were the same. For example, the Irish government was the first in Europe to adopt a comprehensive ban on indoor smoking, was one of the strongest supporters of EU initiatives in this area, and acted as the 'key facilitator' for the working group which developed guidelines for implementing the Convention's provisions on passive smoking. At a meeting of that working group, the European Commission was represented alongside a number of countries that were party to the Convention and representatives of health NGOs (WHO 2007: points 5 and 6).

Policymaking processes do not always follow such a clear multi-level pattern, and the relative importance of each level may vary between issues. For example, issues of health care financing are rooted much more strongly in domestic debates and much weaker at the global level, while the global level is much more important in fisheries issues. Still, the cases in which only the EU level is involved in an issue are rare, so this kind of multi-level policymaking dynamics is likely to be a feature of most EU policy processes.

The second lesson is that these multi-level dynamics make it difficult to distinguish clearly between developments at different levels and to determine in a general sense which level or institution plays the leading role. Rather, debates take place on different levels simultaneously and mutually reinforce (or at least affect) each other. This implies that the crucial political dividing line in these processes is not between institutions at different levels, but between the supporters and opponents of a given policy approach. These supporters and opponents (which could be termed 'advocacy coalitions' following Sabatier (Sabatier and Weible 2007), or 'advocacy networks' following Keck and Sikkink (1998)) are active on all levels, seeking to exploit the institutional differences between the various venues in order to push forward or slow down policy initiatives around an issue. Therefore, rather than asking how different venues or levels of government relate to each other, we are better advised to ask how advocates of different issues and approaches use the available venues to achieve their objectives.

The third lesson is that EU policymaking processes are not confined to EU member states or the international organizations of which the EU is a member. In several of the cases discussed in this book, influential developments took place in countries outside the EU. For example, the US has been a front-runner in the debate on smoking policy; Australia, Canada and the US provided important models of integrated maritime policies; and Norway may be a small country, but in fisheries policy circles it has been both an important player and a source of policy ideas. As mentioned previously, the debates in these various countries are linked together through professional networks in which policy experts exchange and discuss developments and policy ideas, either in person on conferences or through professional publications read within a policy network. Therefore, for an understanding of EU policymaking it is necessary to look beyond the policy networks and policy debates within the EU proper, to include the wider policy networks of which policymakers in the EU are members.

In addition to these lessons on EU policymaking, the analysis presented in this book contains lessons for students of agenda-setting and policymaking in other contexts than the EU. The first lesson mirrors the arguments about EU policymaking made above. These arguments work not only for the EU, but also the other way around: if we want to understand domestic policy dynamics, we need to look at the policy-making processes that take place at the international level and at the developments in policy networks that extend beyond national borders. Often, these processes will contain at least one important key to understanding why and how issues rise on domestic agendas. The second lesson may lead to a different appreciation of the role of venues in agenda-setting. In essence, the concept of venue shopping as developed by Baumgartner and Jones reflects a pluralist perspective on politics in which societal interests use and seek out government venues in order to advance their cause. Certainly, in Baumgartner and Jones' account, venues are in active competition with each other, which heightens their receptiveness to potentially attractive new issues. However, they still react to issues that are brought to their attention, rather than actively developing issues themselves.

In the fisheries case of Chapter 7, there is considerable merit in this type of explanation. Yet in the cases of Chapters 5 and 6, concerning issues that were new to the EU agenda, international policymakers played much more active roles. Rather than merely being 'sought out' by interest groups and national policymakers, organizations and actors such as WHO and the European Commission actively tried to bring together the people working on the same issues, thus to create transnational policy networks which could form the basis for further debates at the international level. In the health systems case, the Commission was even the single most active proponent of a higher status for the issue on the EU agenda, despite member state government reluctance. In each of these cases, the Commission acted as the active 'image-venue entrepreneur' that Wendon (1998) described in the field of social policy. It actively sought to frame issues in ways that would make them amenable to EU action, and to develop institutions that could operate as receptive venues for these issues. Therefore, putting new issues onto the EU agenda involves a two-way relationship between 'venues' and 'venue shoppers', with venue shoppers seeking venues, and venues seeking venue shoppers.

8.3   Agenda-setting and European integration

A key concern among scholars of the EU has been to explain the process of European integration. The central question in this endeavour has been why EU member states have chosen to cooperate, and why they have done so in the policy areas covered by the EU and in the specific form taken by the EU's institutional set-up. A related issue, particularly during the 1960s, was what the process of European integration implied for (the future of) national states in Europe: would they be transcended by the developing European project, or were member state governments still firmly in the driving seat in the process of European cooperation?

The central ambitions of this book are quite different. Rather than reflecting on the issue of European integration as such and its implications for the role of national states, it has sought to analyse the ongoing daily policymaking processes that take place within the EU. In that regard, this study ties in with branches of the literature that seek to understand the EU as a governance system, quite apart from the question of how this governance system has developed and what it is bound to lead to (cf. Rosamond 2000: 105ff.).

Nevertheless, the insights gained in studying the EU as a governance system may aid our understanding of the process of European integration. As seen in Chapter 1, the extent of European integration can be equated with the EU's political agenda: that is, the range of issues that the EU deals with, and the ways in which it deals with them. Hence, if we understand how the EU's political agenda is formed, we should be able to understand better what determines the extent of European integration.

The 'grand debate' on European integration has been dominated by two approaches: the intergovernmentalist approach and the neo-functionalist approach. The two approaches differ in terms of the actors and factors that are thought to determine the integration process. Intergovernmentalists argue that the EU is a cooperation scheme between member state governments (cf. Magnette 2005; Moravcsik 1998), hence those governments determine whether or not to cooperate on a given area or issue. Cooperation will take place only if they agree to cooperate. This decision is based on a cost–benefit calculation, which may be based either on the economic costs and benefits of cooperating, or broader political objectives.

By contrast, neo-functionalists claim a greater role for supranational actors such as the European Commission, the European Court of Justice and European interest groups. By actively seeking new areas of cooperation and strategically exploiting the room that they have to take initiatives, they are able to 'lure' member state governments into cooperating on issues that they had not intended to originally. An important role in this process is played by 'spill-overs' and shifts in loyalty. Spill-overs occur when cooperation in one area makes it logical or beneficial to cooperate in another (Haas 1968: 283ff.; Lindberg 1963: 10–11). In addition, national interest groups may begin to shift their activities and loyalties to the EU in response to the newly created political structures at European level (Haas 1968: 13–14; Lindberg 1963: 9–10). In neo-functionalism's original formulation, these two processes reinforce themselves and each other, leading to a consistent push for further European integration. In later accounts, this deterministic argument has been nuanced considerably in order to account for periods of stagnation in European integration (Rosamond 2000: 62ff.).

As a result, the key debate on European integration has come to revolve around the relative importance of supranational actors and member state governments in that process. Whereas several authors have claimed that supranational actors have been able to move European integration in directions not foreseen or explicitly wanted by member state governments (Burley and Mattli 1993; Sandholtz and Zysman 1989), intergovernmentalists have maintained that ultimately, the process of European integration and the activities of the EU's institutions rest on decisions by member state governments to cooperate in areas where they see mutual benefits (Garrett 1992; Moravcsik 1991; 1998). Others have sought to specify the conditions under which member state governments will delegate tasks and competencies to EU institutions (Pollack 2003).

The empirical material in the previous chapters does not point to a central role for either supranational actors or member state governments. EU-level actors have played important roles in bringing issues to the EU agenda. At the same time, member state governments have been quite capable of drawing the line as to what the EU should be engaged in and what it should not. In addition, the relative importance of different (types) of stakeholders has differed between cases, with a member state government sometimes taking the initiative to place an issue onto the EU agenda, or sometimes the Commission or the European Parliament, or interest groups.

Therefore, the main added value of an agenda-setting approach is not that it yields any decisive 'evidence' for or against one of the existing integration theories. What it does do is to shift the debate away from a number of assumptions that are shared by intergovernmentalists and supranationalists, which may not be the most productive way of looking at European integration processes. This shift in focus is the most valuable contribution to be made by applying an agenda-setting perspective. Two such shifts can be identified. First, much of the debate on European integration has revolved around the question of who is 'in the driving seat': member state governments or supranational actors. From an agenda-setting perspective, this is not a very useful question. Even if we can identify an actor who has taken the initiative to bring an issue onto the EU agenda, the type of actor taking the initiative differs between cases. Moreover, and more importantly, in the vast majority of cases the agenda success of an issue does not depend on a single (type of) actor pushing the issue forward. Rather, it is the combination of actors, some domestic, some European, that determines whether or not an issue will gain sufficient impetus to move forward on the EU agenda. In terms of actual agenda struggles, normally the decisive dividing line is not drawn between EU-level actors and national governments, but between coalitions of actors at different levels of government that share a certain perspective on an issue. These coalitions may include member state and Commission officials, Members of European Parliament, national parliamentarians, domestic and European interest groups as well as academics and journalists, and the dividing lines between coalitions may run across each of these different categories. Therefore, more productive than the question of *who* is determining the EU agenda, is the question: *under what conditions* are actors able to place an issue onto the EU agenda? In some circumstances, the proponents of an issue will be able to place that issue onto the EU agenda, while under other circumstances they are not. Specifying those circumstances may prove a better key to understanding integration processes than identifying specific (types of) actors (cf. Stone Sweet and Sandholtz 1997, with whose approach to European integration the account in this book shows clear affinities).

Second, it is necessary to take a broader view of European integration, placing it within the context of policy debates at domestic level and in other international organizations. Most theories of European integration have tended to explain European integration with exclusive reference to processes within the EU (including the processes that define the position of member state governments in EU decision-making processes). The global level has played a role in these accounts in one of two ways. First, 'globalization' as a process of increased global interdependencies may lead to pressures for European integration, when European firms press for EU initiatives in order to withstand greater global competition (Stone Sweet and Sandholtz 1997: 309). Second, the process of European integration has been placed in the context of the global balance of power, for example in the argument that the creation of the EU should be explained as a response to the bipolar world centred on the US and Soviet Union after the Second World War (Mearsheimer 1990; Waltz 1979: 70–1). In both accounts, developments at the global level are considerations in the calculus of (domestic) European actors, be they economic interests or geopolitically minded governments.

In the agenda-setting approach developed in this book, the global level is important as a set of policymaking venues that form potential alternatives to the EU as well as a source of input into EU policymaking processes. For example, the creation of the Common Fisheries Policy can be understood, both in terms of timing and substance, only in the context of other international cooperation schemes which had been set up at the time that the EU was created (such as RFMOs and a number of separate international agreements) – and the gaps they had left in solving a number of issues. The same is true for the debates on tobacco and alcoholism, which have been embedded in debates in other international venues (such as WHO) and in countries beyond the EU (such as the US).

An agenda-setting approach offers the tools to analyse the interaction between venues at the EU and global levels. After all, when agenda-setting is determined by the receptiveness of venues to certain issues and arguments, political actors face a strategic choice as to where to push for an issue. Whether or not the EU is the most suitable venue for the purposes of an actor depends completely on what that actor wants to achieve, what the EU can offer and whether EU policymakers are likely to take up the actor's claims, relative to what other venues are receptive to and what they can offer. This can be seen not only in the policy areas that were studied in this book but also in entirely different policy areas such as defence policy, where the EU has had to compete with NATO and, on some issues, the Organization for Security and Co-operation in Europe (OCSE). Depending on the types of cooperation that they valued most, member state governments have opted for different mixes of roles for the three organizations, trying to bring some issues onto the EU agenda while preferring other issues to be debated within NATO or the OSCE.

8.4   Bias and responsiveness in EU policy agendas

The final set of debates to which an analysis of agenda processes can contribute relates to possible biases in EU policymaking and democracy in the EU. These debates involve two related points of critique. The first concerns the existence of biases in EU policymaking in the sense that the EU tends to focus on issues of market liberalization. In one of the most thorough and nuanced analyses of these biases, Fritz Scharpf has argued that because of the EU's commitment to breaking down barriers to trade ('negative integration'), it is particularly strong in policies that involve market liberalization. However, because of the difficulties of reaching agreement on decisions to adopt regulatory standards at EU level ('positive integration'), it is much weaker when it comes to policies that protect workers, consumers or the environment. The latter type of policies, so Scharpf argues, are adopted only if they concern issues that do not attract large-scale opposition from member state governments. Generally speaking, this excludes some of the central issues of European welfare states, such as taxation and social insurance policies (Scharpf 1997: 531–3; 1999: 24). As a result, 'European public policy is, in principle, only able to deal with a narrower range of problems, and is able to employ only a narrower range of policy choices for their solution, than is generally true for national policies' (Scharpf 1999: 23). Several observers have made similar observations within the specific fields of EU health policy (e.g Clergeau 2005: 114; Guignier 2004: 99; Moon 1999: 148; Permanand and Mossialos 2005: 51) and, in its early years, EU environmental policy (e.g. Hildebrand 2002: 22; Weale et al. 2000: 42).

The second relates to the 'democratic deficit' in the EU and concerns the limited opportunities for popular representation in EU politics, as well as EU policymakers' weak political accountability regarding citizens and their elected representatives. As a result, EU policymaking occurs in relative isolation from public demands and opinion (e.g. Follesdal and Hix 2006; Mair 2005; Scharpf 1999; Stein 2001).

These two debates are related because (structural) biases in the EU agenda prevent the EU from responding to public demands that fall outside of the limits of its agenda. If, to take a hypothetical example, issues of poverty are banned from the EU agenda, then EU policymakers will not (and cannot) respond to public demands for poverty reduction policies. Therefore, for both debates it is important to understand agenda processes in the EU.

As to biases in the EU agenda, the analysis in this book confirms Scharpf's distinction between types of policies and policy areas. The comparison of EU and US data in Chapter 4 showed that the EU is involved relatively heavily in regulatory issues (covering environmental policy and public health policy), but much less so in health care issues that are related to welfare state arrangements and which have important redistributive implications. On the basis of the case study on health systems, this was explained by the existence of 'vertical blockades' that prevented the issue from reaching the EU's decision agenda. This in itself can be seen as a 'victory' of public opinion, because opinion polls have shown a majority of Europeans to be opposed to an EU role in this area. At the same time, it does lead to a bias on the EU agenda because other EU policies (most notably those relating to the internal market) affect national health systems, but these effects themselves can not be confronted squarely in EU policy debates. This, then, puts clear limits on the extent to which certain popular demands can be addressed.

At the same time, the analysis offers a number of nuances which highlight dynamic developments in the EU's political agenda. As the further analysis of public health documents in Chapter 4 and the case studies of Chapters 5 and 7 showed, the range of aspects and perspectives covered in EU agenda processes tends to broaden over time. This broadening takes place on two levels: individual agenda processes, and the EU agenda as a whole. At the level of individual agenda processes, issues often come onto the EU agenda in terms of market liberalization, but once they become established at EU level, other aspects are added to this. This has been the case for both smoking and alcoholism issues, which in the late 1970s were discussed predominantly in terms of trade barriers (e.g. harmonizing excise duties), but which now are the subject of comprehensive debates. Similarly, fisheries came onto the EU agenda as an issue of economic development and access to foreign waters, but now includes the full range of economic and ecological concerns. This suggests that issues often need to be framed in economic and market integration terms in order to enter the EU agenda, but then political actors succeed in gradually expanding the debate once those issues have gained a foothold on that agenda.

In addition, there are indications that the EU agenda as a whole has become more receptive to non-economic issues and concerns. Again, the analysis of documents in Chapter 4 showed that both among and within the public health subtopics a shift has taken place to more purely health-related issues. A similar shift can be observed in EU environmental policy during the 1980s (cf. Hildebrand 2002: 18–27; Jordan 1999: 10; McCormick 2001: 45–55). These shifts were accompanied by institutional developments within the EU. The creation of DG Environment in 1981 and DG Sanco in 1999 led to the establishment of venues within the European Commission that are receptive to issues related directly to environment and health concerns. As a result, besides the dynamics in individual agenda processes, it has become easier for 'non-economic' issues to gain direct access to the EU agenda.

As to the critique about the responsiveness of EU policymaking to popular preferences, the data on EU policy agendas as well as the case studies suggest that public opinion plays a greater role in EU policymaking processes than might be expected on the basis of the EU's institutional set-up. In fact, in many ways EU policymaking is remarkably responsive to public opinion. For example, the tobacco and alcoholism issues came onto the EU agenda *because* they were on the member state agendas, which in turn reflected changes in public attitudes towards smoking. In the fisheries case, societal changes in perspective on how to deal with fisheries management found their way onto the EU agenda. More generally, the data in Chapter 4 showed that, in the field of environmental policy, the EU agenda has come to resemble the agenda of the US federal government in terms of which issues receive most attention, and the same is true for public health issues. This is remarkable because EU policymakers are relatively shielded from the direct impact of public opinion. This implies that public opinion can affect EU agendas through other channels and mechanisms than direct popular demands at EU level. One such alternative channel is formed by the mechanism through which domestic policies tend to 'trickle up to' the EU agenda. Issues that rise on the agendas of a sufficient number of member states are likely to appear on the EU agenda over time because domestic policymakers will bring them to EU level. Another mechanism is formed by the European Commission's propensity to take up issues that it believes are 'popular' among the member states and European Parliament. It does so because their chance of success is greater and because it allows the Commission to prove its added value vis-à-vis member state governments.

In terms of direct effects, the EU agenda responds not to popular demands but to policy elites at the national and European levels. However, because these policy elites are embedded within a political context that responds more directly to public opinion, EU agendas are affected indirectly by public opinion. This conclusion ties in with recent studies which show that the position of member state political elites on European integration tends to reflect the preferences among their citizens (Carrubba 2001; Steenbergen et al. 2007). Carrubba explained this by pointing out that even if citizens are not actively involved in political debates on European integration, they do have clear preferences on the issue, and politicians are careful to stay within the range of acceptable policies for fear of electoral punishment. Steenbergen et al. showed that the relationship between political elites and their supporters runs both ways, with elites responding to their supporters' preferences and seeking to shape those preferences. All in all, then, the picture presented by these studies is not fundamentally different from what we may observe in domestic politics. Although Carrubba and Steenbergen et al. focused on support for European integration as such, similar mechanisms may be at work in individual policy processes, thus forging a link between public preferences and EU policy agendas.

This analysis has important implications for the debate on democracy in the EU. It suggests that the key issue in democratic reform does not lie with the EU's institutional set-up. Imperfect though this may be, *a priori* it is not an impediment to responsive policymaking. Rather, if one seeks to 'politicize' the EU further, the road to take would be to remove some of the formal restrictions on the EU's competence and allow it to take up a wider range of issues.

This argument about the responsiveness of the EU may invite a number of potential critiques. First, this type of indirect response will occur inevitably with a delay, and therefore EU agendas are less responsive to (changes in) public opinion than domestic agendas. A full test of this point would require a further analysis of the 'stickiness' of EU agendas: that is, the extent to and speed with which EU agendas change in response to changes in public opinion. Such an analysis is likely to find considerable time lags and stickiness. However, the EU is not unique in this regard. Studies of domestic agendas consistently have shown a pattern in which agendas do not respond smoothly to outside influences, but rather change in fits and starts. Long periods of relative stability are punctuated with short outbursts of attention and policymaking activity (Baumgartner, Foucault and François 2006; John and Margetts 2003; Jones et al. 2003; Mortensen 2005). This pattern has been explained through the friction inherent in any political system. It takes time for outside impulses, such as changes in public opinion, to filter through to policymaking venues and, importantly, these impulses need to reach a certain threshold before they are noticed at all. Thus small changes in public opinion are unlikely to cause even a ripple among policymakers, but dramatic changes may lead to a complete overhaul of the policy area (Jones and Baumgartner 2005: 17–21).

The question to be answered about the EU in this regard is whether it shows more friction than other political systems. If so, it would be less responsive to outside impulses, such as changes in public opinion, than domestic polities. Whether this is the case cannot be answered definitively by the data gathered for this study. However, on the basis of the case studies it is not self-evident that the EU shows greater friction than other political systems. In the fisheries case, for example, arguably the EU has been very slow to respond to signs of stock depletion. This also has been the case in domestic polities, as is exemplified by the stock collapses on Canada's Grand Banks. Apparently, this is something that other political systems have found difficult to respond to, and it is something to which public opinion has been slow to respond. Similarly, tobacco control issues have come onto the EU agenda long after they came onto domestic agendas. Yet, in the US, as well, the most far-reaching anti-smoking initiatives have been taken at the local level. Although far from definitive proof of anything, these examples show the need to look at the EU in comparative perspective, and to set its performance against the imperfections that are inherent in any complex, large-scale political system. In addition, the EU is not a static institution. Over the past decades, it has shown an enormous evolution in terms of both the issues that it has taken up and the diversity of policy approaches that it has brought to bear on those issues. Arguably, the responsiveness of EU policymakers to public opinion has become greater over the years, so an analysis of policy processes in the 1980s will lead to different conclusions than an analysis of policy processes in later periods.

Second, a more fundamental critique is that this type of responsiveness does not represent real democracy. It may well be that the EU is not deaf to public opinion and that the 'fits and starts' pattern is characteristic of many democratic political systems, but this still falls short of our normative ideals of democracy. For example, one may argue that for the EU to be democratic, it is not sufficient to respond to public opinion: its main policy choices should be based on open deliberation among citizens or their representatives. Of course, this is a legitimate position to take. Indeed, the argument here is not a call for complacency about the shortcomings of the EU's political institutions. At the same time, we should be careful not to fall into what Laura Cram called the 'Nirvana Fallacy': 'the fallacy of comparing the real world to an ideal world, and thus concluding that the real world is in some way wanting' (Cram 2002: 323). Therefore, this type of critique says little about the EU, or about how it is performing in comparison to other political systems.

In addition to normative reflections on democracy, we are well advised to engage in systematic empirical analysis and comparison of policymaking processes, with a view to determining where the most pressing problems lie in the way that the EU works. This will lead to a more fine-grained and nuanced understanding both of the performance of the EU and the processes and mechanisms that underlie that performance. If anything, this is what this study has sought to show.

Annex 1
List of Interviews

Smoking and alcoholism

21 March 2005	Member of European Parliament
13 June 2005	Official of the Dutch Permanent Representation to the EU
5 July 2005	Representative of the European Public Health Alliance (EPHA)
5 July 2005	Representative of EuroCare
3 May 2006	Member of the European Commission's Alcohol Working Group
2 August 2006	Representative of the European Forum for Responsible Drinking (EFRD)
2 August 2006	Representative of the European Cancer Leagues (ECL)
12 February 2007	Two representatives of the Brewers of Europe
25 September 2007	Official at DG Health and Consumer Protection (DG Sanco)
25 September 2007	Representative of the European Respiratory Society (ERS)

Organization and financing of health care

13 April 2006	Representative of the International Alliance of Patients' Organizations (IAPO)
12 February 2007	Representative of the Association International de la Mutualité (AIM)
13 February 2007	Representative of the European Social Insurance Platform (ESIP)

20 February 2007	Representative of the Standing Committee of European Doctors (CPME)
16 October 2007	Official at DG Employment and Social Affairs
17 October 2007	Official at DG Internal Market

Fisheries policy

14 February 2007	Representative of Europeche
14 February 2007	Representative of Greenpeace – European Unit
14 February 2007	Official at the Spanish Permanent Representation to the EU
25 September 2007	Representative of Europeche
25 September 2007	Official at DG Fisheries
26 September 2007	Official at DG Environment
26 September 2007	Representative of WWF Europe
17 October 2007	Representative of the European Bureau for Conservation and Development (EBCD)

Annex 2
Policy Agendas Topics
Coding Scheme

Subtopics for health policy

Subtopics on organization and financing:

- comprehensive health care reform – includes issues relating to the reform of broader health care systems;
- insurance reform, availability and cost – includes the regulation and availability of health insurance;
- provider and insurer payment and regulation – includes issues relating to the reimbursement and payment of medical providers;
- prescription drug coverage and costs – includes issues relating to the inclusion and exclusion of prescription drugs under statutory health reimbursement schemes.

Subtopics on facilities and professionals:

- facilities construction, regulation and payments – includes issues relating to hospital, laboratory, health centre and nursing home construction, regulation and payment;
- medical liability, fraud and abuse – includes issues relating to malpractice and fraudulent behaviour;
- health manpower and training – includes issues relating to the qualifications, training and supply of health personnel;
- long-term care, home health, terminally ill and rehabilitation services – includes issues relating to nursing homes and other long-term care arrangements.

Subtopics on diseases and medicines:

- regulation of drug industry, medical devices and clinical labs – includes issues relating to the safety of medical and medicinal products and procedures;
- prevention, diagnosis and treatment of specific diseases – includes issues relating to the monitoring, prevention and treatment of specific diseases;
- mental illness and mental disability – includes issues relating to the mentally ill and mental health services;
- other or multiple benefits and procedures – includes miscellaneous medical services, such as dental and vision services;
- research and development – includes issues relating to health research.

Subtopics relating to addictive substances:

- tobacco abuse, treatment and education – includes issues relating to tobacco (including specific taxes);
- alcohol abuse and treatment – includes issues relating to alcoholics (including specific taxes);
- illegal drug abuse, treatment and education – includes issues relating to the prevention and treatment of drug abuse;
- drug and alcohol or substance abuse treatment – includes combinations of both alcohol and drug abuse issues.

'General' subtopics:

- other – includes issues that do not fit any other specific subtopic;
- infants and children – includes issues relating to the health of infants and children;
- general – includes issues that span multiple subtopics.

Subtopics for environmental policy

- drinking water safety – includes issues relating to water pollution in relation to drinking water;
- waste disposal – includes issues relating to solid waste treatment and disposal and sewage treatment;
- hazardous waste and toxic chemicals regulation, treatment and disposal – includes issues relating to the regulation of toxic chemicals

(including pesticides) and hazardous waste (including nuclear waste);

- air pollution, global warming and noise pollution – includes issues relating to air and noise pollution;
- recycling – includes issues relating to the reuse and recycling of materials;
- indoor environmental hazards – includes issues relating to indoor environments;
- species and forest protection – includes issues relating to the conservation of species and habitats, animal welfare and fisheries conservation;
- coastal water pollution and conservation – includes issues relating to the pollution and protection of coastal seas and rivers;
- land and water conservation – includes issues relating to soil erosion and the conservation of water supplies;
- research and development – includes issues relating to environmental research and development;
- other – includes issues that do not fit any other specific subtopic; general – includes issues that span multiple subtopics.

Notes

1 Studying Policy Agendas in the EU

1. The term 'European Union' (EU) was only introduced in the Maastricht Treaty of 1992; so strictly speaking one cannot speak of the 'European Union' before that time. Moreover, many decisions within the EU are formally taken by the European Community (EC), one of its constituent 'pillars'. For the sake of consistency and to avoid the confusion of using different terms for what is essentially one (albeit continuously evolving) organization, the term 'EU' will be used throughout this book to refer to the EU's predecessors (such as the European Economic Community (EEC) and the European Communities) and to European Community (EC) per se, unless there is a specific reason to refer to 'the EEC' or 'the EC'.

2. After George Tsebelis' pioneering work (Tsebelis 1994), a literature has developed around the notion of 'conditional agenda-setting' in the EU (Hix 2002; König and Pöter 2001; Moser 1996; Tsebelis and Kreppel 1998). This literature analyses the ability of EU institutions (Commission, Council and Parliament) to structure the alternatives in formal decision-making procedures. In Mark Pollack's terms, these studies deal with 'formal agenda-setting': that is, the ability of the Commission and the European Parliament to 'structur[e] the choices of the member states in the Council' (Pollack 1997: 121). At that stage, the decision to deal with a certain issue has been made already. By contrast, this book and the literature on agenda-setting on which it builds focus on the processes that precede the introduction of a proposal into the EU's formal decision-making procedures, and that determine the choice of issues for decision-making (which Pollack refers to as 'informal agenda-setting').

4 The Evolution of EU Policy Agendas in Comparative Perspective

1. Bills introduced in the US Congress have a very small chance of making it into law. On average, only around 5 or 6 per cent of all bills that are introduced eventually become law, while more than half never even make it to the floor of Congress. The introduction of a bill serves symbolic purposes for its sponsors in Congress and is a way of communicating policy positions and/or showing off for constituencies. This stands in sharp contrast with Commission proposals in the EU, which almost always become law (even if they undergo substantial modifications along the way). Hence, congressional bills are much closer to European Parliament questions than to COM documents.

2. Entropy is calculated as $\sum P_i(\ln P_i)$, where P_i is the proportion of documents under subtopic i. As logs of zero do not exist, the convention has been adopted that $0*\ln 0=0$ for those subtopics that contained no documents. The maximum possible entropy score for i subtopics is equal to $\ln i$; the normalized entropy score is therefore obtained by dividing the entropy score by $\ln i$.

3. US statutes contain a high proportion of 'symbolic' legislation aimed at raising awareness of certain issues, such as the designation of 'National Alzheimer's Disease Week', 'Ostomy Awareness Week' or 'National Home Care Week'. Over the whole period, this type of legislation makes up 40.7 per cent of all US statutes on health. Most lawmaking activity in this area occurred in the 1980s (from the 97th to 101st Congress), when this symbolic legislation made up around 50 per cent of all health-related legislation, reaching a peak of more than 63 per cent of all health-related legislation in the 99th Congress (1985–6). Because inclusion of these statutes would render a comparison more difficult (and arguably less meaningful), they have been excluded from the analysis, both in Table 4.2 and the remainder of the text.

4. In the policy agendas topics coding scheme, there is a separate subtopic for 'illegal drug production, trafficking and control' under the 'law, crime and family issues' major topic category. Since that major topic is not included in this study, the documents that were coded as part of health policy under the 'illegal drug abuse, treatment and education' subtopic exclusively reflect the health aspects of illegal drug issues.

5   Starting from Scratch: Moving New Issues onto the EU Agenda

1. Documentary evidence of the existence of the pre-draft is provided by two European Parliament questions asked on the subject in 1978 (Questions 249/78 and 798/78) and industry documents that discuss lobbying efforts against it (BAT 1979; Phillip Morris 1979: 7; cf. McDaniel et al., 2008).

6   A Bridge Too Far? The Limits of EU Agenda Expansion

1. In 2005, a new general directive on mutual recognition was adopted, which also included the professions covered by the general directives of 1989 and 1992. However, the five professions covered by the sectoral directives remain outside of this general directive, and remain covered by their own specific directives.

2. This specific example, of course, only applied after the UK had joined the EU in 1973.

3. In the meantime, the OMCs for social protection, pensions and health care have become subject to a process of streamlining that seeks to integrate them into one process (European Commission 2003b). However, this is not directly relevant for the analysis of the agenda processes around health care systems.

7   Changing the Tune: Agenda-Setting Dynamics around Recurring Policy Issues

1. In 1979, ICNAF itself was replaced by the Northwest Atlantic Fisheries Organization (NAFO), which exists to date.

2. In addition, the Green Paper included proposals on animal and public health, sectoral economic policies, the external fisheries relations of the EU and efforts to improve research.

References

Abel-Smith, B. and E. Mossialos (1994) 'Cost Containment and Health Care Reform: A Study of the European Union', *Health Policy*, 28(2): 89–132.

Abel-Smith, B., J. Figueras, W. Holland, M. McKee and E. Mossialos (1995) *Choices in Health Policy. An Agenda for the European Union*, Aldershot: Dartmouth/Luxembourg: Office for Official Publications of the European Communities.

Abbott, K. W. and D. Snidal (2001) 'International "Standards" and International Governance', *Journal of European Public Policy*, 8(3): 345–70.

Albæk, E., C. Green-Pedersen and L. Beer Nielsen (2004) *Making Tobacco Consumption a Political Issue in US and Denmark. The Dynamics of Issue Expansion in Comparative Perspective*, Unpublished Paper, Department of Political Science, University of Aarhus.

Anderson, G. F., P. S. Hussey, B. K. Frogner and H. R. Waters (2005) 'Health Spending in the United States and the Rest of the Industrialized World', *Health Affairs*, 24(4): 903–14.

Arnull, A. and D. Wincott (eds) (2002) *Accountability and Legitimacy in the European Union*, Oxford and New York: Oxford University Press.

Bache, I. and M. Flinders (2004) 'Themes and Issues in Multi-level Governance', in: I. Bache and M. Flinders (eds), *Multi-level Governance*, Oxford and New York: Oxford University Press, 1–11.

Bachrach, P. and M. S. Baratz (1962) 'Two Faces of Power', *American Political Science Review* 56(4): 947–52.

Barnes, C. and K. W. McFadden (2008) 'Marine Ecosystem Approaches to Management: Challenges and Lessons in the United States', *Marine Policy*, 32(3): 387–92.

BAT (1979) *Report about Activities of EEC Task Force*, by Dieter van Specht to ICOSI Executive Committee, Dated 31 January 1979, Bates No. 502135332/5342, available at <http://legacy.library.ucsf.edu/tid/tla29d00>.

Baumberg, B. and P. Anderson (2007) 'The European Strategy on Alcohol: A Landmark and a Lesson', *Alcohol and Alcoholism*, 42(1): 1–2.

Baumgartner, F. R., M. Foucault and A. François (2006) 'Punctuated Equilibrium in French Budgeting Processes', *Journal of European Public Policy*, 13(7): 1086–103.

Baumgartner, F. R., C. Green-Pedersen and B. D. Jones (eds) (2006) 'Special Issue: Comparative Studies of Policy Agendas', *Journal of European Public Policy*, 13(7).

Baumgartner, F. R. and B. D. Jones (1993) *Agendas and Instability in American Politics*, Chicago and London: University of Chicago Press.

Baumgartner, F. B., B. D. Jones and M. C. MacLeod (1998) 'Lessons from the Trenches: Ensuring Quality, Reliability, and Usability in the Creation of a New Data Source', *The Political Methodologist*, 8(2): 1–10.

Baumgartner, F. B., B. D. Jones and J. D. Wilkerson (2002) 'Studying Policy Dynamics', in: F. R. Baumgartner and B. D. Jones (eds) *Policy Dynamics*, Chicago and London: Chicago University Press, 29–46.

Bayer, R. and J. Colgrove (2004) 'Children and Bystanders First: The Ethics and Politics of Tobacco Control in the United States', in: E. A. Feldman and R. Bayer (eds) *Unfiltered. Conflicts over Tobacco Policy and Public Health*, Cambridge, MA and London: Harvard University Press, 8–37.

Beyers, J. (2004) 'Voice and Access. Political Practices of European Interest Associations', *European Union Politics*, 5(2): 211–40.

Birkland, T. A. (1998) 'Focusing Events, Mobilization, and Agenda Setting', *Journal of Public Policy*, 18(1): 53–74.

Botcheva, L. and L. L. Martin (2001) 'Institutional Effects on State Behavior: Convergence and Divergence', *International Studies Quarterly*, 45(1): 1–26.

Bouwen, P. (2002) 'Corporate Lobbying in the European Union: The Logic of Access', *Journal of European Public Policy*, 9(3): 365–90.

Brandt, A. M. (2004) 'Difference and Diffusion: Cross-Cultural Perspectives on the Rise of Anti-Tobacco Policies', in: E. A. Feldman and R. Bayer (eds) *Unfiltered. Conflicts over Tobacco Policy and Public Health*, Cambridge, MA and London: Harvard University Press, 255–74.

Bray, K. (2000) 'Illegal, Unreported, and Unregulated Fishing', in: M. H. Nordquist and J. N. Moore (eds), *Current Fisheries Issues and the Food and Agriculture Organization of the United Nations*, The Hague: Kluwer Law International, 115–35.

Brownson, R. C., M. P. Eriksen, R. M. Davis and K. E. Warner (1997) 'Environmental Tobacco Smoke: Health Effects and Policies to Reduce Exposure', *Annual Review of Public Health*, 18: 163–85.

Burley, A. M. and W. Mattli (1993) 'Europe Before the Court: A Political Theory of Legal Integration', *International Organization*, 47(1): 41–76.

Carr, C. J. and H. N. Scheiber (2004) 'Dealing with a Resource Crisis: Regulatory Regimes for Managing the World's Marine Fisheries', in: D. Vogel and R. A. Kagan (eds) *Dynamics of Regulatory Change. How Globalization Affects National Regulatory Policies*, Berkeley, CA: University of California Press, 118–55.

Carrubba, C. J. (2001) 'The Electoral Connection in European Union Politics', *Journal of Politics*, 63(1): 141–58.

CBD (1998) *Conservation and Sustainable Use of Marine and Coastal Biological Diversity, Including a Programme of Work*, Fourth Conference of the Parties, Decision IV/5, available at <www.cbd.int/marine/decisions.shtml>.

CBD (2004a) *Marine and Coastal Biological Diversity*, Seventh Conference of the Parties, Decision VII/5, available at <www.cbd.int/marine/decisions.shtml>.

CBD (2004b) *Protected Areas (Articles 8 (A) to (E))*, Decision VII/28, available at <www.cbd.int/marine/decisions.shtml>.

Clergeau, C. (2005) 'European Food Safety Policies: Between a Single Market and a Political Crisis', in: M. Steffen (ed.) *Health Governance in Europe. Issues, Challenges and Theories*, London and New York: Routledge, 113–33.

Cobb, R. W. and C. D. Elder (1972) *Participation in American Politics. The Dynamics of Agenda-Building*, Baltimore, MD and London: Johns Hopkins University Press.

Considine, M. (1998) 'Making Up the Government's Mind: Agenda Setting in a Parliamentary System', *Governance*, 11(3): 297–317.

Council (2002) *2440th Council Meeting – Health*, Luxembourg, 26 June 2002, Press Release 10090/02 (Presse 182).

Council (2003) *Joint Report by the Commission and the Council on Supporting National Strategies for the Future of Health Care and Care for the Elderly*, Document No. 7166/03, Brussels, 10 March 2003.

Council (2006) *2733rd Council Meeting Employment, Social Policy, Health and Consumer Affairs*, Luxembourg, 1–2 June 2006, Press Release 9658/06 (Presse 148).

Council of Europe (2003) *The Reform of Health Care Systems in Europe: Reconciling Equity, Quality and Efficiency*, Parliamentary Assembly Recommendation 1626 (2003)1, adopted on 1 October 2003.

Cram, L. (2002) 'The Future of the Union and the Trap of the "Nirvana Fallacy"', *Governance*, 15(3): 309–24.

Damro, C. (2006) 'The New Trade Politics and EU Competition Policy: Shopping for Convergence and Co-operation', *Journal of European Public Policy*, 13(6): 867–86.

Daw, T. and T. Gray (2005) 'Fisheries Science and Sustainability in International Policy: A Study of Failure in the European Union's Common Fisheries Policy', *Marine Policy*, 29(3): 189–97.

De Fontaubert, A. C. (1995) 'The Politics of Negotiation at the United Nations Conference on Straddling Fish Stocks and Highly Migratory Fish Stocks', *Ocean & Coastal Management*, 29: 79–91.

Defever, M. (1995) 'Health Care Reforms: The Unfinished Agenda', *Health Policy*, 34(1): 1–7.

DG Environment (2007) *Guidelines for the Establishment of the Natura 2000 Network in the Marine Environment. Application of the Habitats and Birds Directives*, May 2007, available at <http://ec.europa.eu/environment/nature/natura2000/marine/index_en.htm>.

DG Environment (2008a) *Special Protection Areas – Update of June 2008*, available at <http//ec.europa.eu/environment/nature/natura2000/sites_birds/index_en.htm>, accessed on 31 July 2008.

DG Environment (2008b) *Sites of Community Importance – Update of June 2008*, available at <http://ec.europa.eu/environment/nature/natura2000/sites_hab/index_en.htm>, accessed on 31 July 2008.

DG Sanco (2001) *The Internal Market and Health Services*, Report of the High-Level Committee on Health, 17 December 2001.

DG Sanco (2003) *High Level Process of Reflection on Patient Mobility and Healthcare Developments in the European Union*, Document No. HLPR/2003/16, 9 December 2003.

Dostal, J. M. (2004) 'Campaigning on Expertise: How the OECD Framed EU Welfare and Labour Market Policies – And Why Success Could Trigger Failure', *Journal of European Public Policy*, 11(3): 440–60.

Deep Sea Conservation Coalition (DSCC) (2004) *DSCC Statement to the United Nations General Assembly*, November 2004, available at <www.savethehighseas.org/publicdocs/UNGA_GP_full.pdf>.

DSCC (2007) *For the Protection of Seamounts, Cold-Water Corals, and Other Vulnerable Deep-Sea Ecosystems*, Position Statement, Deep Sea Conservation Coalition, August 2007, available at <www.savethehighseas.org/publicdocs/DSCC_position_2pp.pdf>.

Duina, F. and P. Kurzer (2004) 'Smoke in Your Eyes: The Struggle over Tobacco Control in the European Union', *Journal of European Public Policy*, 11(1): 57–77.

EC (1965) *Council Directive 65/65/EEC on the Approximation of Provisions Laid Down by Law, Regulation or Administrative Action Relating to Proprietary Medicinal Products*, adopted on 26 January 1965, OJ L 22, 9 February 1965, 369–73.

EC (1971) *Regulation (EEC) No 1408/71 of the Council on the Application of Social Security Schemes to Employed Persons and their Families Moving within the Community*, adopted on 14 June 1971, OJ L 149, 5 July 1971, 2–50.

EC (1972) *Actes relatifs à l'adhesion aux Communautés Européennes du Royaume du Danmark, de l'Irlande, du Royaume de Norvège et du Royaume-Uni de Grande-Bretagne et d'Irlande du Nord*, OJ L 73, Special Edition, 27 March 1972, 3–204 (French language version).

EC (1979) *Council Directive 79/409/EEC on the Conservation of Wild Birds*, adopted on 2 April 1979, OJ L 103, 25 April 1979, 1–18.

EC (1983) *Council Regulation (EEC) No 170/83 Establishing a Community System for the Conservation and Management of Fishery Resources*, adopted on 25 January 1983, OJ L 24, 27 January 1983, 1–13.

EC (1986) *Resolution of the Council and of the Representatives of the Governments of the Member States, Meeting within the Council, on Alcohol Abuse*, adopted on 29 May 1986, OJ C 184, 23 July 1986, 3.

EC (1989) *Resolution of the Council and the Ministers for Health of the Member States, Meeting within the Council on Banning Smoking in Places Open to the Public*, adopted on 18 July 1989, OJ C 189, 26 July 1989, 1–2.

EC (1992a) *Council Directive 92/43/EEC on the Conservation of Natural Habitats and of Wild Fauna and Flora*, adopted on 21 May 1992, OJ L 206, 22 July 1992, 7–50.

EC (1992b) *Council Regulation (EEC) No 3760/92 Establishing a Community System for Fisheries and Aquaculture*, adopted on 20 December 1992, OJ L 389, 31 December 1992, 1–14.

EC (1998) *Directive 98/43/EC of the European Parliament and the Council on the Approximation of the Laws, Regulations and Administrative Provisions of the Member States Relating to the Advertising and Sponsorship of Tobacco Products*, adopted on 6 July 1998, OJ L 213, 30 July 1998, 9–12.

EC (2000) *Council Decision 2000/436/EC on Setting Up a Social Protection Committee*, adopted on 29 June 2000, OJ L 172, 12 July 2000, 26–7.

EC (2001a) *Council Recommendation on the Drinking of Alcohol by Young People, in Particular Children and Adolescents*, adopted on 5 June 2001, OJ L 161, 16 June 2001, 38–41.

EC (2001b) *Council Conclusions on a Community Strategy to Reduce Alcohol-Related Harm*, adopted on 5 June 2001, OJ C 175, 20 June 2001, 1–2.

EC (2002a) *Decision No 1600/2002/EC of the European Parliament and of the Council Laying Down the Sixth Community Environment Action Programme*, adopted on 22 July 2002, OJ L 242, 10 September 2002, 1–15.

EC (2002b) *Decision 1786/2002/EC of the European Parliament and of the Council Adopting a Programme of Community Action in the Field of Public Health (2003–8)*, adopted on 23 September 2002, OJ L 271, 9 October 2002, 1–12.

EC (2002c) *Council Recommendation on the Prevention of Smoking and on Initiatives to Improve Tobacco Control*, adopted on 2 December 2002, OJ L 22, 25 January 2003, 31–4.

EC (2002d) *Council Regulation (EC) No 2371/2002 on the Conservation and Sustainable Exploitation of Fisheries Resources under the Common Fisheries Policy*, adopted on 20 December 2002, OJ L 358, 31 December 2002, 59–80.

EC (2003) *Directive 2003/33/EC of the European Parliament and the Council on the Approximation of the Laws, Regulations and Administrative Provisions of the Member States Relating to the Advertising and Sponsorship of Tobacco Products*, adopted on 26 May 2003, OJ L 152, 20 June 2003, 16–19.

EC (2008) *Directive 2008/56/EC of the European Parliament and of the Council Establishing a Framework for Community Action in the Field of Marine Environmental Policy (Marine Strategy Framework Directive)*, adopted on 17 June 2008, OJ L 164, 25 June 2008, 19–40.

ECJ (1978) *Bestuur van het Algemeen Ziekenfonds Drenthe-Platteland* v. *G. Pierik*, Case 177/77, judgment of 16 March 1978.

ECJ (1979) *Bestuur van het Algemeen Ziekenfonds Drenthe-Platteland* v. *G. Pierik*, Case 182/78, judgment of 31 May 1979.

ECJ (1998a) *Nicolas Decker* v. *Caisse de Maladie des Employés Privés*, Case C-120/95, judgment of 28 April 1998.

ECJ (1998b) *Raymond Kohll* v. *Union des Caisses de Maladie*, Case C-158/96, judgment of 28 April 1998.

ECJ (2000) *Federal Republic of Germany* v. *European Parliament and Council of the European Union*, Case C-376/98 of 5 October 2000, ECR-I, 8419–534.

ECJ (2001) *B.S.M. Geraets-Smits* v. *Stichting Ziekenfonds VGZ* and *H.T.M. Peerbooms* v. *Stichting CZ Groep Zorgverzekeringen*, Case C-157/99, judgment of 12 July 2001.

ECJ (2003) *V.G. Müller-Fauré* v. *Onderlinge Waarborgmaatschappij OZ Zorgverzekeringen UA and E.E.M. van Riet* v. *Onderlinge Waarborgmaatschappij ZAO Zorgverzekeringen*, Case C-385/99, judgment of 13 May 2003.

ECJ (2006) *Yvonne Watts* v. *Bedford Primary Care Trust and the Secretary of State for Health*, Case C-372/04, judgment of 16 May 2006.

Edwards, G. (2002) 'Joy Moser, 1921–2001: The Woman Who Gave WHO's Programme on Alcohol its Golden Age', *Addiction*, 97(6): 759–60.

Edwards, G. (2007) 'How the 1977 World Health Organization Report on Alcohol-Related Disabilities Came to Be Written: A Provisional Analysis', *Addiction*, 102(11): 1711–21.

Eggertsson, T. (1990) *Economic Behavior and Institutions*, Cambridge: Cambridge University Press.

Enthoven, A. C. (1985) *Reflections on the Management of the National Health Service*, London: Nuffield Provincial Hospital Trust.

EU Reporter (2005) 'Alcohol and Health', interview with Florence Bertoletti Kemp and Peter Anderson from EuroCare, *EU Reporter eZine*, 12–16 April 2005, 12–13.

EuroCare (2005) *Alcohol Policy Network in the Context of a Larger Europe. Bridging the Gap (Btg): 2004–6*, available at <www.eurocare.org/btg/index.html>, accessed on 4 July 2005.

European Commission (1976a) *Problems Which the Introduction of Economic Zones of 200 Miles Poses for the Community in the Sea Fishing Sector*, Communication from the Commission to the Council, COM (1976) 59, 17 February 1976.

European Commission (1976b) *Future External Fisheries Policy and Internal Fisheries System*, Communication from the Commission to the Council, COM (1976) 500, 22 September 1976.

European Commission (1988) *Proposal for a Council Directive Relating to the Maximum Permitted Blood Alcohol Concentration for Vehicle Drivers*, COM (1988) 707, 30 November 1988.

European Commission (1993) *Commission Communication on the Framework for Action in the Field of Public Health*, COM (1993) 559, 24 November 1993.

European Commission (1998a) *European Community Biodiversity Strategy*, Communication from the Commission to the Council and the European Parliament, COM (1998) 42, 4 February 1998.

European Commission (1998b) *Partnership for Integration. A Strategy for Integrating Environment into EU Policies*, Communication from the Commission to the European Council, COM (1998) 333, 27 May 1998.

European Commission (1999) *Fisheries Management and Nature Conservation in the Marine Environment*, Communication from the Commission to the Council and the European Parliament, COM (1999) 363, 14 July 1999.

European Commission (2000a) *Integrated Coastal Zone Management: A Strategy for Europe*, Communication from the Commission to the Council and the European Parliament, COM (2000) 547, 27 September 2000.

European Commission (2000b) *Application of the Precautionary Principle and Multi-Annual Arrangements for Setting TACs*, Communication from the Commission to the Council and the European Parliament, COM (2000) 803, 1 December 2000.

European Commission (2001a) *Green Paper on the Future of the Common Fisheries Policy*, COM (2001) 135, 20 March 2001.

European Commission (2001b) *Biodiversity Action Plan for Fisheries*, Communication from the Commission to the Council and the European Parliament, COM (2001) 162, 27 March 2001.

European Commission (2001c) *The Future of Health Care and Care for the Elderly: Guaranteeing Accessibility, Quality and Financial Viability*, Communication from the Commission to the European Parliament, the Council, the European Economic and Social Committee and the Committee of the Regions, COM (2001) 723, 5 December 2001.

European Commission (2002a) *The Reform of the Common Fisheries Policy ('Roadmap')*, Communication from the Commission, COM (2002) 181, 28 May 2002.

European Commission (2002b) *Community Action Plan to Integrate Environmental Protection Requirements into the Common Fisheries Policy*, Communication from the Commission, COM (2002) 186, 28 May 2002.

European Commission (2002c) *Community Action Plan for the Conservation and Sustainable Exploitation of Fisheries Resources in the Mediterranean Sea under the Common Fisheries Policy*, Communication from the Commission to the Council and the European Parliament, COM (2002) 535, 9 October 2002.

European Commission (2002d) *A Community Action Plan to Reduce Discards of Fish*, Communication from the Commission to the Council and the European Parliament, COM (2002) 656, 26 November 2002.

European Commission (2002e) *Outcome of the Fisheries Council of 16–20 December 2002*, Press Release, 23 December 2002, available at <http://ec.europa.eu/fisheries/press_corner/press_releases/archives/com02_en.htm>.

European Commission (2003a) *Towards Uniform and Effective Implementation of the Common Fisheries Policy*, Communication from the Commission to the Council and the European Parliament, COM (2003) 130, 21 March 2003.

European Commission (2003b) *Strengthening the Social Dimension of the Lisbon Strategy: Streamlining Open Coordination in the Field of Social Protection*, Communication from the Commission to the European Parliament, the Council, the European Economic and Social Committee and the Committee of the Regions, COM (2003) 261, 27 May 2003.

European Commission (2003c) *Report on the Application of Internal Market Rules to Health Services. Implementation by the Member States of the Court's Jurisprudence*, SEC (2003) 900, 28 July 2003.

European Commission (2004a) *Proposal for a Directive of the European Parliament and of the Council on Services in the Internal Market*, COM (2004) 002, 5 March 2004.

European Commission (2004b) *Delivering Lisbon. Reforms for the Enlarged Union*, Report from the Commission to the Spring European Council, COM (2004) 29, 20 April 2004.

European Commission (2004c) *Follow-Up to the High Level Reflection Process on Patient Mobility and Healthcare Developments in the European Union*, Communication from the Commission, COM (2004) 301, 20 April 2004.

European Commission (2004d) *Modernising Social Protection for the Development of High-Quality, Accessible and Sustainable Health Care and Long-Term Care: Support for the National Strategies Using the 'Open Method of Coordination'*, Communication from the Commission to the European Parliament, the Council, the European Economic and Social Committee and the Committee of the Regions, COM (2004) 304, 20 April 2004.

European Commission (2004e) *Commission Decision Setting Up a High-Level Group on Health Services and Medical Care*, C (2004) 1501, adopted on 20 April 2004.

European Commission (2004f) *Message from Malahide. Halting the Decline of Biodiversity – Priority Objectives and Targets for 2010*, Stakeholders' Conference on Biodiversity and the EU, 25–7 May 2004, Malahide, Ireland, adopted on 27 May 2004.

European Commission (2005a) *Discussion Paper on the EU Strategy on Alcohol*, Prepared for the Meeting of the Working Group on Alcohol and Health on 7 and 8 March 2005, available at <http://europa.eu.int/comm/health/ph_determinants/life_style/alcohol_en.htm>.

European Commission (2005b) *Proposal for a Directive of the European Parliament and of the Council Establishing a Framework for Community Action in the Field of Marine Environmental Policy (Marine Strategy Directive)*, COM (2005) 505, 24 October 2005.

European Commission (2005c) *Promoting Healthy Diets and Physical Activity: A European Dimension for the Prevention of Overweight, Obesity and Chronic Diseases*, Green Paper, COM (2005) 637, 8 December 2005.

European Commission (2006a) *Amended Proposal for a Directive of the European Parliament and of the Council on Services in the Internal Market*, COM (2006) 160, 4 April 2006.

European Commission (2006b) *Halting the Loss of Biodiversity by 2010 – And Beyond. Sustaining Ecosystem Services for Human Well-Being*, Communication from the Commission, COM (2006) 216, 22 May 2006.

European Commission (2006c) *Consultation Regarding Community Action on Health Services*, Communication from the Commission, SEC (2006) 1195/4, 26 September 2006.

European Commission (2006d) *An EU Strategy to Support Member States in Reducing Alcohol Related Harm*, Communication from the Commission to the Council, the European Parliament, the European Economic and Social Committee and the Committee of the Regions, COM (2006) 625 final, 24 October 2006.

European Commission (2007a) *Towards a Europe Free from Tobacco Smoke: Policy Options at EU Level*, Green Paper, COM (2007) 27, 30 January 2007.

European Commission (2007b) *An Integrated Maritime Policy for the European Union*, Communication from the Commission to the European Parliament, the Council, the European Economic and Social Committee and the Committee of the Regions, COM (2007) 575, 10 October 2007.

European Commission (2007c) *Destructive Fishing Practices in the High Seas and the Protection of Vulnerable Deep Sea Ecosystems*, Communication from the Commission to the European Parliament, the Council, the European Economic and Social Committee and the Committee of the Regions, COM (2007) 604, 17 October 2007.

European Commission (2007d) *Recommendation for a Council Recommendation on the 2008 Update of the Broad Guidelines for the Economic Policies of the Member States and the Community and on the Implementation of Member States' Employment Policies*, COM (2007) 803 Part IV, 11 December 2007.

European Commission (2008a) *Proposal for a Directive of the European Parliament and of the Council on the Application of Patients' Rights in Cross-Border Healthcare*, COM (2008) 414, 2 July 2008.

European Commission (2008b) *A Community Framework on the Application of Patients' Rights in Cross-Border Healthcare*, Communication from the Commission, COM (2008) 415, 2 July 2008.

European Commission (2008c) *Introducing Fisheries Management for Marine Natura 2000 Sites*, available at <http://ec.europa.eu/environment/nature/natura2000/marine/index_en.htm>, accessed on 30 July 2008.

European Council (1997) *Presidency Conclusions*, Luxembourg European Council, 12–13 December 1997, available at <http://europa.eu/european-council/index_en.htm>.

European Council (1998) *Presidency Conclusions: Cardiff European Council*, 15–16 June 1998, available at <http://europa.eu/european-council/index_en.htm>.

European Council (2000) *Presidency Conclusion: Lisbon European Council*, 23 and 24 March 2000, available at <http://www.consilium.europa.eu>.

European Council (2001a) *Presidency Conclusions: Stockholm European Council*, 23 and 24 March 2001, available at <http://www.consilium.europa.eu>.

European Council (2001b) *Presidency Conclusion: Göteborg European Council*, 15 and 16 June 2001, available at <http://www.consilium.europa.eu>.

European Council (2001c) *Presidency Conclusions: Laeken European Council*, 14 and 15 December 2001, available at <http://www.consilium.europa.eu>.

European Council (2002) *Presidency Conclusions: Barcelona European Council*, 15 and 16 March 2002, available at <http://www.consilium.europa.eu>.

European Council (2007) *Presidency Conclusions: Brussels European Council*, 21 and 22 June 2007, available at <http://www.consilium.europa.eu>.

European Parliament (2005a) *Report on Patient Mobility and Healthcare Developments in the European Union*, Document No. A6-0129/2005, 29 April 2005.

European Parliament (2005b) *European Parliament Resolution on Patient Mobility and Healthcare Developments in the European Union*, P6_TA (2005) 0236, adopted on 9 June 2005.

European Parliament (2006) *Legislative Resolution on the Proposal for a Directive of the European Parliament and of the Council on Services in the Internal Market*, P6_TA (2006) 0061, adopted on 16 February 2006.

European Parliament (2007) *European Parliament Resolution on Community Action on the Provision of Cross-Border Healthcare*, P6_TA (2007) 0073, adopted on 15 March 2007.

Food and Agriculture Organization (FAO) (1995) *Code of Conduct for Responsible Fisheries*, adopted on 31 October 1995, available at <www.fao.org/fishery/ccrf>.

FAO (2001) *The Reykjavik Declaration on Responsible Fisheries in the Marine Ecosystem*, available at <ftp://ftp.fao.org/fi/document/reykjavik/default.htm>.

FAO (2008) *Regional Fisheries Bodies*, available at <www.fao.org/fishery/rfb>, accessed on 17 July 2008.

Farquharson, K. (2003) 'Influencing Policy Transnationally: Pro- and Anti-Tobacco Global Advocacy Networks', *Australian Journal of Public Administration*, 62(4): 80–92.

Farnell, J. and J. Elles (1984) *In Search of a Common Fisheries Policy*, Aldershot: Gower.

Follesdal, A. and S. Hix (2006) 'Why There Is a Democratic Deficit in the EU: A Response to Majone and Moravcsik', *Journal of Common Market Studies*, 44(3): 533–62.

Franklin, M. (2001) 'European Elections and the European Voter', in: J. Richardson (ed.), *European Union. Power and Policy-Making*, 2nd ed., London and New York: Routledge, 201–16.

Freeman, R. (1998) 'Competition in Context: The Politics of Health Care Reform in Europe', *International Journal for Quality in Health Care*, 10(5): 395–401.

Freeman, R. and M. Moran (2000) 'Reforming Health Care in Europe', *West European Politics*, 23(2): 35–58.

Garrett, G. (1992) 'International Cooperation and Institutional Choice: The European Community's Internal Market', *International Organization*, 46(2): 533–60.

George, S. (2004) 'Multi-level Governance and the European Union', in: I. Bache and M. Flinders (eds), *Multi-level Governance*, Oxford and New York: Oxford University Press, 107–26.

Gilmore, A. and M. McKee (2004) 'Tobacco-Control Policy in the European Union', in: E. A. Feldman and R. Bayer (eds) *Unfiltered. Conflicts over Tobacco Policy and Public Health*, Cambridge, MA and London: Harvard University Press, 219–54.

Gould, E. and N. Schacter (2002) 'Trade Liberalization and Its Impacts on Alcohol Policy', *SAIS Review*, 22(1): 119–39.

Government of Canada (2008) *Backgrounder. The Grand Banks and the Flemish Cap*, available at <www.dfo-mpo.gc.ca/overfishing-surpeche/media/bk_grandbanks_e.htm>, accessed on 6 August 2008.

Government of Spain (2005) *El Ministerio de Sanidad Pone en Marcha una Estrategia Nacional para Prevenir la Obesidad, Mejorar los Hábitos Alimenticios y Fomentar la Práctica de Ejercicio Físico*, Press Release, 10 February 2005, available at <www.msc.es/gabinetePrensa/notaPrensa/desarrolloNotaPrensa.jsp?id=259>, accessed on 24 September 2008.

Government of Sweden (2002) *Preventing Alcohol-Related Harm. A Comprehensive Policy for Public Health in Sweden*, Stockholm: Ministry of Health and Social Affairs.

Gray, T. S. (1997) 'The Common Fisheries Policy of the European Union', *Environmental Politics*, 6(4): 150–8.

Gray, T. S., M. J. Gray and R. A. Hague (1999) 'Sandeels, Sailors, Sandals and Suits: The Strategy of the Environmental Movement in Relation to the Fishing Industry', *Environmental Politics*, 8(3): 119–39.

Green-Pedersen, C. (2007) 'The Conflict of Conflicts in Comparative Perspective: Euthanasia as a Political Issue in Denmark, Belgium, and the Netherlands', *Comparative Politics*, 39(3): 273–91.

Green-Pedersen, C. and J. Wilkerson (2006) 'How Agenda-Setting Attributes Shape Politics: Basic Dilemmas, Problem Attention and Health Politics Developments in Denmark and the US', *Journal of European Public Policy*, 13(7): 1039–52.

Greer, S. L. (2008) 'Choosing Paths in European Union Health Services Policy: A Political Analysis of a Critical Juncture', *Journal of European Social Policy*, 18(3): 219–31.

Gual, A. and J. Colom (1997) 'Why Has Alcohol Consumption Declined in Countries of Southern Europe?', *Addiction*, 92 (Supplement 1): S21–S31.

Gual, A. and J. Colom (2001) 'From Paris to Stockholm: Where Does the European Alcohol Action Plan Lead To?', *Addiction*, 96(8): 1093–6.

Guignier, S. (2004) 'Institutionalizing Public Health in the European Commission. The Thrills and Spills of Politicization', in: A. Smith (ed.) *Politics and the European Commission. Actors, Interdependence, Legitimacy*, London and New York: Routledge: 96–116.

Guiraudon, V. (2000) 'European Integration and Migration Policy: Vertical Policy-Making as Venue Shopping', *Journal of Common Market Studies*, 38(2): 251–71.

Haas, E. B. (1968) *The Uniting of Europe. Political, Social, and Economic Forces 1950–7*, 2nd ed., Stanford, CA: Stanford University Press.

Haas, P. M. (1989) 'Do Regimes Matter? Epistemic Communities and Mediterranean Pollution Control', *International Organization*, 43(3): 377–403.

Harcourt, A. J. (1998) 'EU Media Ownership Regulation: Conflict over the Definition of Alternatives', *Journal of Common Market Studies*, 36(3): 369–89.

Harlow, C. (2002) *Accountability in the European Union*, Oxford: Oxford University Press.

Hatcher, A. (2000) 'Subsidies for European Fishing Fleets: The European Community's Structural Policy for Fisheries 1971–99', *Marine Policy*, 24(2): 129–240.

Hayes-Renshaw, F. and H. Wallace (2006) *The Council of Ministers*, 2nd ed., Basingstoke: Palgrave Macmillan.

Hellebø, L. (2003) *Nordic Alcohol Policy and Globalization as a Changing Force*, Stein Rokkan Centre for Social Studies Working Paper No. 5, April 2003.

Héritier, A. (1996) 'The Accommodation of Diversity in European Policy-Making and its Outcomes: Regulatory Policy as a Patchwork', *Journal of European Public Policy* 3(2): 149–67.

Héritier, A., C. Knill and S. Mingers (1996) *Ringing the Changes in Europe. Regulatory Competition and Redefinition of the State. Britain, France, Germany*, Berlin and New York: Walter de Gruyter.

Hervey, T. K. (2001) 'Up in Smoke? Community (Anti-)Tobacco Law and Policy', *European Law Review*, 26: 101–25.

Hervey, T. K. and J. V. McHale (2004) *Health Law and the European Union*, Cambridge: Cambridge University Press.

Hildebrand, P. M. (2002) 'The European Community's Environmental Policy, 1957 to "1992": From Incidental Measures to an International Regime?', in: A. Jordan (ed.) *Environmental Policy in the European Union. Actors, Institutions and Processes*, London and Sterling, VA: Earthscan, 13–36.

Hilgartner, S. and C. L. Bosk (1988) 'The Rise and Fall of Social Problems: A Public Arenas Model', *American Journal of Sociology*, 94(1): 53–78.

Hix, S. (1999) *The Political System of the European Union*, Basingstoke: Palgrave Macmillan.

Hix, S. (2002) 'Constitutional Agenda-Setting through Discretion in Rule Interpretation: Why the European Parliament Won at Amsterdam', *British Journal of Political Science*, 32: 259–80.

Holden, M. (1994) *The Common Fisheries Policy. Origin, Evaluation, Future*, Oxford: Fishing New Books.

Holm, A. L. and R. M. Davis (2004) 'Clearing the Airways: Advocacy and Regulation for Smoke-Free Airlines', *Tobacco Control*, 13: 30–6.

Hooghe, L. and G. Marks (2001) *Multi-Level Governance and European Integration*, Lanham, MD: Rowman and Littlefield.

International Civil Aviation Organization (ICAO) (1992) *Resolution A29–15: Smoking Restrictions on International Passenger Flights*, available at <http://www.icao.int/icao/en/med/MED_Resolutions.html>, accessed on 20 March 2008.

Imig. D. and S. Tarrow (2001) 'Mapping the Europeanization of Contention: Evidence from a Quantitative Data Analysis', in: D. Imig and S. Tarrow (eds) *Contentious Europeans. Protest and Politics in an Emerging Polity*, Lanham, MD: Rowman and Littlefield, 27–49.

Jacobs, A. (1998) 'Seeing Difference: Market Health Reform in Europe', *Journal of Health Politics, Policy and Law*, 23(1): 1–33.

Joachim, J. (2003) 'Framing Issues and Seizing Opportunities: The UN, NGOs, and Women's Rights', *International Studies Quarterly*, 47: 247–74.

John, P. (2006) 'The Policy Agendas Project: A Review', *Journal of European Public Policy*, 13(7): 975–86.

John, P. and H. Margetts (2003) 'Policy Punctuations in the UK. Fluctuations and Equilibria in Central Government Expenditures since 1951', *Public Administration*, 81(3): 411–32.

Jones, B. D. and F. R. Baumgartner (2005) *The Politics of Attention. How Government Prioritizes Problems*, Chicago and London: University of Chicago Press.

Jones, B. D., T. Sulkin and H. A. Larsen (2003) 'Policy Punctuations in American Political Institutions', *American Political Science Review*, 97(1): 151–69.

Joossens, L. and M. Raw (2006) 'The Tobacco Control Scale: A New Scale to Measure Country Activity', *Tobacco Control*, 15: 247–53.

Jordan, A. (1999) 'The Construction of a Multilevel Environmental Governance System', *Environment and Planning C*, 17(1): 1–17.

Karagiannakos, A. (1996) 'Total Allowable Catch (TAC) and Quota Management System in the European Union', *Marine Policy*, 20(3): 235–48.

Keck, M. E. and K. Sikkink (1998) *Activists Beyond Borders. Advocacy Networks in International Politics*, Ithaca, NY and London: Cornell University Press.

Keohane, R. O. (1984) *After Hegemony. Cooperation and Discord in the World Political Economy*, Princeton, NJ: Princeton University Press.

Keohane, R. O., A. Moravcsik and A. M. Slaughter (2000) 'Legalized Dispute Resolution: Interstate and Transnational', *International Organization*, 54(3): 457–88.

Keohane, R. O. and J. S. Nye (2001 [1977]) *Power and Interdependence*, 3rd ed., New York: Longman.

King, G., R. O. Keohane and S. Verba (1994) *Designing Social Inquiry. Scientific Inference in Qualitative Research*, Princeton, NJ: Princeton University Press.

Kingdon, J. W. (2003 [1984]) *Agendas, Alternatives, and Public Policies*, 2nd ed., New York: HarperCollins College Publishers.

König, T. and M. Pöter (2001) 'Examining the EU Legislative Agenda: The Relative Importance of Agenda and Veto Power', *European Union Politics*, 2(3): 329–51.

Krasner, S. D. (1982) 'Structural Causes and Regime Consequences: Regimes as Intervening Variables', *International Organization* 36(2): 185–205.

Langille, B. A. (1997) 'Eight Ways to Think About International Labour Standards', *Journal of World Trade*, 31(4): 27–53.

Lee, K. and H. Goodman (2002) 'Global Policy Networks: The Propagation of Health Care Financing Reform Since the 1980s', in: K. Lee, K. Buse and S. Fustukian (eds), *Health Policy in a Globalising World*, Cambridge: Cambridge University Press, 97–119.

Leigh, M. (1983) *European Integration and the Common Fisheries Policy*, London and Canberra: Croom Helm.

Leitner, H. (1997) 'Reconfiguring the Spatiality of Power: The Construction of a Supranational Migration Framework for the European Union', *Political Geography*, 16(2): 123–43.

Lequesne, C. (2004) *The Politics of Fisheries in the European Union*, Manchester and New York: Manchester University Press.

Liefferink, D. and M. S. Andersen (1998) 'Strategies of the "Green" Member States in EU Environmental Policy-Making', *Journal of European Public Policy*, 5(2): 254–70.

Lindberg, L. N. (1963) *The Political Dynamics of European Integration*, Stanford, CA and London: Stanford University Press and Oxford University Press.

Link, J. S. (2002) 'What Does Ecosystem-Based Fisheries Management Mean?' *Fisheries*, 27(4): 18–21.

Lord, C. and D. Beetham (2001) 'Legitimizing the EU: Is There a "Post-Parliamentary Basis" for its Legitimation?', *Journal of Common Market Studies*, 39(3): 443–62.

Magnette, P. (2005) *What Is the European Union? Nature and Prospects*, Basingstoke: Palgrave Macmillan.

Mahoney, C. (2004) 'The Power of Institutions. State and Interest Group Activity in the European Union', *European Union Politics*, 5(4): 441–66.

Mahoney, J. and G. Goertz (2004) 'The Possibility Principle: Choosing Negative Cases in Comparative Research', *American Political Science Review*, 98(4): 653–69.

Mair, P. (2005) *Popular Democracy and the European Union Polity*, European Governance Papers, C-05-03, available at <http://hdl.handle.net/1814/3292>.

Mansbach, R. W. and J. A. Vasquez (1981) *In Search of Theory. A New Paradigm for Global Politics*, New York: Columbia University Press.

Marks, G. and D. McAdam (1996) 'Social Movements and the Changing Structure of Political Opportunity in the European Union', *West European Politics* 19(2): 249–78.

Marks, G. and D. McAdam (1999) 'On the Relationship of Political Opportunities to the Form of Collective Action: The Case of the European Union', in: D. della Porta, H. Kriesi and D. Rucht (eds), *Social Movements in a Globalizing World*, Basingstoke: Macmillan, 97–111.

Marks, G. and M. R. Steenbergen (eds) (2004) *European Integration and Political Conflict*, Cambridge: Cambridge University Press.

Martinsen, D. S. (2005) 'Towards and Internal Health Market with the European Court', *West European Politics*, 28(5): 1035–56.

Martinsen, D. S. and K. Vrangbæk (2008) 'The Europeanization of Health Care Governance: Implementing the Market Imperatives of Europe', *Public Administration*, 86(1): 169–84.

Mazey, S. (1998) 'The European Union and Women's Rights: From the Europeanization of National Agendas to the Nationalization of a European Agenda?', *Journal of European Public Policy*, 5(1): 131–52.

Mazey, S. and J. Richardson (2001) 'Interest Groups and EU Policy-Making: Organisational Logic and Venue Shopping', in: J. Richardson (ed.) *European Union. Power and Policy-Making*, 2nd ed., London and New York: Routledge, 217–37.

McCombs, M. and J. H. Zhu (1995) 'Capacity, Diversity, and Volatility of the Public Agenda. Trends from 1954 to 1994', *Public Opinion Quarterly*, 59(4): 495–525.

McCormick, J. (2001) *Environmental Policy in the European Union*, Basingstoke: Palgrave Macmillan.

McDaniel, P. A., G. Intinarelli and R. E. Malone (2008) 'Tobacco Industry Issues Management Organizations: Creating a Global Corporate Network to Undermine Public Health', *Globalization and Health*, 4(2).

McDorman, T. L. (2005) 'Implementing Existing Tools: Turning Words into Actions – Decision-Making Processes of Regional Fisheries Management Organisations (RFMOs)', *International Journal of Marine and Coastal Law*, 20(3–4): 423–57.

McPake, B. (2002) 'The Globalisation of Health Sector Reform Policies: Is "Lesson Drawing" Part of the Process?', in: K. Lee, K. Buse and S. Fustukian (eds), *Health Policy in a Globalising World*, Cambridge: Cambridge University Press, 120–39.

Mearsheimer, J. T. (1990) 'Back to the Future: Instability in Europe after the Cold War', *International Security*, 15(1): 5–56.

Molle, W. (2003) *Global Economic Institutions*, London and New York: Routledge.

Moon, G. (1999) 'The Health of Nations: Structures and Discourses in Pan-European Health Policy', in: F. Carr and A. Massey (eds) *Public Policy in the New Europe. Eurogovernance in Theory and Practice*, Cheltenham and Northampton, MA: Edward Elgar, 146–63.

Moravcsik, A. (1991) 'Negotiating the Single European Act: National Interests and Conventional Statecraft in the European Community', *International Organization*, 45(1): 19–56.

Moravcsik, A. (1998) *The Choice for Europe. Social Purpose & State Power from Messina to Maastricht*, London: UCL Press.

Morishita, J. (2008) 'What is the Ecosystem Approach for Fisheries Management?' *Marine Policy*, 32(1): 19–26.

Mortensen, P. (2005) 'Policy Punctuations in Danish Local Budgeting', *Public Administration*, 83(4): 931–50.

Mörth, U. (2003) 'Framing an American Threat: The European Commission and the Technology Gap', in: M. Knodt and S. Princen (eds) *Understanding the European Union's External Relations*, London and New York: Routledge, 75–91.

Moser, J. (1970) 'World Health Activities Concerning Alcoholism', in: R. E. Popham (ed.) *Alcohol & Alcoholism*, Toronto and Buffalo, NY: University of Toronto Press, 385–88.

Moser, P. (1996) 'The European Parliament as a Conditional Agenda Setter: What Are the Conditions? A Critique of Tsebelis (1994)', *American Political Science Review*, 90(4): 834–38.

Mossialos, E. and W. Palm (2003) 'The European Court of Justice and the Free Movement of Patients in the European Union', *International Social Security Review*, 56(2): 3–29.

Nadelmann, E. A. (1990) 'Global Prohibition Regimes: The Evolution of Norms in International Society', *International Organization*, 44(4): 479–526.

Nathanson, C. A. (2004) '*Liberté, Egalité, Fumée:* Smoking and Tobacco Control in France', in: E. A. Feldman and R. Bayer (eds) *Unfiltered. Conflicts over Tobacco Policy and Public Health*, Cambridge, MA and London: Harvard University Press, 138–60.

Nature (1946) 'International Conference on Overfishing', *Nature*, 157(3992): 578.

Nugent, N. (2004) *The Government and Politics of the European Union*, 5th ed., Basingstoke: Palgrave Macmillan.

Oberthür, S. and T. Gehring (eds) (2006) *Institutional Interaction in Global Environmental Governance. Synergy and Conflicts among International and EU Policies*, Cambridge, MA and London: The MIT Press.

Organisation for Economic Co-operation and Development (OECD) (1994) *The Reform of Health Care Systems. A Review of Seventeen OECD Countries*, Paris: OECD.

Österberg, E. and T. Karlsson (1998) 'Alcohol Policies at the European Union Level', in: E. Österberg and T. Karlsson (eds) *Alcohol Policies in EU Member States and Norway. A Collection of Country Reports*, Brussels: European Commission, 43–75.

Parrish, R. (2003) 'The Politics of Sports Regulation in the European Union', *Journal of European Public Policy*, 10(2): 246–62.

Parsons, S. (2005) 'Ecosystem Considerations in Fisheries Management: Theory and Practice', *International Journal of Marine and Coastal Law*, 20(3–4): 381–422.

Pauly, D., V. Christensen, S. Guénette, T. J. Pitcher. U. R. Sumaila, C. J. Walters, R. Watson and D. Zeller (2002) 'Towards Sustainability in World Fisheries', *Nature*, 418: 689–95.

Payne, D. C. (2000) 'Policy-Making in Nested Institutions: Explaining the Conservation Failure of the EU's Common Fisheries Policy', *Journal of Common Market Studies*, 38(2): 303–24.

Permanand, G. and E. Mossialos (2005) 'The Europeanization of Regulatory Policy in the EU Pharmaceutical Sector', in: M. Steffen (ed.) *Health Governance in Europe. Issues, Challenges and Theories*, London and New York: Routledge, 49–80.

Peters, B. G. (1994) 'Agenda-Setting in the European Community', *Journal of European Public Policy*, 1(1): 9–26.

Peters, B. G. (2001) 'Agenda-Setting in the European Union', in: J. Richardson (ed.) *European Union. Power and Policy-Making*, 2nd ed., London and New York: Routledge, 77–94.

Peterson, J. (1995) 'Decision-Making in the European Union: Towards a Framework for Analysis', *Journal of European Public Policy*, 2(1): 69–93.

Phillip Morris (1978) *The World Health Organization (WHO): Its Work Related to the Activities of the International Tobacco Industry*, 5 January 1978, Bates No. 2010064767/4836, available at <http://legacy.library.ucsf.edu/tid/ume98e00>.

Phillip Morris (1979) *ICOSI. International Committee on Smoking Issues*, April 1979, Bates No. 1003717317/7330, available at <http://legacy.library.ucsf.edu/tid/jhw67e00>.

Pollack, M. A. (1997) 'Delegation, Agency, and Agenda Setting in the European Community', *International Organization*, 51(1): 99–134.

Pollack, M. A. (2003) *The Engines of European Integration: Delegation, Agency and Agenda Setting in the European Union*, Oxford: Oxford University Press.

Pralle, S. B. (2003) 'Venue Shopping, Political Strategy and Policy Change: The Internationalization of Canadian Forest Advocacy', *Journal of Public Policy*, 23(3): 233–60.

Princen, S. (2002) *EU Regulation and Transatlantic Trade*, The Hague: Kluwer Law International.

Princen, S. (2006) 'Governing through Multiple Forums: The Global Safety Regulation of Genetically Modified Crops and Foods', in: M. Koenig-Archibugi and M. Zürn (eds) *New Modes of Governance in the Global System. Exploring Publicness, Delegation and Inclusiveness*, Basingstoke: Palgrave Macmillan, 52–76.

Princen, S. and B. Kerremans (2008) 'Opportunity Structures in the EU Multi-Level System', *West European Politics*, 31(6): 1129–46.

Princen, S. and M. Rhinard (2006) 'Crashing and Creeping: Agenda-Setting Dynamics in the European Union', *Journal of European Public Policy*, 13(7): 1119–32.

Randall, E. (2001) *The European Union and Health Policy*, Basingstoke: Palgrave Macmillan.

Rhinard, M. (2002) *Ideas, Interests, and Policy Change in the European Union: The Mobilization of Frames by Actors in the Agricultural and Biotechnology Policy Sectors*, PhD Dissertation, University of Cambridge.

Richards, J. P. and J. Heard (2005) 'European Environmental NGOs: Issues, Resources and Strategies in Marine Campaigns', *Environmental Politics*, 14(1): 23–41.

Richardson, J. (2000) 'Government, Interest Groups and Policy Change', *Political Studies* 48: 1006–25.

Rich, R. F. and K. R. Merrick (2006) 'Cross Border Health Care in the European Union: Challenges and Opportunities', *Journal of Contemporary Health Law and Policy*, 23: 64–105.

Rochefort, D. A. and R. W. Cobb (eds) (1994) *The Politics of Problem Definition. Shaping the Policy Agenda*, Lawrence, KS: University Press of Kansas.

Roemer, R., A. Taylor and J. Lariviere (2005) 'Origins of the WHO Framework Convention on Tobacco Control', *American Journal of Public Health*, 95(6): 936–38.

Rosamond, B. (2000) *Theories of European Integration*, Basingstoke: Palgrave Macmillan.

Sabatier, P. A. and C. M. Weible (2007) 'The Advocacy Coalition Framework: Innovations and Clarifications', in P. A. Sabatier (ed.), *Theories of the Policy Process*, 2nd ed., Boulder, CO: Westview Press, 189–220.

Sandholtz, W. and J. Zysman (1989) '1992: Recasting the European Bargain', *World Politics*, 42(1): 95–128.

Scharpf, F. W. (1997) 'Introduction: The Problem-Solving Capacity of Multi-Level Governance', *Journal of European Public Policy*, 4(4): 520–38.

Scharpf, F. W. (1999) *Governing in Europe: Effective and Democratic?*, Oxford and New York: Oxford University Press.

Schattschneider, E. E. (1960) *The Semi-Sovereign People. A Realist's View of Democracy in America*, New York: Holt, Rinehart and Winston.

Schmitt, H. (2005) 'The European Parliament Elections of June 2004: Still Second-Order?', *West European Politics*, 28(3): 650–79.

Schrad, M. L. (2007a) *The Prohibition Option: Transnational Temperance and National Policymaking in Russia, Sweden and the United States*, PhD Dissertation, University of Wisconsin-Madison, available at <www.polisci.wisc.edu/users/ schrad/dissertation.htm>

Schrad, M. L. (2007b) 'The First Social Policy: Alcohol Control and Modernity in Policy Studies', *Journal of Policy History*, 19(4): 428–51.

Sell, S. K. and A. Prakash (2004) 'Using Ideas Strategically: The Contest between Business and NGO Networks in Intellectual Property Rights', *International Studies Quarterly*, 48(1): 143–75.

Sheingate, A. D. (2000) 'Agricultural Retrenchment Revisited: Issue Definition and Venue Change in the United States and European Union', *Governance*, 13(3): 335–63.

Sieveking, K. (2007) 'ECJ Rulings on Health Care Services and Their Effects on the Freedom of Cross-Border Patient Mobility in the EU', *European Journal of Migration and Law*, 9(1): 25–51.

Silverman, W. A. (2002) 'The Schizophrenic Career of a "Monster Drug"', *Pediatrics*, 110(2): 404–6.

Simpura, J. (1997) 'Alcohol and European Transformation', *Addiction*, 92(Supplement 1): S33–S41.

Slaughter, A. M. (2004) *A New World Order*, Princeton, NJ and Oxford: Princeton University Press.

Soroka, S. N. (2002) *Agenda-Setting Dynamics in Canada*, Vancouver and Toronto: UBC Press.

Steenbergen, M. R., E. E. Edwards and C. E. de Vries (2007) 'Who's Cueing Whom? Mass-Elite Linkages and the Future of European Integration', *European Union Politics*, 8(1): 13–35.

Steffen, M. (2004) 'AIDS and Health-Policy Responses in European Welfare States', *Journal of European Social Policy*, 14(2): 165–81.

Stein, E. (2001) 'International Integration and Democracy: No Love at First Sight', *American Journal of International Law*, 95(3): 489–534.

Stockwell, T. (2003) 'Classic Texts Revisited', *Addiction*, 98(8): 1173–4.

Stone, D. (2002) *Policy Paradox. The Art of Political Decision-Making*, rev. ed., New York and London: W. W. Norton & Company.

Stone Sweet, A. and W. Sandholtz (1997) 'European Integration and Supranational Governance', *Journal of European Public Policy*, 4(3): 297–317.

Sulkunen, P. (1981) 'Economic Integration and the Availability of Alcohol: The Case of the European Economic Community', *Contemporary Drug Problems*, 10(1): 75–102.

Sydnes, A. K. (2001) 'Regional Fishery Organizations: How and Why Organizational Diversity Matters', *Ocean Development & International Law*, 32(4): 349–72.

Symes, D. (1997) 'The European Community's Common Fisheries Policy', *Ocean & Coastal Management*, 35(2–3): 137–55.

Talbert, J. C. and M. Potoski (2002) 'The Changing Public Agenda over the Postwar Period', in: F. R. Baumgartner and B. D. Jones (eds), *Policy Dynamics*, Chicago and London: University of Chicago Press, 189–204.

Tallberg, J. (2002) 'Paths to Compliance: Enforcement, Management, and the European Union', *International Organization*, 56(3): 609–43.

Tallberg, J. (2003) 'The Agenda-Shaping Powers of EU Council Presidency', *Journal of European Public Policy*, 10(1): 1–19.

Tigerstedt, C. (1990) 'The European Community and the Alcohol Policy Dimension', *Contemporary Drug Problems*, 17: 461–79.

Tigerstedt, C., T. Karlsson, P. Mäkelä, E. Österberg and I. Tuominen (2006) 'Health in Alcohol Policies: The European Union and its Nordic Member States', in: T. Ståhl, M. Wismar, E. Ollila, E. Lahtinen and K. Leppo (eds), *Health in All Policies. Prospects and Potentials*, Helsinki: Finnish Ministry of Social Affairs and Health, 111–27.

Todd, E. and E. Ritchie (2000) 'Environmental Non-Governmental Organizations and the Common Fisheries Policy', *Aquatic Conservation: Marine and Freshwater Ecosystems*, 10(2): 141–9.

Trappenburg, M. (2008) *Genoeg is Genoeg. Over Gezondheidszorg en Democratie* [*Enough is Enough. On Health Care and Democracy*], Amsterdam: Amsterdam University Press.

Tsebelis, G. (1994) 'The Power of the European Parliament as a Conditional Agenda Setter', *American Political Science Review*, 88(1): 128–42.

Tsebelis, G. and A. Kreppel (1998) 'The History of Conditional Agenda-setting in European Institutions', *European Journal of Political Research*, 33: 41–71.

UN (1982) *United Nations Convention on the Law of the Sea*, adopted on 10 December 1982, available at <www.un.org/Depts/los/convention_agreements/convention_overview_convention.htm>.

UN (1992a) *Agenda 21*, available at <http://www.un.org/esa/sustdev/documents/agenda21/index.htm>.

UN (1992b) *Convention on Biological Diversity*, available at <www.cbd.int/convention/convention.shtml>.

UN (1995) *United Nations Agreement for the Implementation of the Provisions of the United Nations Convention on the Law of the Sea of 10 December 1982 Relating to the Conservation and Management of Straddling Fish Stocks and Highly Migratory Fish Stocks*, adopted on 4 August 1995, available at <www.un.org/Depts/los/convention_agreements/convention_overview_fish_stocks.htm>.

UN (2004) *Resolution 59/25*, A/RES/59/25, adopted by the General Assembly on 17 November 2004.

UN (2006) *Resolution 61/105*, A/RES/61/105, adopted by the General Assembly on 8 December 2006.

Van de Steeg, M. (2006) 'Does a Public Sphere Exist in the EU? An Analysis of the Content of the Debate on the Haider Case', *European Journal of Political Research*, 45(4): 609–34.

Van de Ven, W. P. M. M. (1996) 'Market-Oriented Health Care Reforms: Trends and Future Options', *Social Science & Medicine*, 43(5): 655–66.

Vogel, D. (1995) *Trading up. Consumer and Environmental Regulation in a Global Economy*, Cambridge, MA and London: Harvard University Press.

Vollaard, H. (2004) 'Solidarity, Territoriality, and Healthcare: Cross-National Policy Learning in Europe', in D. Levi-Faur and E. Vigoda-Gadot (eds), *International Public Policy and Management: Policy Learning beyond Regional, Cultural, and Political Boundaries*, New York: Marcel Dekker, 267–96.

Waltz, K. N. (1979) *Theory of International Politics*, Reading, MA: Addison-Wesley.

Wang, J. C. F. (1992) *Handbook on Ocean Politics & Law*, New York: Greenwood Press.

Weale, A., G. Pridham, M. Cini, D. Konstadakopulos, M. Porter and B. Flynn (2000) *Environmental Governance in Europe. An Ever Closer Ecological Union?*, Oxford: Oxford University Press.

Wendon, B. (1998) 'The Commission as Image-Venue Entrepreneur in EU Social Policy', *Journal of European Public Policy*, 5(2): 339–53.

World Health Organization (WHO) (1993) *European Alcohol Action Plan*, Copenhagen: WHO Regional Office for Europe.

WHO (1995) *European Charter on Alcohol*, adopted at the European Conference on Health, Society and Alcohol, 12–14 December 1995, available at <www.euro.who.int/document/E57528.pdf>.

WHO (1996) *The Ljubljana Charter on Reforming Health Care*, adopted on 18 June 1996, available at <http://www.euro.who.int/AboutWHO/Policy/20010927_5>.

WHO (2000a) *Tobacco Company Strategies to Undermine Tobacco Control Activities at the World Health Organization*, Report of the Committee of Experts on Tobacco Industry Documents, July 2000.

WHO (2000b) *European Alcohol Action Plan*, adopted at the Forty-Ninth Session of the Regional Committee for Europe of the World Health Organization, 13–17 September 1999, available at <www.euro.who.int/document/E67946.pdf>.

WHO (2001) *Declaration on Young People and Alcohol*, adopted at the WHO Ministerial Conference on Young People and Alcohol, February 2001, available at <www.euro.who.int/eprise/main/who/AboutWHO/Policy/20030204_1>.

WHO (2003) *WHO Framework Convention on Tobacco Control*, Signed on 21 May 2003, available at <www.who.int/tobacco/framework/fctc_en.pdf>.

WHO (2004a) *The Tobacco Industry Documents. What They Are, What They Tell Us, and How to Search Them. A Practical Manual*, available at <http://www.who.int/tobacco/resources/publications/en>, accessed on 17 March 2008.

WHO (2004b) *Global Strategy on Diet, Physical Activity and Health*, adopted by the World Health Assembly in May 2004, available at <www.who.int/dietphysicalactivity/strategy/eb11344/en/index.html>, accessed on 24 September 2008.

WHO (2007) *Elaboration of Guidelines for Implementation of the Convention (Decision FCTC/COP1(15))*, Document No. A/FCTC/COP/2/7, 26 April 2007.

WHO (2008) *Updated Status of the WHO Framework Convention on Tobacco Control*, available at <www.who.int/tobacco/framework/countrylist/en/index.html>, accessed on 15 May 2008.

Wise, M. (1984) *The Common Fisheries Policy of the European Community*, London and New York: Methuen.

Yach, D. and D. Bettcher (2000) 'Globalisation of Tobacco Industry Influence and New Global Responses', *Tobacco Control*, 9: 206–16.

Young, O. R. (1999) *Governance in World Affairs*, Ithaca, NY and London: Cornell University Press.

Zhu, J. L. (1992) 'Issue Competition and Attention Distraction: A Zero-Sum Theory of Agenda-Setting', *Journalism Quarterly*, 69: 825–36.

Zito, A. R. (1999) 'Task Expansion: A Theoretical Overview', *Environment and Planning C*, 17(1): 19–35.

Index